IN THE WAKE OF HEROES

IN THE WAKE
OF HEROES

Introduced by Tom Cunliffe

ADLARD COLES NAUTICAL

B L O O M S B U R Y
LONDON · OXFORD · NEW YORK · NEW DELHI · SYDNEY

Adlard Coles Nautical
An imprint of Bloomsbury Publishing Plc

50 Bedford Square
London
WC1B 3DP
UK

1385 Broadway
New York
NY 10018
USA

www.bloomsbury.com
www.adlardcoles.com

ADLARD COLES, ADLARD COLES NAUTICAL and the Buoy logo are trademarks of
Bloomsbury Publishing Plc

First published 2015
This edition published 2016

British Library Cataloguing-in-Publication Data
A catalogue record for this book is available from the British Library.

Library of Congress Cataloguing-in-Publication data has been applied for.

ISBN: PB: 978-1-4729-3600-4
ePDF: 978-1-4729-1703-4
ePub: 978-1-4729-1702-7

2 4 6 8 10 9 7 5 3 1

Typeset in 11pt Minion Pro by Deanta Global Publishing Services, Chennai, India
Printed and bound in Great Britain by CPI Group (UK) Ltd, Croydon CR0 4YY

To find out more about our authors and books visit www.bloomsbury.com.
Here you will find extracts, author interviews, details of forthcoming
events and the option to sign up for our newsletters.

CONTENTS

Introduction   1

CLASSIC YACHTING   5

EMERGENCY   49

HIGH LATITUDES   69

LONG-DISTANCE CRUISING AND RACING   107

SMALL CRAFT   153

VOYAGES UNDER DURESS   179

WOMEN WRITERS   201

WORKING BOATS   227

Picture Credits   265

Acknowledgements   266

INTRODUCTION

It was at the London Boat Show in January 2004 that my friend Andrew Bray, then editor of *Yachting World* magazine, proposed an idea for a regular feature built around nautical literature. The original plan was to concentrate on exceptional feats of seamanship, and Andrew anticipated the series might run to half a dozen articles. I was delighted with this opportunity, because my study was already lined with a wide-ranging library of maritime titles from which I could draw. As the months passed we began diverging from the foundation plan and started to include passages selected as much for their literary value as for the more obvious attractions of 40ft seas, mutiny and tumbling spars. A year later, Andrew told me that the series was proving popular and asked if we were in danger of running out of material. By then, it was clear that this seemed an unlikely contingency within either of our lifetimes, and so 'Great Seamanship' set course for the indefinite future. Those of us who go down to the sea, whether for leisure, war or commerce, are incomparably blessed with good reading matter. Indeed, I believe that no other sport or form of transport is so richly endowed.

Prodigal antiquarian book-buying had long been a diversion enjoyed by my wife, Ros. Now that she had direct motivation to provide licence for this hitherto private vice, she was to become a well-known figure prowling the dusty corners of coastal bookstores. Today, her online presence haunts their websites, while our own shelves, once merely well stocked, groan under the weight of beautifully written works where the west winds blow, the trades hum, grass skirts sway under moonlit palms and desperate men battle against ice and gale to save not only their ships, but their immortal souls as well.

The idea for this book came from Liz Multon at Adlard Coles Nautical. Why not make a compendium of all the best books drawn from the 'Great Seamanship' columns, she said, for readers to enjoy at their own speed? The plan was so sound I couldn't imagine why we hadn't thought of it before. As I worked through the 120-odd available titles, I realised that, with a few notable exceptions, the best came from before the Second World War. These were the books that sent me to sea back in the late 1960s, when a career addressing British juries threatened to keep my feet dry for a lifetime. Alan Villiers started me off, but it was Erling Tambs who finished the job. If he could buy a fine old boat for so little money and sail away with less, then so could I. And in due course, that is exactly what I did. Many could say the same.

These books are invariably well written, often with that dry brand of humour that pre-dates the current fashion for unloading one's emotions onto anyone who will listen. A theme of self-sufficiency runs through the stories like a golden thread. For the folk of this generation who chose to go deep-sea, the guarantee of salvation did not lie at the touch of an electronic button. They were obliged to fend for themselves with what they had and, if the ship sank, then in the words of the great Colonel HG Hasler, many would have little choice but 'to drown like gentlemen'. Their lives were on the line. Such is the stuff of real adventure.

For this book, I have omitted most of what one might describe as 'mainstream' accounts by such world-famous seamen as Sir Robin Knox-Johnston and Captain Joshua Slocum. This is simply because their writings are so readily available. Some of what a reader will find in the following pages will prove unknown to many. Certain of the books have been elusive to track down. Occasional pages have been culled not from a published book at all, but from a club journal or the yachting press.

Although I have steered away from the occasional rollicking story from the square-riggers that have leavened the stream of material in the magazine, the chapters remain as diverse in mood as the sea itself. To try and create some sort of order from this miscellany, the book is divided into sections. The definitions of what these may be are loose, particularly when it comes to 'Emergency' and 'Working Boats', but while I may not have entirely succeeded, at least I have tried.

In the context of the 21st century it may seem unfashionable to award women writers their own section, but just as it can be unwise to judge the morality of a century ago by the mores of today, it should be understood that when these ladies put pen to paper, the sea was very much the realm of men. Women were a rarity on boats. Those prepared to leave their perspective to posterity in book form were veritable pioneers. Therefore, we honour them with a division to themselves, and fascinating reading it makes.

Each chapter is preceded by a paragraph or two, which I hope will explain something of the author and the circumstances of what follows. Where the account is a reconstruction taken from different areas of a book, I have inserted a sentence or two to tie together what might otherwise be disjointed extracts. Occasionally I have edited the core text to fit the current medium. All this is to give the reader easier access to the wild and wonderful world that follows.

Finally, I would advise anyone who enjoys a particular passage to go out, find an original copy of the book itself and dive in. I am currently rereading Henry Plummer, the New Englander who sailed a 23ft sloop to Florida in winter with his son and his cat in 1912–13. The wry, self-effacing humour is pure Yankee. Last night, tucked up snugly in bed around midnight, I was with Henry when he piled up on the frozen mud in a snowbound creek somewhere in Carolina. His comments were so pithy that I burst out laughing, which woke my wife. Had I been reading today's paper I would have suffered a major earful for my pains. When I explained that it was only Captain Plummer up to his tricks again she turned over with a smile and went back to dreaming about which website to plunder for new treasures in the morning. The supply never seems to end.

Tom Cunliffe
www.tomcunliffe.com

CLASSIC YACHTING

Paid hand Tom Diaper

A day's racing in the Solent RT Pritchett

Fitting out John Scott-Hughes

Storm in the Atlantic Scott Cookman

The old Britannia Anthony Heckstall-Smith

A rough ride in the Dover Strait DR Collins

A racing bet Rayner and Wykes

PAID HAND

Tom Diaper
Tom Diaper's Log
Robert Ross 1950

Little is written about the lives of the paid hands on yachts from the Golden Age before the Second World War. Tom Diaper's Log *was first published in 1950 from a lightly edited handwritten manuscript dedicated to his granddaughter Doreen, 'For her kindness to me'. It traces his life from his birth as a fisherman/yacht hand's son in 1867, until 1939. He probably wrote the memoir in 1947, two years before he finally let slip his cable. This remarkable account tells of hard times looking for work, glory days racing against the Kaiser at Kiel, and finally finding a quiet, steady job with a considerate owner.*

We join Tom Diaper now aboard the 23-metre Shamrock. *These enormous yachts were the largest gaff cutters ever seen, and were effectively the precursors of the later J-class. She is bound for New York to play her part in the America's Cup contest of 1920. The account is fascinating for the insight not only into what went on delivering these mighty yachts between race courses – when their owners were seldom on board – but also into the language and thought processes of a true professional hand.*

For 1920, I had shipped in the *Shamrock* 23-metre as second mate under my brother, Alf Diaper, who was the skipper of her. We started on the 5th February to make her ready to cross the Atlantic to act as trial-horse to train and tune up the *Shamrock IV* for the American Cup. She went over in 1914, only the war came on. The *Shamrock* 23-metre was not one of the *Shamrocks* built for the Cup, but built to race around the British coast regattas.

The *Shamrock* 23-metre was over at Camper & Nicholson's yard. Jim Gilby, the mate, was getting her ready with the port watch for the crossing under her ocean rig while I with the starboard watch was packing all her racing gear – sails, spars, and all the halyards, etc. – and labelling it to go across in one of the Cunard boats. Quite a big job it is to pack a 23-metre racing gear, but we managed to get it done by the 1st April, and the *Shamrock* was launched and moored off Southampton. The next day we went for a short sail with the owner on board. Sir Thomas Lipton and his guest, Lord Delaware, wished us a good and quick voyage across the Atlantic then, with 'God speed you,' they went on shore.

Diaper and his shipmates had a rough time working the Shamrock *down to Falmouth, where they were held up by the weather for over a fortnight. After a false start they finally got away, still with a headwind…*

We made the first leg of our journey to Ushant, when we put her on the other tack, the wind beginning to increase and the sea getting up. We kept tacking her up to the windward till the third night out of Falmouth, no one getting any rest, it was so rough. I went on watch at midnight when an able seaman asked me to take a look around the forecastle. I did, and quickly got the captain and navigator to look also. This is what I saw.

An iron stanchion in the centre of the forecastle, which was a deck support, was starting to bend, which should not have been, but the pounding of her long bow and the heavy seas pounding her deck was causing that – and not only that. The fishplate what ran around each side of the ship underneath the covering board was half-inch steel plating and it was bending the port and starboard in line across the deck with the iron stanchion, all bending together. Myself, having had more experience than anyone in that class of ship, warned them that if we kept on pounding her bow in such a storm much longer, the *Shamrock* would not reach America. Why not then turn back and wait for a better chance of luck and a fair wind? The skipper and navigator together said, 'We dare not turn back for Sir Thomas Lipton wants this boat in America.'

I myself answered, 'To h—with Sir Thomas! He looked out for himself not to be here with us. There are twenty-two of us on board, and sixty-eight in England depending on us. What will they all do if we are lost? The owner cannot look after them, and you know the boat is no good to save us. Now will you listen to me this once, for I have had a lot of experience in this kind of craft. It is 12.20 and I will try to keep her going until 2 a.m. If it is no better by then I will turn her round and make for the first port we can reach in safety. The only way you will get this boat to America is by running away from this storm. I will take the blame, if there is any.'

So that was agreed on. They went below, being worn out by their long watch on deck in the gale. The strain had told on the skipper, who was ill; it was physically impossible for him to carry on longer on deck. At fifteen minutes before 2 a.m., I called an able seaman, saying, 'Go below, see the first mate, tell him to get all hands out and make ready to turn the ship round.'

So when the first mate came on deck, he said, 'The skipper wants you, the weather is worse now, Tom.'

I replied, 'At times it's a devil of a lot worse.'

The skipper said, 'What is it like on deck, Tom? It is hard enough below.'

I said, 'It's that bad, skipper, that I have warned the watch to just rope themselves, for you have a hard job to see the big ones coming. Skipper, it will be a risky job turning her in this hurricane.'

'Are you going to wear or gybe her, Tom?'

'No, neither. I am going to stay her' (or, in plain words, tack her round) 'and I am steering her.'

To the navigator, I said, 'After I get her round, I will see what is on the log and keep her north-east course till I report to you.'

The skipper gave me a tot of whisky; 'I don't want this to buck me up, only for good luck,' I said. Then I went on deck and saw the first mate.

I said, 'Jim, I will take the wheel, for I am going to sail her until everything is ready for tacking.'

'Yes, Tom,' he answered.

'Now, you, Jim,' I said, 'go forward to the main rigging. Have a rope to put around you for safety and when I call out to you, you will be looking for a dark spot in the waves. Call out like hell, "A dark spot, Tom." Then I will, if I have enough way on and the ship answers all right, lee-ho, and every man for himself.'

So only a short space of time had gone by, and I had offered up a short prayer for guidance and safety in the job I was going to do – the same as I had always done since I started going to sea, to the only One up above Who can see you safely through anything, good or danger, if you ask Him – when the mate's voice came, 'A dark spot coming, Tommy.'

'All right,' I answered, 'and every man for himself.'

Now every man was at his station and everything went just like clockwork. We got that ship round, in spite of the mountainous seas and a hurricane of wind and dark as a dungeon, as well as if we were on a mill-pond, without shipping a pail of water, or breaking a rope yarn. That was the time that Sir Thomas Lipton ought to have been with us, trying to cross the Atlantic. So having got her round, I set the course north-east, and went below to report to the navigator, and had the oil bags put over. Then, turning to the captain I said, 'I don't think a tot of whisky would hurt the men. It will act like medicine. I will enter it in the official log as such.'

'Well, Tom,' he said, 'I reckon you all deserve it; you all done a good job. I nearly thought I had got into the Solent.'

But I answered; 'It was a bit too jumpy to think that! But we had a lucky turning.' We drank our tot and then the watch below turned in, or lay down somewhere to try and get some rest. I returned to my watch on deck, but, owing to the wind veering more to the west and making the heavy seas coming more on the quarter, we could not make a true north-easterly course for Falmouth. The navigator was a bit worried, and the skipper too, but I said, 'We shall make Dartmouth, what's the odds? We can get repairs done there.'

When we did get there we looked a proper wreck on deck. The lashings had pulled the stem-pieces away from the two eighteen-foot lifeboats, all the plank ends had pulled away from the stems, and both boats had to be made seaworthy.

We stayed till the repairs were finished in about a week, repairing the mainsail which we had partly blown away, and then we made a fresh start from which we did not turn back.

This time the Shamrock *made an uninterrupted 22-day passage and completed her job.*

The continuation of Tom Diaper's log leaves no doubt about the sheer scale of these mighty gaff cutters, but the writer's pithy observations on Shamrock IV's *failure to lift the America's Cup are really illuminating. Penned many years after the event, they are undiluted by tact, political correctness, or concern lest he upset his employer. Boat-for-boat,* Shamrock IV *was said to have stood a good chance against the defender* Reliance, *but after establishing a 2-0 lead, she lost 3-2. For the races, Sir Thomas had decided to have her steered by an amateur, which represented a major break with tradition. Most of* Shamrock IV's *hands were hardcore Essex professionals and both crews took a dim view of this meddling with their business. Despite the well-known rivalry between the Solent and Essex, Tom Diaper – a Southampton man to the quick of his fingernails – sides unambiguously with the men from the Colne and the Blackwater. Perhaps when confronted by misguided owners, it came down to 'All for one and one for all'.*

The Customs cleared us and we were towed to City Point Yacht Yard to change the ocean gear into the racing gear that had arrived before us. We were rigged in a week, all but the topmast. We had to leave that on deck; with it up we was one hundred and seventy-five feet from the deck to the top of the topmast, too tall to go under Brooklyn Bridge.

We were soon ready to help tune up the *Shamrock IV*. We had some races together. She had three out of five against us, but she did not win the cup – too many amateur sailing masters. In fact, I have before me now a photograph out of a New York newspaper with the *Resolute* catching the *Shamrock* up quick, when it ought to be the other way about – the *Shamrock* leaving the *Resolute* behind. The *Shamrock* lost the cup where she ought to have won it. In fact, Sir Thomas Lipton and Lord Delaware came on our *Shamrock* on November 27th, and said he had done wrong to lose the cup. Our crew was the one that ought to have been on *Shamrock IV*. He would have taken any odds on it, but he found out too late.

Many thanks to the Diaper Heritage Association for permission to print this article.

A DAY'S RACING IN THE SOLENT

RT Pritchett
Yachting Volume No. 2
Badminton Library 1894

This rare account by RT Pritchett, from the Badminton Library's Yachting
Volume No. 2 *(1894), offers an insight into life on board a big day-racer in
the late Victorian era. The relationship between the owners – noble, royal or
just plain wealthy – and the supremely professional paid hands who sailed
the majestic craft is shown here to be one of affection and respect on both
sides. Pritchett is a guest aboard a 40-rater. The rule that created these yachts
generated rapid development and ultimately favoured boats whose speed
outshone their seaworthiness. In 1906 it was superseded by the International*

Rule, but in this, its heyday, the rater system gave the world great sport and vessels of extraordinary beauty.

Along with Mr Pritchett, we join the 70ft cutter Queen Mab *after breakfast one August morning. The hands are in the final stages of preparation for the day's racing.*

Cowes in the early morn is not generally known to visitors. The 'wood and brass work' is now in full swing, for this admirable function must be completed by eight bells. If cleanliness be next to godliness, surely yachts have very much to commend them, with their spotless decks, bleached runners, and immaculate canvas. As our tender stands out towards the yachts, the craft increase in size as the water deepens. First the small raters are passed. Then the French yachts are reached, for of late years the burgee of the French club is often seen at Cowes, and the American flag is more frequent than of yore. The Guard-ship now looms. The Royal yacht *Victoria and Albert* is at her buoy. Eight bells strike. Immediately the morning flutter of bunting flies to the mastheads, where all the burgees should arrive simultaneously, taking the time from the flagship.

By this time we see *Queen Mab* basking and glistening in the bright morning sunshine, in perfect repose, yet rather fretting to be off. Having come alongside very carefully, without touching the varnish, we are soon on board, and find all in motion. The business of the day has begun.

The preliminary functions are completed, such as sending the gig away with the superfluous gear of squeegees, mops, oars. The 12ft dinghy is already lashed over the skylight, with the stem wedged up to the coaming abaft the companion. The crew are going aloft to 'string down' on the throat halliards; gradually, the mainsail peak rises, and the sail soon becomes fairly set.

In joining a racer there is nothing so comfortable as being on board in good time. With a flying start it is very important to be under way to the minute, especially in light winds and with a tide running, such as the swill in Cowes Roads generally is. It is no joke for a boatman to catch a racer once under way, to say nothing of the anathemas of the owner, and the skipper's suppressed comments.

Soon comes the welcome of the owner of *Queen Mab*, Col. T. B. C. West. The forties are a prominent class and justly so; they emphasise the sport of class racing over handicaps.

The crew are immensely keen. Should an old adversary not be getting under way, the why and wherefore will be at once discussed. The headsails have now been set, and we are pirouetting about waiting for the preparatory gun. There is no doubt that wonderful skill, dexterity and firmness shown in the handling of the various craft.

Now comes the full excitement of the start. 'First gun, sir; fifteen minutes to go!' is the word. All is now extra wariness, sometimes fourteen yachts under way, manoeuvring, and keenly watching each other. 'Blue Peter, sir, five minutes!' is next heard. The owner, watch in hand, by the skipper, records the fleeting moments as they pass, calling out the minutes: at length it comes to 1 min., 50 secs., 40 secs., 30 secs., 20 secs. 'How much, sir?' 'Ten seconds'; then 'Let her go!' and she goes – with her cranse iron over the line directly after the gun.

A good start is a grand beginning. So long as one is leading, no explanation is required why the good ship is not showing her best form, or how it is that she is not in her right trim. By this time the fleet is getting sorted; with a good sailing breeze the large craft draw out ahead in many cases; the large cutters are started, say, a quarter of an hour ahead, and the forties together. In 1892 the forties were very strongly represented, *Thalia*, *Reverie*, *Queen Mab*, *Corsair*, *Creole*, *Varuna*, *White Slave*. This gave most interesting sport, far preferable to handicapping, which is only adopted to bring vessels of different tonnage together. A curious instance of this occurred at Cowes, when *Irex*, *Genesta*, and *Lorna* all came in together within five minutes, and having brought up, stowed canvas and dined, it was discovered that *Sleuthhound* was coming in, almost saving her time allowance of about 53 min. It is certainly most uninteresting to the spectators on shore to see the first fine craft come in close together, and returning from afternoon tea to perhaps discover that the real winner is just sailing in round the flag-boat and getting the gun.

That *Queen Mab* will hold her own with the best is a point upon which we feel happily confident, her racing flags being proof of her capacity – thirty-six is the number she showed at the end of the season. *Varuna*, also a new boat this year, designed by Mr. G. L. Watson with a Watson bow, as in *Mab*, was a beautiful craft, really perhaps the designer's favourite. These bows, with those in *Corsair* and others, elicited sighs and groans from the old school of yachting men; for what with the schooner bow, the Viking bow, the inverted Roman nose bow, the bottle-nose bow, the Fife bow, and the canoe bow, one's idea of what a bow should be became somewhat confused. However, overhang forward carries the day up to 200 tons. *Corsair*, 40-rater, designed by Mr. Arthur Payne of Southampton, was a grand boat, with less beam than *Mab*, beautiful counter, long boom, very workmanlike all round. *Thalia* was a fine craft, by Fife of Fairlie, a splendid sea boat. Many is the good race Mr. Inglis has sailed in her, with Carter, who sailed *Britannia*, 1893, at the tiller.

We live in an age of rapid development; 1892 becomes ancient history in 1893, still it seems sad that when one has a good vessel like *Thalia*, she should so soon be outclassed. Fashion always runs to extremes; now that fashion has attacked yachting, the belle of one season is extinguished in the next. 'Sic tempora et naves mutantur.' *['Thus change both times and ships' – Ed.]*

The westerly wind turned out very light, and without a good sailing breeze racing becomes peaceful repose. Much interest, however, is felt in the performance of *Irene*, designed by Mr. G. L. Watson for Prince Henry of Prussia, who was at the tiller all day, heart and soul in it, longing for a breeze, and probably keeping up the old superstition by giving an unintentional whistle for one; but still it would not come. At 4 hrs. 0 min. 35 secs. *Queen Mab* came in the winner, *Thalia* taking second prize.

For real racing, a true wind such as we had in the race for prizes given by the Royal Southampton Yacht Club is indispensable. This was a small but sporting muster. *Iverna* and *Meteor* were sent away at 10.45 a.m. The forties, *Corsair*, *Queen Mab*, and *Thalia*, were despatched at 11 a.m. to a perfect start and a whole-sail westerly breeze, *Mab* crossing two seconds after the Blue Peter was hauled down. The gun missed fire. We hailed the Committee Boat, 'Are we all right?' when the pleasant echo returned, 'All right, go on,' and away we went.

It was a fine reach down from Southampton, the three close together in single file. Passing Calshot Lightship we hauled our wind and stood over for Cowes, feeling the westerly breeze which came sweeping up from the Needles; below Egypt we went about and took our jumps merrily – a nasty sea; our working topsail relieved her somewhat – for *Corsair* and *Thalia* were carrying jackyarders. It was a grand beat down to Lymington; the rain was heavy, but the sun came out; and the Lymington mark boat was rounded. As the mark boat was near all were astir. 'Get your gear on your spinnaker boom, my lads, and top him as soon as you can. Will you take the time, sir, of *Meteor* and *Iverna* rounding?' Before this our masthead man George had gone aloft by an acrobatic performance which is always interesting to the beholder: on the port tack with his port foot on a hoop, and the starboard foot on the sail. George was a good compact cheery hand, and must have been born for this particular function.

By this time we are round. 'Down spinnaker boom, and all aft, my sonnies!' Skipper Parker seems to smile upon his pet. At this time bread and cheese and beer are served out, and form a very pleasant pendant to 'all aft' except the look-out, who took his mid-day in solitude by the unfilled foresail. A splendid dead run from the Lymington mark back to Cowes now takes place. See! *Corsair's* spinnaker is suddenly taken in, Sycamore, her skipper, having discovered that her mast was sprung, and he therefore went into Cowes. We were now cracking on for the Warner, our enjoyment only once disturbed by a hail from the look-out, 'Boat right under bow, sir,' and in the same breath, 'Only a photogger, sir,' and on we sped.

Rounding the Warner *Thalia* carried away her throat halliards, but soon continued the race. Rounding mark-boats and lightships is thrilling work, and beautifully it is done on *Queen Mab*. It is delightful to see the judgement and decision, and how cheerily the hands haul on to the mainsheet; truly this is sport and excitement not easily beaten.

It is generally supposed that racing yachts are cleared out below; it is so in America, but not here. Everything is in its place, and when the steward appears at the companion with the welcome words, 'Lunch, sir!' we find that all is well – but look out for the swinging table: touch that and there will be a ghastly crash. The 40-rater has the owner's cabin and the lady's cabin, with a very comfortable one for a guest, to say nothing of accommodation for sea bachelors who do not require shore luxury. The ladies' conning tower is generally the top step of the companion, but in the *Seabelle* Mrs. Taylor had an arm-chair swung like a gimbal compass, in which she knitted comfortably at whatever angle the yacht might be in a seaway.

After lunch we are close-hauled lying for Calshot Castle, hissing through it with a pleasant swish of spray, ever and anon making some of the hands duck their heads as they lie up to windward. Many is the dry remark and cheery yarn that one hears under these circumstances;

not many words but much to the purpose, old recollections are revived, and there is always something to be learnt. Each hand is on the look-out in calm weather, scouring the horizon for a wandering catspaw, or in bad weather, watching the other craft to see how they take it. To note the skipper's face is a study; his eye on every leach and every sheet, keen and ready for any emergency, entirely absorbed in 'her', how she is going and how he can best cosset her. Such was the impression left of Ben Parker at the tiller of *Queen Mab*, who had sailed for some years under Tom Diaper.

It was a merry close haul back from the Warner to Southampton Water, with a beat up to the Committee-boat. We get the 'gun', that great joy at the end of a good race. 'Down foresail,' and round she comes. The cheering is over, so now to clear up. Unlash the dinghy and fill in the Declaration. The gig is by this time alongside, and it must have been delightful to the owner as he stepped into her to look up and see five winning flags flying – five first prizes in five starts in one week.

FITTING OUT

John Scott-Hughes
Sailing Through Life
Richard Clay & Co 1947

John Scott-Hughes, from Seaview, Isle of Wight, was a total seaman from another age. He was born in 1893 and after an early life on deep water in just about everything that floated – commercial and yachting, steam and sail – he discovered he could write. His success was assured when, in 1933, he was appointed Yachting Correspondent of The Times. *He kept the job until a few months before his death in 1960, by which time he had authored several books. He was already a master mariner when he started writing, and he served in the Second World War as a Lieutenant Commander RNVR. Scant information is available on his home background, but whatever this may have been, he certainly found a ready acceptance among the seamen and fishermen/yacht crews of his day.*

In his highly readable volume Sailing Through Life, *published in 1947, he mentions attending a meeting with 'Sir Philip Hunloke, representing*

*the King, and Mr Sopwith, representing himself'. He also describes his
early years as an apprentice paid hand and the influence on his life of
his messmates in various focsles. It is to this period that we turn as he
describes joining and fitting out* Czarina, *a three-masted topsail schooner
yacht, before the First World War. The comments on the skipper from this
man who had walked with the mighty are pure lower deck. They come at
the end and are well worth waiting for. The magical world he takes us to is
only a century away, but it may as well be on Mars…*

'Iwouldn't try for no square-rigger, not if I was you. Floating
workhouses. That's what most of 'em are. Besides, you can get your
sail-training in a big yacht pretty much the same. If you must have sail,
try yachting. Yachting in summer, deep-sea in winter – see what I mean?
Half-and-half like…'

So had said Banjo Bob on my first ship, the P&O Indian Transport
SS Dongola where I served a voyage as a boy seaman. His advice led
me straight to Marvin's Yard at Cowes, the favourite winter berth
for the big British yachts for a century and more. The yard was an
especially remarkable sight in the decade before 1914. On the early
spring day in 1912 when I boarded my new ship, the *Czarina*, there
lay in the port, unless my memory is much at fault, the *Sunbeam, Lady
Torfreda, Whyte Ladye, Boadicea, Modwena, Miranda, Cetonia, Oceana,
St. George, Lamorna, Semiramis,* and *Valhalla,* the last-named being
an outstandingly magnificent vessel, a full-rigged ship of 1490 tons,
manned by a crew mustering not far short of 100 hands. This was keeping
fine company. But the *Czarina*, in which Banjo Bob's introduction had
secured me a berth, was a beauty also. Square-rigged forward, carrying
a t'gallant-sail and single topsail, she was a three-masted schooner of
just on 500 tons. She was thus of the same rig and much the same size
as the celebrated *Sunbeam*; indeed, the pair so closely resembled each
other in every way as to be regarded as sister ships. Sisters or not, a
kinship of a sort did exist, because the *Czarina*'s owner, the Hon. Albert
Brassey, was a brother of Lord Brassey of the *Sunbeam*.

The *Czarina* had been laid up for the winter in so thorough a fashion
that she appeared as no more than a long, slim hull in which were stuck
the three stumpy lower-masts, stripped of all rigging.

Thus when the crew joined all was to do, and for a lad so ignorant as I, no experience could be more fortunate. In the *Dongola* when any considerable weight had to be shifted the cry was, 'Steam on the winch!' In the schooner there was only muscle and sinew ('Armstrong's patent'), but soon I was learning what prodigies could be performed by sling and lift and purchase by men who knew how. There was another thing. When the fall of the powerful four-fold purchase was taken to the capstan and the capstan bars shipped and we began to 'Walk her up, boys!' the men started singing.

In steam you do not sing, even on jobs which 'go with a song', as when the anchor is coming in, if it is being heaved in by steam.

When the three separate topmasts had been swayed aloft and fidded in position, the standing rigging was set up. Before the introduction of bottle-screws it was held proper that rigging should have some give in it, such as is afforded by stout tarred lanyards rove through *lignum vitae* dead-eyes. In its way the setting up of the main rigging is a major job of sailorizing, calling for the employment of tackles and frappings and rackings and what-not to secure that just-so degree of tautness when (in a favourite focsle phrase) 'everything bears an equal strain'.

Scraping the masts to prepare them for their coats of varnish was one of our earlier tasks, and so soon as I had been shown how to give a knife a scraping edge, up I was hauled in a bos'n's chair to the mizzen topmast truck; and days and days did I spend up there, it seemed to me, and even now I can recall the look of the grain and the smell of the shavings from that flawless column of finest Oregon pine. The other spars, the square-sail yards, the booms and gaffs, were prepared on shore, the spar under treatment being laid across trestles set out on the strip of grass which, pleasantly, bordered the dock, running under our bowsprit and figure-head.

This figure-head, by the way, was the image in ivory paint and gold-leaf of some Czarina, crowned and robed, to whose features the artist had imparted an expression of marked serenity and sweetness. I do not claim that it was the handsomest figure-head along the river. Some of the other ships carried massive figures, divinities of gigantic proportions whose draperies were swept aft as far as the fore-rigging.

All the same we were proud enough of our Czarina, possibly the more so because not a few yachts sported the 'fiddle-head', a compromise between the figure-head proper and the unadorned bow which was soon to be the vogue.

Another of the grass-plot jobs was the overhauling of the patent blocks, of which there seemed to be an uncountable quantity in infinite variety, but all to be stripped and greased and have their ash or elm 'shells' scraped and varnished. When the schooner had been laid up in the autumn every block had a label attached, describing its purpose and its position; and it may be guessed with what bewilderment, not to say dismay, I would finger a tally with a name such as 'Maintopmast preventer backstay tackle, lower'.

To speed the date of commissioning we were given the services of a professional rigger from Marvin's. He was an old, old chap, said to be going on for ninety, small and bowed, with a fringe of white whisker running under his chin from ear to ear. Although suffering so badly from cataract that he was not far off total blindness, he was still a superb craftsman, both in rope and wire. So long as he began on the right touch he could continue and finish faultlessly. This was 'marlinspike seamanship' as an art! I tried to profit, while I stood all those long hours beside him, fetching and handing his tools and gear, the serving-board and mallet, greenheart fids and marlinspikes, parcelling, tarred twine, but if I did learn anything at all it was from what is called 'visual instruction', I suppose, for the old man would be thinking his own thoughts, and a whole morning or afternoon was likely to go by without a word from him.

Of all the sailorizing jobs, the most important, as I have said, was the setting up of the standing rigging. Before the introduction of bottle-screws, lanyards and dead-eyes was the only method (some hold that it is still the better). Tarred Italian hemp, three-stranded, was always used. Because the strands of the rope were laid-up right-handed, the lanyard had to be rove right-handed through the deadeyes so that the turns should remain in the rope; thus in the port rigging the stopper knot, a Matthew Walker, of the standing part must be at the after-hole of the upper dead-eye, becoming as it were the forward hole as the riggers progressed to the starboard side. When rove, the lanyard was set up by purchase, using two luff tackles, 'luff-upon-luff', the hauling part of the purchase being taken to the capstan and walked round by the watch until the Mate cried 'Enough!...', the judgement of that 'Enough!' being crucial, as it is in matters beside.

At length came the day when, the hundreds of blocks having been shackled on alow and aloft and the running-gear rove through them, the sails were brought on board to be bent on. For stowing below or in a sail-loft a sail is commonly made up along its longest edge, and it will be appreciated that in a lofty ship this edge or side is of goodish length. Moreover, a mainsail of the size carried by the *Czarina* weighs near a ton; so that to see a dozen men staggering on board with this long bundle of sail slung from shoulder to shoulder was likely to put one in mind of some fabulous snake of prodigious proportions and, happily, dead!

Finally – final at least of the jobs inboard – we restored the deck. Of first-quality yellow pine, a beautiful wood of close grain, each plank was thicker in depth than the side which showed. So that the deck planking might run straight for the length of the vessel from stem to stern, the planks were laid on the 'gun-stock' principle; which is to say that each outer plank was notched into the covering-board, which, outside of all, followed the curve of the ship's sides. Thus these notches in the covering-board resembled in shape a series of gun-stocks. A feature about this kind of join, by the way, is the extra wide seam, known as a 'devil', calling for extra pitch to 'pay' it with; hence the saying, 'The devil to pay and no pitch hot', of which nowadays we remember only the first half.

To bleach the deck oxalic acid was used (some yacht skippers, with a blank cheque for expenses, used lemons, by the hundredweight). Next we scrubbed and scrubbed and scrubbed, all day long, and all day long the next day until the deck was as white as a hound's tooth, as a yacht's deck should be, a pleasure to tread and a delight to the eye. And this perfection was maintained throughout the commission. In our skipper's scale of moral values a blemish on the deck was worse than a stain on the character.

The *Czarina's* fitting-out had been supervised by the two mates, both first-rate sailormen. Captain Fryer did not join until the last week, when we were giving the topsides a final coat of glossy black-enamel paint. Captain Fryer had had command deep-sea in sail. Very tall, very burly, with long grey Viking moustaches, he walked his poop to windward like a lord. In manner and character, however, he was a bully (a fact of course discovered by the crew in the first five minutes), and in his clipper ships, unrestrained by the presence of an owner, he must have been a tyrant. And there is no denying that there was some unholy gloating in the foc'sle when he put the ship ashore, which happened at Cowes, of all places, and during Cowes Week, of all times.

The weather had been wild all week, blowing from the southwest each day, near gale force at times. We got under way towards the end of the week, all the same, and under short sail stood eastward up the Solent with a party of the owner's friends on board. When the ship was put about to return to the Roads she was struck by a heavy squall. Captain Fryer luffed her hard, as he needs must do. But having very little sea-room – for we were within a biscuit-toss of the Brambles – the schooner worked to windward as she luffed in the way a smart vessel will, and in far less time than it takes to tell she ran hard on the shingle with a jar that nearly whipped the masts out of her. In five minutes the squall passed, exposing us to the view of all Cowes.

Helped by a rising tide, the tugs had her off not many hours later, but for days afterwards the old man was like a raging lion.

Many thanks to Jennifer Scott-Hughes, daughter-in-law of John Scott-Hughes.

STORM IN THE ATLANTIC

Scott Cookman

Atlantic: The Last Great Race of Princes

Wiley & Sons 2002

The 1905 Transatlantic Race was not the first such event, but it set the standards. Earlier competitions had come and gone, but it was 1905 that produced the weather, the yacht and the man.

Wilson Marshall's schooner Atlantic *and her captain Charlie Barr will be remembered long after her owner is forgotten. They made the passage from Sandy Hook to The Lizard in 12 days and 4 hours at an average of 10.32 knots, a record that stood unchallenged until very recently. But there was a lot more to this race than Barr. A precedent was created that obliged owners to be on board rather than leaving the actual passage to their paid crews and 'hired gun' skippers. Originally promoted by Sir Thomas Lipton, it was hijacked by Kaiser Wilhelm of Germany in search of prestige on the high seas. To Kaiser Bill's frustration, the top German entry* Hamburg *came in* second, but 11 yachts started and finished. These included the 'tiny' 108ft Burgess-designed schooner Fleur de Lys, owned by the aristocratic New York surgeon, Lewis A Stimson, and crewed for the event by fishermen from Gloucester, Massachusetts, under the redoubtable Captain Bohlin. Together with his guests and notably his daughter Candace, Stimson took far more part in the race than most of the gentlemen.

In his book Atlantic (published in the United States by Wiley), Scott Cookman describes the events and history with swashbuckling gusto and scholarly accuracy. His work is required reading for all who love the sea. Below are two extracts from the race itself.

THE storm struck *Fleur de Lys* 500 miles due east of St. John's, Newfoundland. They were passing to the north of the Flemish Cap, easternmost thumb on the outstretched palm of the Newfoundland fishing banks, just after midnight on May 25. The light southeast breeze carrying them suddenly vanished, the way a ship's cat did when frightened. In its place, a fresh breeze (17 to 21 knots) commenced blowing out of the northeast. To fishermen like Captain Bohlin and his crew, it stank: like seasick vomit, bilge water, kerosene lamps. Any easterly wind in those latitudes generally brought heavy weather, and hell with it. Generally, the harder it blew, the bigger the hell it was bringing and the faster it would arrive. This one came in screaming. It intensified hourly: strengthening at first into a strong northeast wind (22 to 27 knots) that raised seas into rank after rank of drenching, oncoming 13-foot waves, then morphing into a near gale that moaned through the rigging and brought 20-foot breakers out of the darkness.

By 3.00 a.m. it was blowing force 9: a violent gale strong enough to flatten fences, strip shingles off roofs and branches from trees; driving waves 2½ stories high at *Fleur,* and turning the night white with spindrift. Bohlin fought it, stubbornly reefing but not hauling down canvas, attempting to hold as close to his racing course as he could. But little *Fleur* was soon taking such a brutal pounding that even Tommie Bohlin finally threw in his hand. Conditions had to be life-threatening for him to do that. A wall back at Gloucester City Hall was inscribed, like a war memorial, with names of Gloucestermen lost in battle with the sea. On average, thirty-two new townsmen's names, painfully fresh, went up every year. None of them, pridefully, were Bohlin's crew. He knew in the soles of his boots when the limit had been reached. He hauled down the mainsail, set the outer jib and trysail, and hove to.

The gale raged all day. And the next day. And the day after, but Bohlin didn't remain hove to for long. As soon as the wind hauled around to the northwest, though still blowing up to 40 knots, with 22-foot following seas, he steelily upped the mainsail and foresail again. Kiting along, rolling and plunging, *Fleur* logged 242 miles that day, averaging 10 knots, her best speed so far. But it was a very rough, dangerous ride. Little *Fleur*, the shortest, narrowest, lightest vessel in the race, with less keel under her than any other, took a bone-rattling beating.

It got much worse on May 27. The northwest wind strengthened again from a gale to a strong gale; howling at a sustained 47 knots, with gusts exceeding 55 knots. 'Sea is very heavy,' Bohlin scribbled in his noon log entry. 'The main boom goes into the slings often, for half its length. Lee side often full above the main ropes. Helmsman has been lashed [to the wheel] now two days.' Shortly after noon, the wind carried away *Fleur*'s jib. At dusk it ripped the big foresail off its boom. At 9.00 p.m. the following seas began breaking over the port quarter and sweeping the decks, but 'Cap'n Tommie' was bronco-busting before the wind, under double-reefed sail, at up to 14 knots.

The boat was under the crest of the huge wave surging in off the port beam – not the stern quarter – before anyone fairly saw it. It smashed into the main rigging like a landslide, knocking *Fleur* on her beam ends and burying the boat in black water. All four seamen on watch forward were washed aft to the mainsheet, gouged by every chock, cleat, and hatchway on deck and knocked senseless. They were stopped from washing overboard only because they were hurled square into the quartermaster and the first mate lashed to the helm.

Bohlin was on deck before *Fleur* recovered, stepping on bodies to grab the wheel. All hands, including the cook and the steward, scrambled on deck to bring the boat under control while Dr. Stimson and his male guest dragged the injured below. All six men were in shock, retching salt water and bleeding profusely. Candace Stimson draped them in comforters she ripped from the bunks of the guest staterooms. Her father, who was one of the finest trauma surgeons of his day, went to work, his daughter assisting. One seaman was coughing blood: most of the ribs on the right side of his chest were broken. Two had multiple cuts and gashes, some requiring up to thirty stitches apiece to close. The other three had severe lacerations and contusions. Dr. Stimson patched them up, made his way topside on the rolling, wave-washed deck, and shouted Bohlin the news: six hands down, half of *Fleur*'s crew.

It did not seem to alarm him. 'Hell, Doctor,' he shouted back, 'their wives whip 'em worse than that at home.'

With *Fleur* back under control, hammering before the gale under reefed sail and still logging 12 knots or more, he was in his element. His Gloucestermen would bounce back. Until they did, Dr. Stimson told him, he and his guests would stand their watches, while Candace stood hers at the helm.

The same violent storm struck all six leading yachts in the race on May 25, including the *Atlantic*. By 4.00 p.m. conditions were so awful that Barr hauled down every stitch of canvas but fore and mizzen trysails. Under these bare storm sails, he continued driving *Atlantic* before the gale at 11 knots, taking a brutal beating. Throughout the first watch that night (8.00 p.m. to 12.00 a.m.), he logged that the vessel 'rolled violently.' The world's foremost yacht racing skipper didn't use that kind of phrase lightly. If Barr called it violent, it was horrifically so. He made the same notation at the end of the middle watch (12.00 a.m. to 4.00 a.m.), again at the end of the morning watch (4.00 a.m. to 8.00 a.m.), and again at the end of the forenoon watch (8.00 a.m. to noon). He never left the deck.

The crew had then been battling the gale for some thirty-three consecutive hours. They had made sixteen sail changes in that time; repaired and reset *Atlantic*'s raffee; rigged and tended four oil bags; worked pumps to rid the ship of water; and been knocked nine ways to Sunday standing watch in pile-driving seas and spindrift so blinding they could scarcely see. They couldn't keep it up much longer. Despite oilskins and boots, they were soaked through and shaking. With the air temperature at 50°F and a 40-mile-per-hour gale raging, the wind-chill on deck was a subfreezing 26°F.

The owner Wilson Marshall and his guests hadn't bargained on anything remotely like it. Below decks, where they'd been the entire time, everything was amplified and made worse by the fact that they couldn't see what was going on. They could hear the wind screaming at the *Atlantic*'s long masts and heavy spars. The breaking seas thudded against the thin deck above their heads like a besieging army pounding to get in. Leaks had sprung everywhere; jets of black water spurting in from boarded-over skylights and portholes, parted seams and battened hatches and doors. The saloon was ankle-deep in sloshing sea. Almost all the hanging lamps had shattered and gone dark.

From behind – always from behind – echoed an incredible, incessant boom. It jacked the boat up by the stern, wrenched her almost on her beam ends, and plunged her down-wave to a neck-snapping stop. Above all the terrible noises, it was the nonstop thrumming and vibration in the rigging – a devil's harp – that had Wilson Marshall shaking. The gale obviously wasn't moderating in the least. His prized *Atlantic* was being smashed. His guests were terrified. His crew was exhausted and at the breaking point. Yet Captain Barr continued to run her before the wind. It was all too much. The only reasonable thing to do was heave to and ride out the storm.

There are two starkly different accounts of what happened next. Marshall's was that Barr made his way below to see him as the gale intensified and said, 'Commodore, if we are going to lay to, we must do it now or not at all.' Reportedly Marshall looked at him thunderstruck and said, 'Captain Barr, I am racing.' Reputedly Barr's reply was 'That is all I wanted to know, sir.'

Everything screams against this account. It has Charlie Barr leaving the helm of *Atlantic* at the height of a full gale, something he had not done for two days. One can scarcely imagine him doing so unless he was ordered to, and even then reluctantly. It has the most accomplished racing skipper of the day, perhaps ever, deferring to a novice yachtsman whether or not to heave to in the middle of a transatlantic race. What's more, it has Marshall – who despite being the vessel's owner and former commodore of the Larchmont Yacht Club, was no more than a passenger aboard – insisting he's racing, which he certainly wasn't. He wasn't even on deck.

The more plausible account has Marshall popping his head out of the companionway and shouting at Barr in no uncertain or polite terms to heave to at once. Fifteen feet from his head, the lee rails of the boat were fully under water that was climbing the deck. Overhead the screech of canvas and screaming rigging was deafening. About the only intelligible utterance he could have made was an order to heave to. For Barr, lashed with his quartermaster to the wheel and fighting to hold her before the wind, it was the last straw. 'You hired me to win this race,' he shouted back, 'and that is what I intend to do.'

The fact that Charlie Barr made good on his statement in the finest of style is now embedded both in legend and history. At sea, the manic driving and competitive spirit of the race is well exemplified by this exchange, but the human comrade factor, the reaction of lesser mortals than Barr, is best captured by the closing words of the chapter:

After crossing the finish line, all the yachts continued past the dangerous rocks at the Lizard and skirted the wild Cornish coast up the English Channel, coming to anchor in the Solent between Southampton and Cowes. It was the first time most of them had laid eyes on each other since leaving Sandy Hook. When they did, a remarkable thing happened.

As *Ailsa* sailed up Southampton water, a sailor aloft in the foremast of *Hildegarde* made her out and hailed the deck. 'By the time we had got abreast of her,' Stevenson, a journalist on board, wrote, 'all hands had lined up along her starboard rail. Caps and yells filled the air till we had passed by and edged up on *Endymion*, who repeated the honor.' Anchoring well up in the harbor alongside *Sunbeam*, the spontaneous salute was repeated and then echoed from every other racer in the fleet. It was heartfelt and universal. At that moment considerations of wealth, rank, and privilege evaporated. It was fellow sailors, after a hard-fought battle with the sea, welcoming one another home. When little *Fleur de Lys* limped in she looked a fright. Under patched rigging and sails stood Captain Bohlin, Dr. Stimson, Candace, and her bloodied, bandaged Gloucestermen. Half-smashed dories were stacked on deck, and her pumps were discharging water over the side. A British sailor in one of the first boats that pulled aboard whistled at the damage, then saw Miss Stimson on deck and respectfully took off his cap. 'You must 'ave 'ad it something rough,' he said. Candace Stimson just smiled.

THE OLD *BRITANNIA*

Anthony Heckstall-Smith
Sacred Cowes
Allan Wingate 1955

His Majesty's Yacht Britannia *was a 102ft cutter designed by GL Watson and built in 1893 for the Prince of Wales, later Edward VII. She was radical in form, with 10,000 sq ft of sail and a spoon bow, rather than the clipper bow or straight stem generally favoured in those days. Her wholesome lines were undistorted by any rule and she proved to be one of the most successful racing yachts of all time. By the close of her 'coming-out' season she had 33 firsts from 39 starts. In her second, she won all seven big-class races on the French Riviera, before returning to trounce the 1893 America's Cup winner* Vigilant. *For years, her prize money paid for her upkeep and it soon made a measurable dent in the £10,000 she had cost to build.*

Britannia *was much loved as well as technically capable. Sailors and the common people alike adored seeing her black hull smoking by in the heavy weather she thrived on. Right into the 1930s she continued to carry home the silverware under her new owner, Edward's son George V, 'The Sailor King'. Her helmsman was often her sailing master, Sir Philip Hunloke, while Anthony Heckstall-Smith helped make up her regular afterguard. Anthony was the son of Brooke 'Bookstall' Smith, author, Editor of* Yachting World *and secretary of the Yacht Racing Association, which gave us all the International Rule and the 'metre boats'.*

In the first of these two extracts from Anthony's book Sacred Cowes, *he describes a remarkable race aboard the old yacht in the King's absence. In the second, he offers an unusual insight into the characters of the Sailor King and his Queen, as well as a priceless peep at life in Cowes with the Bright Young Things in the mad years following the First World War.*

On August 17th, in 1933, I sailed in *Britannia* at Babbacombe Regatta on a day when she defeated all her rivals that were many years her junior. I went aboard at Brixham and we sailed across Tor Bay to Babbacombe in a nice breeze, accompanied by three other yachts of the Big Class – W. L. Stephenson's *Velsheda,* Hugh Paul's *Astra,* and *Shamrock* V then owned by Tom Sopwith.

By the time we arrived at the starting line, the wind had freshened considerably and, shortly before the start, we received a signal from H.M.S. *Sutton,* our escort vessel, to say that a gale was predicted. We saw, too, that both *Velsheda* and *Shamrock* were reefing their mainsails in preparation for a blow. However, as time was short and Hugh Paul, in *Astra,* had evidently decided to carry a whole mainsail, Phil Hunloke chose not to shorten sail.

Our course was a triangular one of 45 miles – three times round three five-mile legs. By the time the starting-gun fired, ominous black clouds had rolled up over the cliffs above Babbacombe and the wind had already freshened considerably.

'We shall be for it before the day's out,' I said to Phil. And for it we certainly were!

Soon after we came onto the wind, a few seconds ahead of *Shamrock,* Phil was calling for the sheets to be eased as *Britannia* was beginning to wallow. The third leg of the course gave us a reach, with the wind a little for'ard of the beam, into the starting line. Now *Britannia* heeled to a tremendous angle with the water up the companion deck house. Phil, waist deep in water, was having difficulty steering her. Blinded by driving spray, he shouted to the second mate to give him a hand at the wheel, and called for a lashing to be tied round his waist to keep him from being swept overboard. We were travelling at fourteen knots and under the press of her whole mainsail and in the savage gusts of wind that crashed down from the high cliffs, the old yacht was practically unmanageable. Her entire lee deck was under water and her main boom, with the sheet eased, but a few inches from the water. In a cloud of flying spray, we tore through the pleasure boats, hollering at them to keep clear of us and leaving them pitching and rolling in our wake. We had to bear up to sail through the line at the end of the first round.

'She won't bear up!' Phil shouted as he and the second mate forced the wheel over, the pair of them half buried in foam. Then, with a crack, the clew of the jib carried away, mercifully easing the sorely pressed ship.

Now, our nearest rival, *Shamrock*, was minutes astern of us, so, in the gale and rising sea, Phil refrained from taking any chances and did not even set the spinnaker off the wind. Now, too, *Velsheda* and *Astra* had retired from the race; the latter having carried away most of the hanks on her mainsail.

Soon after we rounded the weather mark more than five minutes ahead of *Shamrock*, which was lying over almost on her beam ends, I saw her mast go over the side with a mighty splash. So the old *Britannia* was the only one left in the race.

'I can't give up!' Phil yelled to me above the whistle of the wind, but I knew that he was dreading that reach into Babbacombe Bay and those terrible squalls screaming down from the cliffs.

'Pray God they'll stop us at the end of this round!' I yelled back.

That second reach back to the line was a mad, thrilling nightmare. As Phil wrote of it afterwards: 'I could hardly steer her; although the mainsheet was eased right off, she kept coming up into the wind. We seemed like a toy boat which one often sees on the 'Round Pond,' and we had little more control than the owners of these models have once they have started them off on their course.'

I confess there were moments when I thought the old *Britannia* would charge on and on right up on to the beach as she tore along in a hissing white mist of spray. There were times when Phil and the second mate at the wheel, and old Albert Turner, the skipper, crouching beside them, disappeared altogether in a welter of foam that rose in great plumes from the lee rigging. Looking over the weather rail, I could see almost the whole length of *Britannia*'s copper-sheathed bottom, for in some of those wild squalls she was over on her beam ends.

I think we all must have prayed very hard that the Committee might stop the race, for as we roared through the line, the 'S' flag broke out on the Committee boat and the finishing gun fired at the same instant.

We anchored in Babbacombe Bay, and went below for a drink, and in the saloon, Phil said to me: 'You're a writer, so sit down now and write a telegram to the King at Balmoral telling him how splendidly the old boat won and how she outsailed all the young 'uns.'

Phil was enormously pleased with himself and not without reason, for never have I seen a yacht more skilfully and courageously handled than *Britannia* was that day.

I filled several of the special long white telegraph forms with my account of that race to *Britannia*'s owner. As Phil read the last page, he said: 'The Privy Purse will probably make the devil's own fuss about paying for this!'

'But think how pleased the King will be,' I said.

Phil laughed as he signed the last page. 'You're right,' he said. 'To hell with the expense!'

I think everyone – not excluding Phil Hunloke – was somewhat afraid of the King for he was a stickler for discipline, at times sharp tempered and quick to express disapproval. He was, too, old fashioned in his outlook and a stern critic of the modesty and manners of the Bright Young People who were a curious product of his reign. I remember well an occasion when, quite unwittingly, some of the prettiest and nicest girls at Cowes incurred his displeasure. Aquaplaning behind fast motor-boats was just then becoming the rage and Poppy Baring (now Mrs. Peter Thursby) and some of her friends were experts at this new and exhilarating sport. One afternoon when Queen Mary was at tea at Nubia House with Lady Baring, she heard Poppy, Lady Mainwaring and their friends discussing the thrill of riding a plank in the wake of a speedboat. Her Majesty expressed her interest and asked that when they next went aquaplaning, they should do so near the *Victoria and Albert* so that she might watch them.

The following afternoon, Poppy and Glanaris Mainwaring, looking delightful in the latest Jansen bathing dresses, sped round and round the Royal Yacht, riding the wash of a fast Garwood speedboat, called

Gee-Wiz, steered by Claude Grahame-White, while Queen Mary stood on *Victoria and Albert*'s deck waving her appreciation. But as they flashed close under the gilded stern in a cloud of flying spray, engines roaring, Lady Mainwaring espied the King looking through a porthole. That same evening, Sir Richard Williams-Burkeley, then Vice-Commodore of the R.Y.S. and Lady Mainwaring's father, received a sharp note from his Admiral expressing his disapproval of young ladies in bathing dresses performing aquabatics round the Royal Yacht, as well as his rooted dislike for noisy motor-boats whose duty it was to keep well clear of the *Victoria and Albert* at all times.

Some days later, when Sir Harry and Lady Mainwaring were dining aboard the *Victoria and Albert*, the King referred to the incident again and it was evident from his remarks that not even Queen Mary had dared to tell him that the 'disgraceful exhibition' had taken place at her command.

Except in the finest weather, Queen Mary did not like the sea. She was a poor sailor and inclined to be nervous when *Britannia* heeled over at a steep angle in a fresh wind. But, possibly because he believed that his people enjoyed seeing the Queen racing, the King sometimes insisted that she should accompany him. This he did in the summer of 1923 when he visited the Clyde regattas on the thirtieth anniversary of the launching of *Britannia*. Throughout the whole of the two weeks of the Royal visit, the weather had been wild. But one morning conditions had sufficiently improved for Her Majesty to sail in *Britannia*. Soon after the start of the race, however, storm clouds rolled down from the mountains surrounding the Firth and wild squalls of rain and wind swept the Clyde. Half way round the course, when the crew were fighting to lower the jib-topsail in the rising wind, the sheet of this sail ran out and the sail itself flew out to leeward like a huge kite at the end of the flailing wire that lashed about wildly, threatening to decapitate everyone who tried to recover it. The Queen, who had been sheltering in the deckhouse, had gone below to the ladies' cabin, where the noise and confusion over her head must have been alarming. My father, who was aboard at the time, said that everyone was fearful for the King's safety, since nothing Hunloke or anyone else could say would stop him working with the crew to recover the jib-topsail sheet. When finally, with the yacht close-hauled, the sail was secured, the King said to Hunloke: 'Send someone below to find out how the Queen is.' One of the hands dived down the companionway. A few minutes later, he returned on deck and came face to face with the King. 'Well, how is Her Majesty?' he asked.

Flustered, the man pulled off his sou'wester.

'Well, what did she say?' the King shouted above the whistle of the wind. 'Speak up!'

'Her Majesty said, "Never again, she's d****d if she will,"' the sailor stammered, to the huge delight of his master.

A ROUGH RIDE IN THE DOVER STRAIT

DR Collins
Sailing in Helen
Edward Arnold 1947

Nautical literature never ceases to surprise, with Sailing in Helen *by Mr DR Collins a notable example. I found a copy of this obscure, slim volume in an antiquarian bookstore in the summer of 2012. Previously having been unaware of its existence, I read it from cover to cover and had a day of pure joy. The author is a young man in the 1930s who has a few pounds and an ailing hair-cream business. His heart just isn't in his work and, in a moment of optimism, he buys the ancient 10-ton yawl* Helen. *She is too big and he can't afford to run her, but neither he nor his readers are disappointed as he makes his early forays to sea. Later in the book, he gives up work as a bad job and heads off on an abortive trip to Madeira. His crew are gloriously decadent – 'The Colonel' eats only nuts and raisins, which he ships in a huge trunk*

*lashed to the foredeck, while Alex is a Russian ne'er-do-well who has
spent most of his life in jail.*

*Like Collins' business efforts to date, this trip too is a failure, yet the
man's spirit is indomitable. Destitute, owning nothing but his tiny yacht,
he is loaned a room in Sussex and a 9ft x 4ft shed. Here, financed by a
£50 overdraft from Barclays, he makes and markets products he modestly
describes as 'scent' under the name of Goya. After the war, 'scent' became
'perfume' and the rest is history.*

*We now join him and two friends on his first 'foreign' venture. Helen
has made it to Calais. It's Easter and, as so often happens to those of us
who like to make an early start in our annual plans, it is blowing great
guns and they are surrounded by Job's comforters. Undeterred, they press
on out to sea, homeward bound in weather that should have kept them on
the mooring shelling their festive eggs. Collins' handling of an ugly decision
as Dover is approached gives us a hint of the man he was to become, while
the black comedy of the arrival in Ramsgate shows just how far he had
still to go.*

ON Easter Monday it was blowing a gale from the south-west. In
talking or writing about sailing most people exaggerate bad weather
and, unless you know the person concerned, you have no idea whether
his idea of gales coincides with your own, or with the official definition.
This really was a gale, force seven, with gusts up to force eight, on the
Beaufort Scale. We checked it with the Air Ministry by telephone when
we were back in London.

We had definitely decided to return to Dover that day, but the wind
whistling through the shrouds, a black, wild sky, and the miniature
breaking seas inside the harbour caused the inevitable conference of doubt.
The main snags were that we did not know how hard it would be blowing
outside and that, because I had no real idea how sound *Helen* was, I had no
clue about how much bad weather she would stand without breaking up.
I remembered an awful story the owner of *Diana*, a fifteen-ton converted
smack, had told me about a passage from Boulogne to Ramsgate. One of
the waterline planks had sprung away from the stem for a distance of about
eight feet. He had stuffed the hole with mattresses and completed the trip
in a waterlogged condition. The yacht was probably a good deal younger
than *Helen*, whose age I had not then been able to discover.

Looking back, I can now see that the most valid reason for not attempting the crossing was my own lack of experience, but in my ignorance I did not doubt my ability to muddle through, and neither, apparently, did Buzz or James. Had I been more experienced, it would certainly not have occurred to me to sail.

In the middle of our pyjama-clad discussion over breakfast in the cabin we heard the swish of a passing yacht. I looked out to see a white twelve-tonner, close reefed and with storm jib set, running out towards the entrance. The incident decided us. If she could manage the trip then so could we. Breakfast and dressing were hurriedly completed. James wedged everything movable down below securely in position, whilst Buzz and I put storm lashings on the mizzen, which I did not propose to use, and tied down two reefs in the mainsail. I had no storm jib, so we reefed and lashed down the staysail in order that it could quickly be set if my number two jib carried away. A phrase that I had read in some square-rigged book kept running through my head – 'blew right out of the bolt ropes.'

At this period of her career and for another year or two, until I got quite brave about throwing iron over the side, *Helen* was very over-ballasted. She was admittedly very stiff, but she behaved in a seaway rather like the proverbial half-tide rock. A previous owner, I was informed, was very keen on ballast and had made a practice of adding a hundredweight or two each year. Her freeboard forward was about two feet, but it tapered away to no more than a few inches aft.

In the midst of our preparations for sea we were hailed by a woman standing on the deck of a motor yacht anchored quite close. 'Are you thinking of going out ?'

'Yes.'

'My husband's just been ashore to see the harbour master. He says that once you're clear of the lee of Gris Nez the seas will be too bad for a small ship.'

'Thanks awfully, I think we'll just see what it's like.'

'Please don't.'

I gave her a cheery wave to terminate the conversation. It was very nice of her to be concerned but at the time I was inclined to resent an additional element of doubt being introduced to my vacillating mind. We were just beginning to shorten in the anchor chain when the white twelve-tonner came in again. It was another mental setback.

'What's it like outside?' I shouted as she sailed past.

'Bloody awful.'

There followed five more minutes of indecision before we agreed that, as we were all set, we might just as well have a sail and see what it was like outside. We could always run in again, or else go along the coast to Dunkirk.

Up came the anchor, inches deep in the most filthy black slime. It was quickly lashed down, there was no need to wash it off; the Channel would do that job for us. We hoisted the jib, it flapped and kicked heavily for a few seconds before *Helen* came round and we were racing between the piers to the sea.

As soon as we were clear of the harbour the wind set up an appalling howl in the rigging and drummed in our ears. For the first few miles the seas were not bad. We were certainly getting very wet but nothing heavy came on board. Half an hour after we sailed I went below to set a course, it was work that would have been better done before we started. I was just beginning to feel extremely sick in the muggy atmosphere of the cabin when there was a terrific roar of breaking water and *Helen* lurched far over to starboard. I looked up apprehensively and saw the light blotted out to a dim green as a whole sea broke over the ship. Water poured through from cockpit to cabin. I rushed up, half expecting to find one of the other two had been swept away, but luckily they had been able to hang on and were smiling through the water pouring off their heads and oilskins. I abandoned all attempts at navigation and took over the tiller.

Buzz started working *Helen's* back-breaking, up-and-down, old pump. There was water over the cabin floor but I did not know how much of it had come in via the cockpit or how much she was leaking. I kept on thinking of how little freeboard she had aft. It could not be more than eight or nine inches and there was already that depth of water sloshing about below. We took it in turns to pump, but about forty-eight strokes was all any of us could manage at a time. Our backs ached, our hands blistered, we felt sick. We never succeeded in reducing the level to below the floorboards until we were nearly in port, but at least we were holding our own.

In spite of the force of the wind it turned out to be a glorious day. Bright sunshine set off the magnificence and beauty of the roaring crested seas, and as we got further and further across the cheerfulness of achievement caused us to forget our earlier uneasiness. I had not sufficient knowledge to work out mentally the tide so I steered in the general direction of Dover and hoped for the best. About three and a half hours after leaving Calais we were again swept and drenched by an entire sea breaking over the ship. Nothing carried away. *Helen* staggered, the lower part of her mainsail filled with water, but she rapidly recovered, and seemed to shake herself free of the weight that was trying to pin her down.

Soon after the second real drenching we sighted the South Goodwin light vessel away on the starboard bow, so we brought her up onto the wind and found she would just lay the course for Dover. Half an hour later, about three miles from Dover breakwater, the position did not look quite so cheerful. The seas were breaking right across the south entrance and I did not look forward to the prospect of sailing through; the risk of being swept onto the lee breakwater was too great. The eastern entrance was almost equally impracticable, for I would have to beat through it and then face a dead beat across a mile of open harbour to the dock entrance. She might have done it, but it was blowing extremely hard and the consequences of missing stays in the entrance would probably have been conclusive, so I decided to square away and run for Ramsgate. I had never been there before and had no chart of the place, but Dover was clearly impossible.

We were soon in the lee of the South Foreland and the fair wind, after having sailed close-hauled, gave us the usual impression that its strength was less. I remembered having read that there was a large area of soft mud in the middle of Ramsgate harbour and that there were often boatmen available who would run a line out to a buoy for incoming yachts. It hardly seemed likely that anyone would be sculling around in that wind, so, before we got in, I asked Buzz to go forward and get the anchor ready.

As we approached the stone piers, Buzz was prepared to anchor, to take in the jib, or to pass a line to a boatman if one was available. We shot in between the Bank-holiday-tripper-laden piers at a frightening speed and I was amazed to see a boatman within a few yards of a succulent-looking mooring buoy. I shot *Helen* up into the wind and yelled to Buzz to take in the jib and pass the man a line. Buzz misunderstood and started letting go the anchor. I couldn't leave the tiller in case *Helen* fell off the wind and sailed into the mudbank, but, in the din of whistling wind and flapping banging canvas, Buzz heard my frantic shouts. He stopped veering cable and sprang to the jib halyard, placing his foot inside the coil on deck as he did so. The sail came half down and filled, blowing off to starboard; Buzz was pulled off his feet by the tangled coil. I left the tiller to run forward and give him a hand, but *Helen* payed off and started sailing smartly at the waiting boatman. It looked for a minute as if we were going to ram and sink him, but James shoved the tiller down just in time and the man ran a line to the buoy for us. The passage had taken just under six hours.

Back in London I discovered that, apart from one fifty-ton motor yacht, *Helen* was the only boat to cross the channel that Easter Monday. As there were between twenty and thirty English yachts in Calais and Dunkirk it was a great triumph for the old boat. I was very pleased, later on, to see in the *Yachting World* a photograph of *Helen* 'putting out alone.'

I had arranged with another friend to come down to *Helen* for the following week-end. He telephoned me on Tuesday and said, 'I suppose we'll go over to Calais by steamer and fetch her back.'

'No,' I replied. 'Ramsgate by train.'

A RACING BET

Rayner and Wykes
The Great Yacht Race
Peter Davies 1966

On 11 December 1866, the 200-ton schooners Fleetwing, Vesta *and* Henrietta *took the starting gun off Sandy Hook, New York, to race to the Isle of Wight across the winter North Atlantic. All three were crewed entirely by professionals. The only owner on board was James Gordon Bennett the younger, son of the newspaper tycoon. The race was born out of a drunken argument in a New York club over the relative merits of centre board and deep-keeled yachts. The two young playboys who owned the shoal-draughted* Vesta *and the powerful, heavy-displacement* Fleetwing *each bet $30,000 that his yacht would beat the other across the Atlantic. Sitting quietly in the corner was Bennett, who asked humbly if the other two might accept a further $30,000 in the pot if he were to enter his* Henrietta *in what had become a serious challenge. The two promptly agreed, because it was well accepted that while their yachts were the fliers of their day,* Henrietta *was slow but steady. As it turned out, they reckoned without Bennett's superior experience as a yachtsman. Realising*

that this was no ordinary event, Bennett invited his skipper to stand down for the duration and hired Captain Samuels, late of the Black Ball Line North Atlantic packet clipper Dreadnought, *to drive his yacht. Samuels'* Dreadnought *had set the Atlantic record for a sailing vessel of 12 days to Liverpool. He turned out to be the key factor.*

The race was run in heavy, largely fair winds. The hard-bitten professionals managed well, but tragedy stalked this ill-found enterprise in the form of a typical mid-Atlantic winter storm. We join the Henrietta *in the calm before the madness began. Much of the narration on board Bennett's vessel is thanks to Stephen Fisk, a reporter sent on board by Gordon Bennett the elder to make sure nothing was missed when he published the story after the event. Fisk was keen to sail and had been obliged to sidestep a subpoena to a court hearing by smuggling himself aboard in a champagne case. Such was the spirit of the day.*

A BOVE all things, Captain Samuels knew the sea. He had learned his lessons the hard way and was never caught with too much sail set in an untimely storm. In the race, however, a certain amount of caution had to be sacrificed. In trimming *Henrietta* for the storm Captain Samuels had reefed right down: he had left only a double-reefed foresail and a fore staysail – the ultimate storm canvas for a schooner before the gaff sail was taken in and a trysail set so that the ship could be brought head to wind to heave to. But this was a perfectly judged trimming. *Henrietta* kept going: two hundred fragile tons against the tremendous swell whipped up by the north-west winds of the past two days, which was now meeting the new seas being driven up from the south-west by the storm. In the heart of the conflict between the two opposing seas she rode on. Huge cliffs of water formed as giant waves met. The cliffs stood poised above her, shutting out the world, then came crashing down. Broached again and again beneath the seas the little ship remained buoyant, driving on under her sparse canvas as the wind tore through the shrouds and she was hurled up the slopes of waves that towered over her highest spars.

'On deck,' Fisk wrote, 'even in the early part of the storm, which hit us about 4 p.m., the driving rain and spray enclosed us completely like a watery curtain. But soon it seemed that we were driving *through* the sea rather than over it. It was hard to understand how any vessel could endure the tremendous walls of ocean that fell upon us. Below, the servants were hurled about as if shot from great catapults. Those of the guests who were in their berths could only cling like grim death to the sides to prevent themselves being dashed to the cabin floor, which was awash with the seas that had seeped in and which no doubt would have flooded us out had Captain Samuels not had the foresight to have holes bored in the floor to drain them away.'

Even for a short while such conditions must have been unpleasant if not alarming, though Fisk says that 'everyone was good humoured'. One of the gentlemen kept all who would or could listen amused with an ebullient narrative concerned largely with Josie Wood and Madame Restall, with his horseracing ventures built up as a background. Stories about well-favoured madams and high-class abortionists were probably just the right sort of diversion for lightening the tensions of an Atlantic storm, although there was certainly no neglect of the ship by Captain Samuels or any of his crew in consequence. They all spent, according to Fisk, 'a very jolly day despite the increasing danger'.

But the storm continued hour after hour, its force increasing rather than diminishing. All that could be done to trim the ship for her battle had been done. If there were faults in her design or construction they could not long remain unrevealed; but any such revelation could hardly be less than disastrous.

At 8.40 p.m. 'we were boarded', says Captain Samuels with characteristic understatement, 'by a very heavy sea over the quarter, completely burying us, filling the foresail and stoving in the ship's boat'.

This was in fact so heavy a sea that the yacht canted right over and her upper shrouds went under. Fisk says, 'The groaning of timbers was like the fearsome shrieks of some demented soul in the depths of the ocean. Everything not lashed or fixed fell and rattled about in the ship like dice in a box. Crockery that was not in racks smashed all round us. We ourselves were flung to our backs – at least, I was, having no handhold of anything – and were suddenly looking at a vertical cabin floor, with spikes and paraphernalia rattling against an equally vertical *ceiling*. It was the first time the ship had canted over so far and not an experience I would care to repeat, though I suppose all true sailors must know it well and consider it an experience to be treated with nonchalance.'

When Samuels went on deck he found that the storm had increased in violence. He made up his mind. The ship could no longer be driven through the storm. He gave the order to heave to. Fisk said that the operation of fetching the storm trysails from the cabin and laying the ship's head to the wind under close canvas reminded him of the bringing forth of a pall for a funeral. 'A pause in a race like this seemed like the burial of all our hopes. Nevertheless it was some consolation to be informed by Captain Samuels that in his thirty years' experience he had never seen a vessel that could face such a gale so long, and it was charitable to hope that our rivals were having better weather than ourselves. Once hove to, the yacht rocked lazily and pleasantly; the waves rushed and the winds howled fast, but did not disturb her.'

It is sad but true that in such circumstances once a ship heaves to she tends to stay rocking lazily and pleasantly, making no progress at all. And it was so in this case. By midnight the gale had died and the sky was clear and bright with moonlight. But not until six the following morning was *Henrietta* under way again; and not until nine could Samuels write in his log, 'Freshening wind, ship beginning to step off again, set squaresail'.

George Osgood's *Fleetwing*, though 120 miles to the south of *Henrietta*, was lashed by the same storm. Captain Thomas was as well prepared as Captain Samuels and by four o'clock in the afternoon he too had reduced his canvas to a double reefed foresail and fore staysail.

Fleetwing, true, was a more powerful and slightly heavier yacht than *Henrietta* (230 as against 205 tons); but this would not have made a great deal of difference against the battering of such tremendous seas. Also, she and her crew had had to press on through a longer spell of bad weather than had her rivals, so far; she had lost her jib-boom early in the race; one member of the crew (Sean Kelly) suffered a minor injury; and the pumps had had to be brought into action to drain her flooded cockpit. And Ernest Staples had felt gloomy about their inability to hold divine service on Sunday through press of weather – 'which might have obviated our later troubles'. Whether it would have done so is conjectural; but there is no doubt that the later troubles now hit them.

At 9 p.m., twenty minutes after *Henrietta* was boarded by that giant wave that buried her completely, a similar huge sea hit *Fleetwing*. The watch was at that time in the cockpit – six of them sheltering on the weather side and two forcibly holding the helm under control. The deluge crashed down upon the forward part of the ship and swept all eight of them overboard. Peter Wood and Thomas Hazleton, the two men at the helm, summoned up the strength to keep their grasp of the wheel's spokes. But the sea defeated them. They were washed astern as the sea crashed over the ship, each still clutching the spokes that had been wrenched from their sockets.

There must have been cries of alarm and despair, but these would have been inaudible in the shrieking wind and the crash of the sea hitting the ship. Ernest Staples, who gives a retrospective account of the disaster, says, 'I was below at the time, lighting my pipe and talking – shouting were the better word in that great gale – to Captain Thomas. We heard and felt the great concussion caused by the striking of the sea and rushed on deck with all the speed the shuddering of the ship allowed. The sight which met our view was a most affecting one. The cockpit, which but a few minutes before we had seen filled with the watch, was now clean swept of every living soul, and the deck and pit, from the main rigging aft, completely covered with water.'

Under the weight of the sea the ship had keeled over until her upper shrouds were covered. But she did not capsize. As soon as she had righted herself Captain Thomas gave the order to heave to. The watch below came quickly on deck and every possible effort was made to recover the lost men. Miraculously, two of them had managed to lay hold of the trysail as they were swept from the cockpit; the sail had come adrift and they were perilously suspended over the side of the ship with the sea threatening to beat them to death against the hull. But with a tremendous effort and some astonishing acrobatics the rescuers managed to haul them aboard. They were Pieters, a Dutchman, and Smith, a nondescript. For what it was worth in the continuing pitching of the ship in the unabating storm, they were given brandy and extra blankets and told to dry out before the stove in the cabin. Their rescuers, plus the officers and guests aboard *Fleetwing,* then spent the next five hours hove to and searching, by means of such storm-lanterns and lifelines as they could muster, for the remaining six men. In vain. Peter Wood, Thomas Hazleton, Sean Kelly, Patrick McCormick, Matthew Brown, and the negro Lincoln Massy, were lost. Massy's jeremiads after the loss of *Fleetwing*'s jib-boom may have been depressing. Captain Thomas was certainly right to stifle them before they depressed everyone aboard and jeopardized the stimulus the race demanded. But they had proved to be prophetic. And now, with six men and five precious hours lost, *Fleetwing*'s sails were bent and she started off again. Ironically, the storm had died with the men. The sky had cleared, the sea had fallen; there were stars and a moderate breeze as she gathered speed at 2 a.m. on Thursday, 20 December, changed her course to north-east, and ran off before the wind.

Amazingly, one might say miraculously without risk of exaggerating, the three hard-driven schooners made landfall off the Bishop Rock on Christmas Eve and brought up off Cowes within around 12 hours of one another. Henrietta *won the race, flashing past the Needles shortly before sunset on Christmas Day, her blue lights and rockets signalling her arrival off the Royal Yacht Squadron in the early evening.* Fleetwing, *followed by* Vesta, *anchored in the small hours of Boxing Day.* Henrietta's *time was a remarkable 13 days, 22 hours and 46 minutes. It was not until 1905 that another Yankee schooner, the* Atlantic *under the legendary Captain Charlie Barr, was to better this with a run of 12 days and 4 hours in the rather more official Kaiser's Cup Transatlantic Race (see pages 25–30).*

The so-called 'Great Yacht Race' had shown that a big centre-boarder could hold her own with deep-keeled craft. It made young James Gordon Bennett a fortune in wager money and cemented the reputation of Captain Samuels, but the price paid in human life was shocking. The celebrations and general bonhomie among the gentlemen with scant regard for the poor lost sailors and their families as described in Rayner and Wykes' book can only be described as disturbing to a modern reader. Little seems to have been said at the time, but history indicates that the greatest lesson learned from this race should have been obvious before it ever happened. The North Atlantic in winter is not a playground, especially for young gentlemen who do not care to sail it themselves, preferring to send their paid crews to hazard their lives in pursuit of another man's wager.

EMERGENCY

Stranded! Martyn Sherwood

Dire straits aloft Frank Mulville

Desperate driving Erling Tambs

STRANDED!

Martyn Sherwood
The Voyage of the Tai-Mo-Shan
Rupert Hart-Davis 1957

In February 1933, the engineless 54ft ketch Tai-Mo-Shan *was driven ashore on Crooked Island in the Bahamas where recent tidal waves and hurricanes had washed away most sources of sustenance and income, and where mechanised assistance was not to be had.*

The boat was on the way home to England from China. Her crew were four young officer submariners and a surgeon-lieutenant of the Royal Navy, all on a hard-argued, half-pay sabbatical from the Admiralty. The story of the stranding is a typical one from the days of vessels powered by sail alone, with high-calibre seamen forced into a bad decision by abnormal circumstances. Anchored on what unkindly turned into a lee shore in darkness, they attempted to beat clear of the unlit anchorage, but missed stays after touching the sandy bottom at the critical moment.

Her rescue is a fine example of the pre-war 'can-do' attitude in circumstances where, to quote Martyn Sherwood, the MO and writer, 'owing to the extreme poverty of the natives, little help, other than plenty of manual labour, could be expected from them'. When we join them, the

9ft-draught yacht has already spent nearly a fortnight lying on her bilge up the beach. The crew and the local villagers are poised for a desperate final effort to heave her off.

*T*HURSDAY *22 February 1933*
Today we started with high hopes, three jacks and a number of rollers and planks. Now the evening has arrived, we are still here, ready for bed and talking over ways and means to defeat these confounded sand-flies. We started off this morning by placing all three jacks under her stern, in order to lift her sufficiently to get a roller and skids under her keel. This entailed setting them in position within a very confined area between the rudder and the ship's bottom, with water frequently washing over our heads. The rollers under the bilge were easier. The skids were two-inch planks placed fore-and-aft under the rollers, preventing them from sinking into the sand.

We then set two of the jacks up against the stern and, with the help of the villagers, screwed up on them while hauling on a purchase attached to hawsers. These ran out via a cable to our anchors. The hawser was soon bar taut and we waited anxiously for the jacks to reveal a sign of motion. The long line of natives who stretched away up the beach past our encampment kept a steady strain on the hawser. Suddenly laughter rang out; these natives had fallen to the ground as the hawser came home with a run. Examination detected a broken link in the cable. We rejoined the cable with a shackle and off we started again. If only she would lift up on the rollers, she had to go!

We waited impatiently during the overhauling of the purchase. The villagers, feeling the effects of the hot sun, were beginning to take less interest in the proceedings. Their efforts suffered in consequence. The wind also determined to defeat our optimism and began to freshen from seaward. Another pull, another sickening wrench, and again a slackening of everything. This time a seven-inch hawser had parted. This capped our efforts, and we decided to talk over our next step. Meanwhile, on the 'blind' or seaward side of the boat, a dozen men were given the job of prizing under the keel. This entailed getting the point of a long pole under the keel and then, by sitting along its length, assisting the jacks to lift. They were sitting in a row, obviously blessing their luck at having such an easy number, when, with a loud snap, the pole broke in two and all of them were flung ignominiously into the sea. 'Out of sight, out of mind' was never more applicable, for until the dripping figures began to appear one by one around the stern, we had forgotten their presence. They all laughed; everybody does, here!

Before going to bed to-night we have decided to enlist the help of the captain of the local schooner *Louise*, offering him a sum to get her off in twenty-four hours. He seems a good fellow and well able to take charge of the native labour. To somebody's plaintive cry of 'Mind my fingers, boss,' he replied, 'Why? You've plenty more!'

Friday, 23rd February
Captain Collie of the *Louise* got busy early. The plan was to haul *Tai-Mo-Shan*'s bow round instead of trying to heave her off stern first, as we have been attempting until now. By about noon he had the bow well jacked up and several rollers and skids under the foremost end of the keel. He also placed two jacks under her port bow to help push it to seaward. She was listed heavily to port, but the weather luckily has remained fine and the sea calm.

Despite repeated haulings we did not get the initial start on her, though the jacks have moved her bow slightly to seaward. Two anchors were laid out on the starboard bow, the inner end of the cable being joined to the purchase by the remains of the seven-inch hawser. This again parted.

It is now 9 p.m. and all is quiet except for the chirping of crickets in the bush behind this camp. A bright moon lights up our boat lying on her side some twenty yards from where I am stretched out on the sand, with an oil lamp to enable me to write up this diary. It is high tide at 1 a.m. and all the men are to be here by then.

Saturday, 24th February
I am extremely glad, as, indeed, we all are, that as I write at 1 p.m. the bow no longer points up the beach but inclines slightly out to sea. The raucous shout of Ben Gibson, a huge native, 'O.K. Haul away' is drifting into my tent, a true indication of the spirit of confidence which has taken possession of everyone.

The excited chatter of the women makes concentration difficult, while the men all have that 'I-told-you-so' air, even though they have been here since one o'clock this morning. High tide was at about 3.30 a.m. and by 2.30 we were getting ready for it. The men pulled with a good will, but despite the tackle which we used to get the maximum results, we were getting pretty desperate by 5 a.m.

'Can we move that bow?'

'No, sir!'

We decide to keep on for a few more minutes. The marvellous happens. She starts. No, it can't be true! Must be the dawn deceiving us. We lean a stick against the port bow, a few inches protruding above the gunwale. Can it be true that those inches are decreasing? Let's move nearer for a clearer view in this cursed half-light. I wish that man would pull on this rope instead of cursing us. My fingers ache and feel as though I can never straighten them again. I wish I had not cursed Arthur, the cook, for being late this morning. He is next to me on the rope. He eyes me furtively, rather sulkily, but he too is pulling, pulling.

I hear Philip's voice somewhere at the back, 'One, two, six, HAUL AWAY!' I didn't know he could raise such a roar; I see George's scarlet sweater over Arthur's shoulder moving forward, backward, forward, backward. A shout, a cheer, as the stick falls. 'She moves!' is shouted by everyone. 'Hold it and rest,' shouts Captain Collie...

As the tide ebbs, this potential breakthrough is brought to a halt, and little progress is made for the remainder of Saturday. Sunday passes in further frustration as the anchors, laboriously laid to seaward, consistently fail to hold. Finally, they are relaid far out among some rocks with the aid of a borrowed extra cable. Here, they conveniently become immovably foul.

Monday, 26th February

I have been sleeping at the village, where I usually walk with Ben Gibson. He is a great hulking man, rather morose, who needs careful handling. However, he is a polite host, though he always manages a request for a gift of food or rope.

We have had wonderful moonlit nights, and trudging through the sand with weary feet, I have been refreshed by the absolute beauty of the evenings. The starlit sky and silvery sea, the long stretch of yellow sand and the palm-trees silhouetted against the sky make a scene which the most matter-of-fact person could not fail to note.

Each evening I would stop at Ben's house and smoke a cigarette, while one of his daughters was sent to get two glasses of water. This water is a great delicacy, as a tidal wave had sent the wells brackish, but Ben has installed a tank and is able to drink pure rain-water. He is a great Seventh-Day Adventist who adheres strictly to the letter of the Bible. Even a door damaged by a hurricane has been repaired by a coloured sheet which illustrates the doings of Jeroboam.

This morning I again became the village caller, and, having awakened my host and his two sons, I proceeded to the house of an elder called John. A wood-fire luckily filled the kitchen with smoke and served to hide my astonishment when 'Poppa' remarked to his family that he was 'kind of feeling' that we were going to get off this time, and that he would not meet our crew again until we were in Heaven! I felt that such God-fearing people are somewhat better-equipped to enter those realms than one so ill-prepared as myself. However, I am glad to say that the first half of his prediction came true!

We have had another tiring day. The boat finally came off into deep water fairly easily, but having got clear of the beach with a heavy list, we found one plank on the port side crushed in. While we were patching the damage, the wind freshened considerably and threatened to blow from seaward. We had to work our way out through the passage in the reef, which necessitated both skilful placing and frequent shifting of the anchors, by which we hauled ourselves out. We had to keep the list on the boat to get her through the shallow water by attaching anchors to the end of the starboard spinnaker boom. At one period, owing to a delay in tripping the anchors, we became rather anxious, and were relieved when we finally anchored well clear to seaward of the reef.

By dark, the *Tai-Mo-Shan* 'beach settlement' had ceased to exist, though most of it still remained on the upper deck. Supper was a very cheerful meal and Captain Collie came along with three of his crew. The natives of these islands were brought over as slaves from West Africa, and to-night Captain Collie himself told us the following story. He said that his great-grandfather lived in West Africa, and that the British found out that he was very fond of peanuts. They laid a trail of them, and grandpa found them much to his liking. One day he came to the end of the trail, and there he found some British officials, holding out a bag of peanuts. Captain Collie explained that his great-grandfather popped his head into the bag to obtain what he wanted. No sooner had he done so than a string was pulled tightly around his neck. He was finally released in the Bahamas, told to start a new life, and that in future his name was Adam Collie. That, the Captain explained, is how his family got their name and their home.

Tai-Mo-Shan *completed her voyage none the worse for her ordeal. The King himself honoured her arrival home with a letter of congratulations. The longevity of her construction was confirmed when she appeared on the brokers' listings for sale in the Mediterranean in 2005. During the Second World War, her crew repaid the Navy and the nation with four DSOs and a VC.*

DIRE STRAITS ALOFT

Frank Mulville
Dear Dolphin
Ashford Press Publishing 1991

The late Frank Mulville was a man whose modest exterior belied the passions that drove him to a life outside the experience of ordinary mortals. Following a childhood in London and on the pampas of Argentina he was apprenticed into the Merchant Navy. Torpedoed in 1943, he then served with the Royal Naval Volunteer Reserve until peace left him struggling to settle down. He worked as a window cleaner, journalist, salesman, cookery demonstrator and brush manufacturer. He was also a socialist and a member of the Labour Party and wearing this hat, as it were, he sailed his 40ft Looe Lugger Girl Stella *to Cuba shortly after the communist revolution to throw his own labour on the line assisting the people's struggle for survival. After losing this vessel in the Azores, he continued voyaging with* Iskra, *a smaller 1930s gaff cutter in which, with his third wife, Wendy, he cruised the Atlantic from the Arctic Circle to Buenos Aires.*

In 1980 sales of his books were slack, so Mulville loaded Iskra *with his output and made a single-handed commercial voyage to the United States in order to offer 'Books for sale – Genuine Atlantic copies!' Crossing the Gulf Stream, a peak halyard block carried away leaving little choice but to go aloft. This apparently insignificant event turned into one of the toughest challenges of his life. He describes it in his book on* Iskra's *voyaging,* Dear Dolphins. *The book is more than a yarn of the sea. As Mulville examines his inner motivations in its pages, it offers his readers a window into their own souls.*

BERNARD Shaw believed that only fools learn by experience – the wise don't have the experience because they are cunning or careful enough to evade it. But experience leaves something of value behind with us, if not wisdom at least an understanding which it is difficult to obtain without it. I would not wish to be without the recollection of what happened to me on the twenty-fourth day of the passage, although it came near to taking my life.

I have often been aloft before without difficulty, but not in the Gulf Stream. It is easy enough on the mooring in some quiet creek, or even at sea on a calm day, but here everything was different and I knew that once up the mast I would be thrown from side to side like a toy monkey on a stick. I took the sail down with a sick feeling of disquiet and got ready to climb the mast.

I hooked the bosun's chair to the throat halyard and made sure I had my knife with me, on a lanyard round my neck. I shackled the top of the chair to a shroud; this would help to stop me from swinging like a pendulum and crashing against the mast. The shackle would slide up the stay as I went up. As soon as I was above the deck *Iskra* seemed to come alive. Every movement she made was multiplied in its violence as I went higher. At ten feet above the deck the chair wound itself round and round the stay – it took ten minutes to unwind it. My legs and arms were squeezed between the shrouds and the chair, raising red, painful weals. At fifteen feet the shroud converged with the mast and I was dashed against it with astonishing force. Every wire stay I clung to was wrenched out of my hand, the other hand held the fall of the halyard. I gained height inch by inch, getting tired fast. By the time I got to the crosstrees I was nearly exhausted. I was shaken by the movement like a rat in the jaws of a terrier, lacerated where the wire stays cut into my legs and arms, bruised where I had been hurled against the mast. Then I saw that the chair was foul – I couldn't move it any higher because the fall of the topping lift was behind it. 'Fuck,' I said. No one answered. I tried to undo the shackle and free the chair but I couldn't get it undone. I looked up – the block was six feet above my head.

If I had been a wiser seaman I would have given up, come down the mast, thought the job through and then tried again. But I am not. I have a streak of obstinacy which will not allow me to stop doing something I have started until I have finished it. Sometimes it's a good streak, sometimes it isn't.

I decided to make the chair fast, climb out of it, stand on it and so reach the block. I doubled the fall of the halyard round the top of the chair and put a half hitch in it. Then I struggled upwards, holding on to the mast and crosstree. When I tried to stand on the chair it wobbled

and shot away from under my feet so that I almost fell. Then I got my feet on it and stood up. As high as I reached, my hand was inches below the block. I climbed out of the chair and stood on the crosstree. 'Got you, you bastard.' I pulled the block down, paused for a second to look round, standing on the crosstree, clinging for my life to the mast. It was overcast; if anything the sea was more lumpy. As *Iskra* rolled and pitched I looked down on the waves, then the deck with its untidy confusion of ropes and sails swung across the screen of my vision, then the sea the other side, inverted like a crazy upside-down film strip.

I started to climb back into the chair. It had got itself turned round and round the shroud again, but this time with the fall of the halyard twisted up with it. I could reach it with my foot from where I stood on the crosstree. Each time she rolled to starboard I managed to kick the chair and persuade it to unwind itself a turn. By the time I got it free I was beyond what I had previously thought of as a state of exhaustion. Somehow I got myself back into it, through the tangle of ropes that now held it in a kind of cocoon. Now all I had to do was to untie the fall of the halyard and lower myself down again. Soon it would be over. Now I was being thrown about more because I no longer had the strength to steady myself. I no longer cared as long as I got down to the deck again. I slipped the halyard and began to lower. Slowly the chair descended. Then it stopped and I couldn't shift it down another inch. I looked below me – the fall of the halyard had wound itself round one of *Iskra's* sidelight screens and was as securely fast as if I had tied it there myself. I pulled and jerked at it with the last of my strength but it was fast.

I thought as clearly as my battered head would allow me to think. I was in some danger, I was very weak, the skin on my arms and legs was raw, I doubted whether I was strong enough to climb out of the chair again. I looked up towards the horizon and saw a ship steaming past *Iskra* quite close. I saw no one on deck, no sign that I had been seen. Just as well, I thought, there wasn't much they could do for me. If I climbed out of the chair and slid down the mast or the shrouds I would leave all my halyards behind, leave myself no means of hoisting sail or of climbing the mast again without great difficulty. Why not shift the chair from the throat to the peak halyard which was still free, attaching a line to the block so that I could pull it down when I got to the deck?

I cut *Iskra's* flag halyard which was there beside me and tied it to the block, then I started to change the chair to the peak halyard block, pulling up the slack to take the weight, raising myself a few inches, enough to free the chair from the throat halyard and hook on the peak. Now at last I was clear of this mad tangle – all I had to do was lower away. Then *Iskra* ran into the wash of the ship. I could see the rolling waves from my perch aloft. Suddenly all was confusion and turmoil. The mast began to whip from side to side with extraordinary force; I was swung twenty or thirty feet back and forth every few seconds when she rolled and pitched. My hands were torn free of the mast, shrouds, halyards, my head crashed against the mast. I lost consciousness.

When I woke up I was hanging upside down by my feet which were caught round the ropes of the bosun's chair. I remember looking down at the sky, at the top of *Iskra*'s mast, seeing the horizon below me as she rolled and as I swung from side to side, showing a clear line of sea which swung in and out of my view. I thought, 'This is the end – I shall never get out of this; if I can free my feet I shall drop on my head on the deck or drop overboard, *Iskra* steaming slowly away from me.' Then my hands, stretched out over my head, downwards, came against *Iskra*'s starboard shrouds. Instinctively I gripped them. I twisted my feet and both of them came free of the chair. I swung through 180 degrees in a perfect arc like a circus clown on a trapeze and my feet came to rest exactly on *Iskra*'s sidelight screens. I found myself standing there, quite overcome with astonishment, looking down at the deck no more than six feet below me. I said, 'I'm alive, I'm alive, I'm alive, I'm alive.'

Catastrophically for Mulville, these events left him so exhausted that he let fly his peak halyard while lowering the mainsail in the routine gale that arrived the following day. After hours of self-torment, recrimination, and sheer denial of the horror of going aloft again, pride prevails. His tiny dolphin figurehead takes the place of his conscience and speaks out…

This was no way to arrive in a new country, limping in under a jury rig because I was too inept to climb the mast. 'Just get on and do it,' said the dolphin.

This time I used my head. I put on the heaviest pair of trousers I had, a thick shirt with long sleeves, shoes and socks. I hooked the chair to the throat halyard again. This time I didn't shackle it to a shroud; and this time I left the storm trysail set and this time I dropped the fall of the halyard overboard with a winch handle fast to it so that it would sink into the sea as I hauled myself up. It wouldn't foul this time unless a whale took it. This time it was easy. When I swung with *Iskra*'s roll I fell harmlessly into the soft folds of the sail. If my leg came against the stays, even with the old sores, I hardly felt it through the trousers. I climbed quickly to the crosstrees with the end of the halyard tied to the chair, reached up and threaded it through the block. Then I let myself down and as I came, the fall of the throat halyard came up out of the sea. When I got back to the deck I was laughing and shaking with fright all at the same time. A breeze came up from the north-east. I set my beautiful mainsail again and soon *Iskra* was bowling south with everything set, right up to her big white topsail.

I was through Purgatory – everything was different. The sky came blue, the sea a pale aquamarine. Gulls wheeled round *Iskra*'s wake as she pointed for the Nantucket light with a spanking fair wind behind her.

DESPERATE DRIVING

Erling Tambs
The Cruise of the Teddy
Rupert Hart-Davis 1950

Years ago I cruised far and wide with my family in an old sailing pilot cutter. Despite her age the boat proved a faithful friend who never let us down in many a long summer. She did, however, suffer from a few age-related habits.

It's a well-known maxim that 'harbours rot ships and men'. After prolonged spells in port – especially in hot weather – the topside planking would shrink away from the caulking so that, while bottle-tight at her berth, she leaked literally like a basket as soon as she heeled over. Usually, time would resolve this as the boards slowly absorbed water and took up, but on one occasion we came very near to sinking in Long Island Sound after a month alongside. Aboard was a distinguished American yachtsman, and setting him ashore without getting his trousers wet was a close-run thing. The cabin sole was afloat and we were pumping with all we had, including the engine whose cooling inlet I had redirected to the bilge, but we barely kept pace until we doused our canvas and brought her back to an even keel.

I chuckled therefore as I read Erling Tambs' rousing tale about voyaging in a pensioned-off 40ft Norwegian pilot cutter, designed and built 80 years ago by the great Colin Archer. The Cruise of the Teddy is inspirational, as the Tambs family hack their way around the Pacific, accompanied by their dog, named 'Spare Provisions' with typically Scandinavian gallows humour. Unlike me, they had no engine when their seams opened, but Tambs was not the man to pussyfoot around. With true seamanlike instinct, he saw that his only chance of saving the ship and her people was to throw caution to the stong tradewind and let her give all she had.

After reading this, let nobody claim that real Colin Archers are slow…

OFF Tahiti, 1931

On the occasion of this memorable departure the wind blew westerly in the harbour, as is often the case when the trade wind is strong from SE outside. The westerly wind inshore is really an eddy forming under the lee of the high mountains. Thus at the outset we had to beat against a head wind, which compelled us to make several tacks before we cleared the inner reef and could lay the passage.

In the meantime the wind had been gradually abating, dying out entirely as we were approaching the pass, on either side of which a tumultuous sea broke heavily over the reef. Having lost steerage way we were helplessly at the mercy of the currents. Fortunately, fed by the enormous masses of water breaking into the lagoon, the current raced swiftly seaward, whirling *Teddy* through the gap in a breathless five minutes. I heaved a profound sigh of relief when the reef was cleared and the thunder of the huge breakers no longer sounded so threateningly near.

Yet on our little *Teddy* conditions were none too pleasant. A calm belt lay between us and the trade wind which, sweeping down from over the mountains and promontories of Tahiti, struck the sea level in a sharply defined line half a mile to seaward – half a mile of tumbling tossing seas, which it took nearly an hour to traverse, assisted, as we were, only by occasional catspaws from various directions.

However, little by little we approached the edge of the trade wind, but as we drew nearer I fell to wondering if it would not, perhaps, be wiser to shorten canvas. We carried all our usual working kites, mainsail, jib and staysail. By all appearance the trades were blowing with great force, causing a great commotion in the sea.

All at once we were involved in the turmoil. The gale struck us like a blow. For one anxious moment *Teddy* heeled over at a dangerous angle. Lanyards cracked and I almost expected the rigging to go overboard, when, righting herself again, she was off.

Examining the lanyards I found that two strands had carried away at one place of the aftermost starboard lanyard, but that otherwise they seemed in fair condition. A foot of hemp rope lashed along the broken part was all that was required to render them secure. To be sure, the press of canvas was rather severe, but the wind was on the quarter, every inch of sail was drawing, and old *Teddy* simply flew over the waves. My heart swelled with pride at the sight.

Meantime, circumstances would not allow me much time to admire the boat. Presently I discovered that the cabin floor was awash. We were evidently making some water.

Before leaving Tahiti I had noticed that the planks above the waterline had shrunk considerably and, accordingly, I was prepared to do some pumping at the start, trusting at the same time that the frequent wettings which the boat would receive at sea would soon cause the planks to swell and render our ship tight again. However, I had not taken into account the possibility of striking it so unconscionably rough at the very start.

I pumped. Pumping our *Teddy* is at any time hard work, particularly hard when the boat is rolling and plunging in a turbulent sea. The pump is a simple device, its principle consisting of a heavy piece of leather at the end of a stick, but very efficacious, giving at least a gallon of water at each stroke. Yet my pumping did not seem to avail. The cabin floor was still submerged.

Having exhausted myself, I went down into the cabin to survey the situation. Imagine my consternation, when I discovered that even while I had been pumping, the water had risen three or four inches above the floor. I ran into the forepeak, looking for the leakage. There, to my horror, daylight showed through every seam, and whenever the boat dived into a sea, the water shot in from both sides, transforming the place into a shower bath. This was decidedly worse than I had expected.

Back I rushed to the pump. My fatigue was forgotten. I was pumping for our lives now, up and down, up and down. Yet the water crept slowly upwards, inch by inch. My wife strove hard at the tiller with baby Tony beside her in the cockpit. They depended on me for their safety. I pumped faster. The surroundings danced before my eyes; every muscle in my body was aching, but pump I must.

Then the pump carried away, and I sank down on the cabin top, defeated. Below, the water was washing over the first step of the companion. I realized that the deeper *Teddy* came into the water, the more her open seams would be permanently submerged and the faster she would sink. What could I do? I had no means of repairing the pump.

Teddy, as though she sensed the peril, sped gallantly on, doing surely ten knots. The boisterous seas she pushed impatiently aside. Moorea loomed ahead. This was a race against time. We had to make that island, or drown.

I looked below and was horrified; the water had risen over the benches on the leeward side. Although painfully aware that we already carried rather more canvas than was safe, in my desperation I hauled the trysail out of the sail bunk and set it spinnaker-like to windward. It was a frantic struggle, but I succeeded.

How that sail pulled! Onward *Teddy* flew like a bolting racehorse. I had not the time to log her speed, but I am convinced that she did eleven knots or more. Oh, she was grand!

In the cabin the water splashed about, wetting and ruining one thing after another. It rose inch by inch, a surging mass of rusty water in which at times became visible cushions, books, pulpy biscuits, saucepans, clothing – all the unpretentious things that formed part of our daily life. I noticed them indifferently; greater things were at stake, the lives of my wife, my boy and my boat.

The dog, wet and miserable, cowered forlornly in the companion. She whined pitifully, whenever I looked at her, but even Spare Provisions was of minor consideration then. Presently she came on deck; the water had risen above the companion floor.

I could not keep my eye off that terrible water rising stealthily and inevitably down below. Again and again I would look at my watch and at the island looming ahead; again and again I would try to calculate our chances, swinging between hope and black despair.

The water had established a connection between the sail locker and the cabin; it rushed in and out with the motion, pounding against the bulkhead in the companion and throwing spray on deck. It had formed into an additional danger, increasing with every moment; I feared lest the wash of the water should impair our speed. We could not afford to slow down.

Long since the leeward bunks were soaked. Presently the mattresses were afloat. The water crept up the sides, splashing against the deck. It rose. It rose.

But already the nearest point of the island was abreast. My hopes rose as I edged in towards the reef. However, soon I changed our course again, striking straight for the entrance to Papetoai Bay. The roar of the breakers warned me how utterly futile would have been an attempt to swim ashore. As yet the huge and shifting weight of water inside did not seem to affect the speed of my boat. She rushed onward through blurred visions of sizzling foam, swaying with a deliberate gravity under the heavy burden of her canvas. As the shore sped past, my confidence gradually returned. Only three or four miles more and we would be saved. We would make it, if only the wind did not abate.

A fierce squall struck us. *Teddy* travelled all the faster for it. I could not help laughing. The strength of my boat occurred to me as something immensely funny. I am afraid that the new-born conviction of our safety had put me a bit off my balance. Already the pass was plainly visible.

Off the entrance I had a hard struggle, when the trysail had to be stowed. Then, after a heavy jibe, we shot through the foam-bordered reef passage into the smooth haven of Papetoai Bay. A native in a pirogue was fishing in the lagoon. We picked him up on the way and secured his pilotage to a beautiful little cove near the head of the bay. The anchor was dropped, a stern rope passed ashore and made fast to a cocos palm. I looked at the watch: we had travelled more than twenty miles in one and three-quarter hours. Nor had there been any time to spare. *Teddy* lay very low by the head. In the forepeak the water reached up to my chest, and even in the cabin the surface was on a level with the table. One half-hour longer at sea would have finished us.

Now the danger was over. No longer exposed to the continual duckings of the sea, the boat drew water only through the seams which were submerged by the surplus weight of the flood inside, although surely that was bad enough, and we lost no time in starting to bale out the water. Terii, the native, assisted in our toil. Passed hand to hand, three large buckets were permanently in action for three and a half hours, before the water level was at last brought down to the cabin floor; by rough estimate I calculated that we had baled out more than twenty tons of water; at the outset we must have been dangerously close to the point where our combined efforts at baling would have been insufficient to keep the boat afloat…

…When on the following day I surveyed the boat, I found that the topsides had shrunk to within an inch or two of the waterline. Now that the paint which had covered the seams had been washed away, I discovered places where I could almost push a lead pencil through the seams. No wonder she was leaking!

I think that particular experience has taught me a lesson…

HIGH LATITUDES

Tricky navigation Rockwell Kent

Ice all round Lord Dufferin

Icebound off Franz Joseph Land John Gore-Grimes

Aground in the High Arctic HW Tilman

On the rocks Desmond Holdridge

The Last Unknown Alvah Simon

TRICKY NAVIGATION

Rockwell Kent

N by E

Brewer and Warren 1930

Rockwell Kent (1882–1971) was an American artist, writer and political activist who expanded his curriculum working as a lobsterman, a ship's carpenter and a dairy farmer. His art is often identified with the school of American Social Realists and the great muralists of the 1920s and 1930s. In 1929, he sailed from the American East Coast to Greenland with skipper Arthur S Allen, Jr., and 'the mate' in the brand-new gaff cutter Direction. *Today, such voyages are, if not commonplace, at least no longer regarded as foolhardy. In those days the trip was pioneering. Reading between the lines of Kent's voyage account in his beautifully illustrated book soon makes it clear that the skipper makes some shaky judgement calls following Kent's admirable work in the navigation department. One such came while he was cruising in intermittent but dense fog up the Great Northern Peninsula of Newfoundland. The sort of incident that ensues has become rare in our GPS-assisted world, but it was once every sailor's nightmare.*

Rockwell Kent's English is outrageous, yet contrives uniquely to transmit the essence of an artist's mind.

*J*UNE *23 1929 – Great Northern Peninsula of Newfoundland – 49° 35N 58° 00W*

No change; thick fog, fair wind; and a near mountain wall of shore, veiled as the presence of Jehovah. The compass was our eye by night and day.

We might have questioned the judgement that laid our course so near the shore. We didn't. The momentary glimpses of it thrilled us; we were there for that. 'Live dangerously' might have been our motto. And in further token of it we set our spinnaker, in order, it might seem, that if we struck we'd strike all standing.

It was the end of my morning watch. We were in the vicinity of Bonne Bay and logging five knots in a heavy sea. The skipper relieved me. The fog had lifted somewhat, revealing a far stretch of coast. Where this at its most distant point was silhouetted against the sky appeared a promontory that sloped seaward in a graceful, far-tending curve. It appeared lost in the murk of the horizon rather than ended there; so that either through the form's suggestion of continuance or by actual vision I concluded that land lay across our course; and with much conviction I called it to the attention of the skipper. He differed. The fog rolled in upon us and we held our course.

It was some hours later in the afternoon. I had come out of my forecastle to look at the fire and inspect the baking beans. 'Good,' I thought as I licked the spoon, 'but maybe a little more molasses.' So I added it. I looked at the clock. Only three-thirty! And just then the top of the companionway was pushed open.

'Cupid,' said the captain very quietly, 'better come on deck and take in the spinnaker.'

I jumped for the deck. Thick fog, and wind; there, off the starboard bow a hundred yards away, the land! We had to manoeuvre.

'Rocks to port!' Steady. We'll pass between.

Then suddenly there loomed a line of reefs across that way; and everywhere except astern were rocks. A hunted animal cornered by dogs; we felt like it, we must have – though there was little thinking done of how we felt.

There were just two moves left; tiller hard down and chance to tack, or gybe and risk the starboard reef by driving near it. Split seconds now. We wore round. For an eternal instant we drove straight at the land. Then, caught aback, the mainsail filled, lifted the boom and hurled itself and everything to port. We trimmed sheet frantically, close. We gathered way. And the sea, lifting our wake, mingled it with the back wash of the surf.

Meanwhile the half lowered spinnaker was proclaiming confusion. We drew it, struggling, to the deck and bundled it; and as swiftly as the fog shut out the land we breathed again with the relief of danger passed.

'Listen! What's that?' It's nothing.

I am on the bowsprit. Listening. Peering into the obscurity of that fog with an intensity that is the sublimation of my fear. Then suddenly, incredibly, a spot of lightness creeps into the plane of gray, a line of white – moving, and gone, and there again.

'Land on the starboard bow!'

We come about. The low reef drops astern. The fog encloses us. Anxiously we sail, in silence.

This time we hear it, booming; see it! 'Land to port! – ahead!' Again about.

And always, standing there on the tip end of the bowsprit, seeing nothing of the management of the boat, having no bearing on anything, it is to me the wind that shifts and the land that comes toward me out of the fog, and retreats again. Lifted one moment high above the water, swiftly and gently lowered till my feet are touching it, soothingly swaying I seem rocked in space. A Heavenly movement! Like the dreams of ether it transcends the peril of the hour.

And that peril, the desperation of it since the first moment we encountered land, seemed by each futile tack to draw more closely and inevitably round us. Blindly we beat about beset by reefs and scarcely sea-room for manoeuvring. We realized it. We were trapped.

And then it happened, when the intervals at which we met the land had become monotonous in their even recurrence, and sailing about at all seemed merely a senseless postponement of inevitable disaster, that as we peered and listened there came to us a sort of sensory annoyance as at the delaying of one beat in an established rhythm. The expected didn't happen. Slowly, it dared to dawn on us that the whole thing was over. That we were clear of it. At sea!

'How about,' said the cook, sticking his head at this juncture out of the cabin, 'a good, hot plate of beans?'

Having been spared from the rocks of Newfoundland, the boys sail on into the fog. Three weeks later, they burst out of it off Greenland to face one of the classic dilemmas of the traditional navigator. The sun appears, but this can generate only a single position line at any one time. A good pilot could hang his hat on that to within a mile or two, but Kent's sole remaining navigational input after days of bad visibility was a shaky estimated position. The question was how to produce a fix. The hitherto esoteric Kent now comes up with a fine example of precise lateral thinking to which the technical aspect of his narrative does no favours. Quite how he manages a 'longitude' at 1500 hours remains a piece of artistic licence. What is sure is that he couldn't supply the latitude they really needed on that north-trending coast. However, whether the sun sight generated a true longitude or a line running diagonally across the chart doesn't actually matter. He fixed the yacht with the sight he reduced and a second 'wavy line' guesstimated as three miles from the coast. He confirmed his whereabouts by observation and by using his converging course as a sort of infinitely transferable line of position, and he got it right.

July 14 1929 – West Greenland – 63° 20N 51° 35W
We seemed, as we advanced, to be emerging from the fog into an area of clearer atmosphere; and into that grimness which had been our mood crept presently an almost exultant expectancy as though we should for certainty at last and now behold the glamorous country that we'd climbed the latitudes to reach.

And then it came – not suddenly, nor close, nor frighteningly, but gradually from a long way off, low islands and a long low coast, gray in a silver mist. And as we stared, it all at once grew bright, and shafts of sunlight streamed down through the mist illuminating patches of the land and the white surf along its shore. 'And this is Greenland,' we thought, 'so wild and beautiful!'

And yet the clouds were even then resolving into forms so lofty as to dwarf the land and we sat staring speechlessly at a blue barrier of granite mountains rising to cloud wreathed, snow-topped peaks four thousand feet and more above the sea.

Between the summits, here and there, appeared the far, white snowfield of the inland ice. Glaciers curved stream-like down steep valleys or hung suspended on the mountain sides. Granite and ice; and over the stony hills of the broad foreland sparse vegetation turning green with summer.

And with the knowledge of being at last at the threshold of Greenland came, momentously, the question, where!

Charts picture in two dimensions what to the eye at sea appears in one. Those most fantastic indentations and projections of the shore on which the navigator would depend to get his bearings show as the straight unbroken line of where the sea's plain cuts the land. No wonder then that with the panorama of that coast before our eyes and every promise on the chart of here and there a settlement and everywhere, almost, a bay or anchorage, we were as lost as if no charts had ever been.

But, just as upon our determination to make the land there had followed that spectacular unveiling of it, so now in our most need to know our whereabouts the sun came out; and in that moment the heavy fog that lay over the sea lifted and revealed for the first time in days a clear horizon.

I jump for the sextant, catch the sun and draw it downward toward the western ocean rim.

The mate stands by the chronometer.

'Ready!' I call.

The seconds pass. The crimson sun declines toward an emerald sea; nearer and nearer, 'Now!' I cry.

And the mate writes on a slip of paper: 3 h. 47m. 23.9s.

And even as I leave the deck the day grows dark again.

It's latitude we need; the sight and calculations are for longitude. I figure carefully. With longitude 51° 35' West as the result, I go to the chart. Assuming us to be three miles from the shore I draw the line of our course. The intersection of that with the line of longitude gives our position. We're less than fifty miles from Godthaab!

Shortly after this navigational coup, Direction's skipper made another bad tactical decision that ended with the loss of the boat in a remote fjord the following morning. The remainder of Rockwell Kent's book is a wondrous mix of legend and traveller's tale. If you can find a copy of the Brewer and Warren (New York) edition of 1930/31, the artwork alone will repay the investment.

ICE ALL ROUND

Lord Dufferin
Letters from High Latitudes
Oxford University Press 1910

The year 2006 saw 150 years since Lord Dufferin pioneered Arctic yachting in his schooner Foam. *With him were a crew of paid hands, Mr Wyse the skipper, Dufferin's friend the Doctor ('Fitz'), and his lordship's inimitable valet, Wilson. This unlikely team made it to around 79°N under conditions of some extremity.*

The text below is taken from Letters from High Latitudes, *a collection of epistles His Lordship wrote originally to his mother. He has clearly censored the descriptions of some of his runs ashore accordingly – which of us hasn't done the same? – but his Victorian deadpan humour shines through, especially in his portrayal of events at sea. Ashore, the social conditions of his day were so far removed from our own that when Dufferin was invited to a function by local dignitaries in Iceland, he found himself able to communicate more than adequately in Latin, a language that in those days all civilised people had in common. As a preamble to the main story, he narrates an incident during the final dinner on board before sailing from Arctic*

Norway, Fortunately for us, he abandons the ablative absolute and sticks to plain English.

THE very day we left Hammerfest our hopes of being able to get to Spitzbergen at all received a tremendous shock. We had just sat down to dinner, and I was helping the Consul to fish, when in comes Wilson, his face, as usual, upside down, and hisses something into the Doctor's ear. Ever since the famous dialogue which had taken place between them on the subject of seasickness, Wilson had got to look upon Fitz as his legitimate prey; and whenever the burden of his own misgivings became greater than he could bear, it was to the Doctor that he unbosomed himself. I guessed, by the look of gloomy triumph in his eyes, that some great calamity had occurred, and it turned out that the following was the agreeable announcement he had been in such haste to make:

'Do you know, Sir?' – This was always the preface to tidings unusually doleful.

'No – what?' said the Doctor, breathless.

'Oh nothing, Sir; only two sloops have just arrived, Sir, from Spitzbergen, Sir – where they couldn't get, Sir – such a precious lot of ice two hundred miles from the land – and, oh, Sir, they've come back with all their bows stove in!'

Undeterred, Foam and her mixed bag of a crew sailed northwards to Bear Island (approximately 74N 19E) about 150 miles short of Spitzbergen, where they ran into the predicted wall of horizon-to-horizon pack ice. The rest of the story speaks eloquently for itself, but remember that the yacht has neither engine nor GPS and that radar and any sort of radio were still generations away in the unforeseeable future. Neither does she benefit from even the most basic electricity. It may also help to bear in mind that she was probably the first non-commercial vessel ever to penetrate these deserted waters, and that if she were to come to grief her crew's chances of survival were very slim indeed.

What was now to be done? If a continuous field of ice lay 150 miles off the southern coast of Spitzbergen, what would be the chance of getting to the land by going further north? Still, unpromising as the aspect of things might appear, it would not do to throw a chance away – so I determined to put the schooner round on the other tack, and run westwards along the edge of the ice until we found ourselves again in the Greenland Sea. Bidding, therefore, a last adieu to Mount Misery, as its first discoverers very appropriately christened one of the higher hills in Bear Island, we suffered it to melt back into the fog, and with no very sanguine expectations as to the result, sailed west away towards Greenland.

During the next four-and-twenty hours we ran along the edge of the ice nearly due west. It was weary work, scanning that seemingly interminable barrier and listening to the melancholy roar of waters on its icy shore. At last, after having come about 140 miles since leaving Bear Island, the long, white, wave-lashed line suddenly ran down into a low point, and then trended back with a decided inclination to the north. Here at all events was an improvement; instead of our continuing to steer WxS, or at most WxN, the schooner would often lay as high up as NW, and even NWxN. Evidently the action of the Gulf Stream was beginning to tell, and our spirits rose in proportion. In a few more hours, however, this cheering prospect was interrupted by a fresh line of ice being reported, not only ahead, but as far as the eye could reach on the port bow – so again the schooner's head was put to the westward, and the old story recommenced. And now the flank of the second barrier was turned, and we were able to edge up a few hours to the northward, only to be again confronted by another line, apparently more interminable than the last. But why should I weary you with the detail of our various manoeuvres during the ensuing days? They were too tedious and disheartening at the time for me to look back upon them with any pleasure. Suffice it to say, that by dint of sailing north whenever the ice would permit, and sailing west when we could not sail north, we found ourselves on the 2nd of August in the latitude of the southern extremity of Spitzbergen, though divided from the land by about fifty miles of ice.

All this while the weather had been pretty good, foggy and cold enough, but with a fine, stiff breeze that rattled us along at a good rate whenever we did get a chance of making any northing. But lately it had come on to blow very hard, the cold became quite piercing, and in every direction except the south, a blaze of iceblink illuminated the sky. A more discouraging spectacle could not have met our eyes. The iceblink has a luminous appearance, reflected on the heavens from the fields of ice that still lie sunk beneath the horizon; it was therefore on this occasion an unmistakable indication of the encumbered state of the sea in front of us.

I had turned in for a few hours of rest and release from the monotonous sense of disappointment, when 'a voice in my dreaming ear' shouted '*Land!*' and I awoke to its reality. I need not tell you with what greediness I feasted my eyes on that longed-for view, the only sight – as I then thought – we were ever destined to enjoy of the mountains of Spitzbergen!

The whole heaven was overcast with a dark mantle of tempestuous clouds that stretched down in umbrella-like points towards the horizon, leaving the clear space between their edge and the sea illuminated by the sinister brilliancy of the iceblink. In an easterly direction, this belt of unclouded atmosphere was etherealized to an indescribable transparency, and up into it there gradually grew a forest of thin lilac peaks, so faint, so pale, that one could have deemed them unsubstantial spires of fairy-land. The beautiful vision proved only too transient; in one short half-hour mist and cloud had blotted it all out, while a fresh barrier of ice compelled us to turn our backs on the very land we were striving to reach.

Although we were certainly upwards of sixty miles distant from the land when the Spitzbergen hills were first observed, the intervening space seemed infinitely less; but in these high latitudes the eye is constantly liable to be deceived in the estimate it forms of distances.

The next five days were spent in a continual struggle with the ice, and in Fitz's diary the discouraging state of the weather is pithily expressed:

'August 2nd. – Head wind – sailing westward – large hummocks of ice ahead – hope we may be able to push through. In evening, ice gets thicker; we still hold on – fog comes on – ice getting thicker – wind freshens – we can get no farther – ice impassable, no room to tack – struck the ice several times – obliged to sail South and West. Things look very shady.'

Sometimes we were on the point of despairing altogether, then a plausible opening would show itself as if leading towards the land, and we would be tempted to run down it, until we found the field so closely packed that it was with great difficulty we could get the vessel round – and only then at the expense of collisions, which made the little craft shiver from stem to stern. Then a fog would come on – so thick, you could almost cut it like a cheese – and thus render the sailing among the loose ice very critical indeed: then it would fall dead calm, and leave us muffled in mist, with no other employment than chess or hopscotch.

Ever since leaving Bear Island, Wilson had been keeping a carnival of grief in the pantry, until the cook became almost half-witted by reason of his jeremiads. Yet I must not give you the impression that the poor fellow was the least wanting in pluck – far from it. Surely it requires the highest order of courage to anticipate every species of disaster every moment of the day, and yet to meet the impending fate like a man. Was it his fault that fate was not equally ready to meet him? His share of the business was always done: he was ever prepared for the worst; the most critical circumstances never disturbed the gravity of his carriage, and the fact of our being destined to go to the bottom before tea-time would not have caused him to lay out the dinner-table a whit less symmetrically. Still, I own, the style of his service was slightly depressing. He laid out my clean shirt of a morning as if it had been a shroud; and cleaned my boots as though for a man on his last legs.

This was the cheerful kind of report he used invariably to bring me of a morning. Coming to the side of my cot with the air of a man announcing the stroke of doomsday, he used to say, or rather toll,

'Seven o'clock, my lord!'

'Very well; how's the wind?'

'Dead ahead, my lord – *dead*!'

'How many points is she off her course?'

'Four points, my lord – full four points!' (Four points being as much as she could be.)

'Is it pretty clear? eh! Wilson?'

'Can't see your hand, my lord!'

'Much ice in sight?'

'Ice all round, my lord – ice all ro-ound!' – and so exit, sighing deeply over my trousers.

Yet it was immediately after one of these unpromising announcements that for the first time matters began to look a little brighter. The preceding four-and-twenty hours we had remained enveloped in a cold and dismal fog. But on coming on deck I found the sky had already begun to clear;

and although there was ice as far as the eye could see on either side of us, in front a narrow passage showed itself across a patch of loose ice into what seemed a freer sea beyond. The only consideration was whether we could be certain of finding our way out again, should it turn out that the open water was only a basin without any other exit. The chance was too tempting to throw away; so the little schooner gallantly pushed her way through the intervening neck of ice where the floes seemed to be least huddled up together, and in half an hour found herself running up along the edge of the starboard ice, almost in a due northerly direction. And here I must take occasion to say, that during the whole of this rather anxious time, my master – Mr. Wyse – conducted himself in a most admirable manner. Vigilant, cool, and attentive, he handled the vessel most skilfully, and never seemed to lose his presence of mind in any emergency.

Soon after, the sun came out, the mist entirely disappeared, and again on the starboard hand shone a vision of the land; this time not in the sharp peaks and spires we had first seen, but in a chain of pale-blue egg-shaped islands floating in the air a long way above the horizon. This peculiar appearance was the result of extreme refraction, for later in the day we had an opportunity of watching the oval cloud-like forms gradually harden into the same pink tapering spikes which originally caused the island to be called Spitzbergen: nay, so clear did it become, that we could easily trace the outlines of the enormous glaciers that fill up every valley along the shore.

Towards evening the line of coast again vanished into the distance, and our rising hopes received an almost intolerable disappointment by the appearance of a long line of ice right ahead, running to the westward, apparently, as far as the eye could reach. To add to our disgust, the wind flew right round into the north and, increasing to a gale, brought down upon us not one of the usual thick Arctic mists to which we were accustomed, but a dark, yellowish-brown fog.

For the whole of that night did we continue beating up along the edge of the ice, in the teeth of a whole gale of wind. At last, about nine o'clock in the morning – but two short hours before the moment at which it had been agreed to abandon the attempt – we doubled a long low point of ice and there, beyond, lay open sea! You can imagine my excitement.

'Turn the hands up, Mr. Wyse! Bout ship!'

Up comes the schooner's head to the wind, the sails flapping with the noise of thunder-blocks rattling against the deck, as if they wanted to knock their brains out – ropes dancing about in galvanized coils, like mad serpents and everything to an inexperienced eye in inextricable confusion, till gradually she pays off on the other tack. The sails stiffen, the staysail sheet is let go and, heeling over on the opposite side, again she darts forward over the sea like an arrow.

'Stand by to make sail! Out all reefs!' (I could have carried sail to sink a man-of-war!) and away the little ship went, playing leapfrog over the heavy seas, and staggering under her canvas, as if giddy with the same joyful excitement which made my own heart thump so loudly.

In another hour the sun came out, the fog cleared away, and above the horizon grow the pale lilac peaks, warming into a rosier tint as we approach. Ice still stretches toward the land on the starboard side; but we don't care for it now. The schooner's head is pointing ExS. Clearer and more defined grows the outline of the mountains, some coming forward while others recede; the articulations of the rocks become visible and now, at last, we glide under the limestone peaks of Mitre Cape, past the marble arches of King's Bay on the one side and the pinnacle of the Vogel Hook on the other, into the quiet channel that separates the Foreland from the main.

It was at one o'clock in the morning of the 6th of August, 1856, that, after having been eleven days at sea, we came to an anchor in the silent haven of English Bay, Spitzbergen.

ICEBOUND OFF FRANZ
JOSEPH LAND

John Gore-Grimes
The Irish Cruising Club Journal
1998

Much is written in today's journals about surviving fearsome gales and gigantic Southern Ocean greybeards. A different area of expertise altogether is that of small-yacht ice navigation. So far, no textbook exists to guide those who are drawn by this call of the ultimate wild. Nonetheless, a few acknowledged authorities have led the way. One of the big names is the unstoppable John Gore-Grimes, whose 'day job' in those days was to practise law in Dublin.

In this account from The Irish Cruising Club Journal *of 1998, he describes being locked in the ice while bound for the near-impossible destination of Franz Joseph Land, north of Novaya Zemlya in the Russian Arctic. He and the crew of* Arctic Fern, *a purpose-built Najad 441, tackle their situation with exemplary seamanship and the high spirits that are the trademark of the club.*

A T 1700 on Friday 31st July we were at 77°49'N 55°37'E and by 1100 on Saturday morning we were completely stopped at 78'13'N 55°09'E. It had been a sunny sleepless night as we worked our way from lead to lead, successfully breaking through some thick ice barriers with spinnaker pole and the heavy stainless steel emergency tiller. In fifteen hours we had covered about 26 miles but then we ran out of leads. We found a small pool and anchored *Arctic Fern* to the ice.

On our first day wet fog rolled in which was to remain with us for the duration of our captivity. I walked over to look at some ice hummocks and it was clear that these were the winter pressure ice. Using the binoculars I could see no evidence of recently formed pressure ice which is easily recognisable by the jagged pieces of blue ice which are forced upwards. The old winter pressure ice still had a covering of snow on it. This was good news because the constant fear for the ice navigator is that your vessel will become trapped between two large floes which may have been forced into contest against each other. When the edges of the two floes meet and have no other route to take, the ice is forced upwards with colossal energy to create the hummocks which are littered all about this frozen ocean. The lack of recently formed hummocks was only of small consolation because pressure ice can occur at any time to make a mockery of Kevlar, steel or, indeed, any materials made by man.

We did not stray too far from *Arctic Fern*. The fog and the hummocks offered good camouflage for roaming polar bear. Although we were entirely surrounded and unable to move, the first 24 hours were quite pleasant because we were moored in a pool with the anchor well buried in ice about five feet above the water. This was a relatively good place, but nothing in ice remains relatively good for long.

Robert cooked a splendid dinner, but before the first plate was on the table the devil took me and I opened two bottles of Chablis. The inevitable followed with two more and, as Dutch courage started to take effect, there was mention of a swim. Merryl and Andrew, who are people of a lunchtime disposition, took a few paces backwards and allowed the two Gore-Grimes and the Pendleton to continue on their merry way. As we left the water each of us would have qualified as *alto soprano* in the Vatican boys' choir, but Merryl found a bottle of Jagertee and poured it into hot mugs of tea. We were soon ourselves again – back to *basso profundo* and thinking all the while what good anti-freeze Chablis Premier Cru is.

We drifted around in the ice for the next five days, with our furthest east at 55°43'8. It rained heavily on Sunday 2nd August, with visibility down to a cable or less. No sooner were we settled below when the ice began to grind against the hull. The noise is ugly, but motivating.

We punched holes in the skirts of underwater ice at one-foot intervals. It was slow, laborious work and it took two people to operate the heavy spinnaker pole, using it as a manual kango hammer. Eventually a large sheet of ice would break away and shoot to the surface. This was not a perfect solution but we found that by sinking a broken lump and pushing it under the sea ice we could stow it away quite neatly. Our aim was to allow the surface ice to lie close to the hull without any protruding underwater ledges. As far as possible, and this was by no means always possible, we aimed to have a clearance of two to three feet along one side, while the other lay with fenders out against sheer ice with no underwater protrusions.

In between hacking ice we tried either to read or rest but the intervals did not permit tedium. Some slumbers were rudely interrupted and we noticed that they often produced weird, multicoloured, speed-of-lightning dreams. You knew you had them but you could not quite remember the details. If the intervals were slightly longer, some of us occasionally enjoyed the luxury of big-screen, stereo, erotic dream fantasies which were all too quickly obliterated by the cold reality of hacking more ice away from the hull.

At 0015 on Monday 3rd August Merryl came into my cabin to tell me that there were bears outside. They were about 150 feet from the boat on a piece of ice which touched our topsides. There was a mother and a young cub. I climbed out through the aft cabin hatch and sure enough they were there looking magnificent. The mother gave a growl and then yawned. The yawn is usually a sign that the polar bear is not feeling unduly aggressive. The cub was very close to the boat and looked playful. I was extremely nervous. In 1989 I had put my rifle sight to a bear's head but I could not pull the trigger. There seemed no sense in having a gun. That is correct if you have a strong boat to hide in, but if you lose the boat and are trekking across ice, an old rifle might be very useful indeed.

Fifteen minutes later Andrew fired a flare. He did not aim it at the bears but the noise and the smoke sent them running across the ice.

We had a second visit from a lone bear at 2336 on Monday night. We were much calmer on this occasion, confident in the knowledge that we could drop into the cabin and secure ourselves if the bear came on board. We stood on deck and he came close and growled. It was not a menacing growl, but we fired a flare and there was the usual noise and smoke. The bear was unimpressed. Eventually I growled at him and he looked at us and walked off slowly. He probably thought, 'How pathetic!'

Wednesday 5th August was our most troublesome day with heavy ice attacking the hull beneath the surface. We had to haul the boat into a new position not more than a cable away, but the movement of the floes was completely unpredictable. They were so large that instead of moving in a uniform direction, they were frequently turned around by a neighbour which could be as much as half a mile off. There was a lot of hacking and pulling with ropes and once or twice we had to drive the boat at the ice at full revs. The result usually gave us a half-hour's respite but then it was back to work again.

On Thursday 6th August it was foggy and there were still no leads in sight. A big old yellow bear suddenly pulled himself out the water onto the ice. What we had thought was all ice pool was in fact a deepwater lead. I gave this bear the biggest growl that I could muster and it seemed to work because he jumped back into the water, swimming south down a lead. 'Thank you Mr. Bear'. He had shown us a possible way out of our ice prison. As we hauled in the anchor I thought to myself that I should try the growl out on a judge or two in the Dublin Courts.

We followed our yellow bear for a while once we had freed ourselves from our ice harbour. When we finally left him behind, we had five hours of tortuous twisting and turning through heavy floes. The crew worked the spinnaker pole in turns. It was hard, but there was not a single complaint. The thought of open water was sufficient motivation to keep hammering at the ice in order to secure our freedom.

By 1700 we were in relatively open water, headed towards Nord Kapp of Norway, so we made a tank full of water and everyone enjoyed hot showers. Clean again, with fresh clothing, we had just agreed unanimously that the best thing about ice in the Arctic Ocean is getting out of it, when all of a sudden we were again surrounded. By 2200, just ten hours after our departure from our last ice cloister, we were caught in another one. It allowed no escape and in poor visibility it simply enveloped us in a most unmannerly fashion. We were stuck again. There were no large floes but just many pieces of ice jammed in very close proximity. There was a mighty ocean swell and the drama was exaggerated as great walls of ice rose and fell all around us. The height from top to bottom was approximately 15 feet but the peaks of each heavy swell were well separated so that the moving ocean did not cause the closely packed ice to grate against the hull of the *Arctic Fern*.

It was a foggy night and one watch followed the next with little possibility of moving out of this disagreeable scene. At 0715 on Friday 7th August, however, Andrew called me from a deep, dreamless sleep to report open water no more than three cables away. I came on deck, peered into the fog and confirmed this. The boat was still entirely surrounded by ice, so we wondered how we would penetrate it and effect our escape. The ice was well broken, however, and you certainly would not think of walking on it, so we started up the trusty Yanmar and moved out slowly at 1,000 revs, dashing ice aside with the crew on the bow assisting with the spinnaker pole. One hour later we were free again and this time our freedom was permanent. By 0900 Nico's entry in the log read, 'Only melted icebergs now. They are so melted that they are invisible.'

John Gore-Grimes goes on to describe the homeward-bound passage to Ireland via the Lofoten Islands and Stornoway. He concludes with a deceptively profound remark that could well be extended to all mixed-weather yacht cruising:

Much can be said about high latitude sailing, but for me the best part of it is returning home and remembering all the fun and the good bits. The bad bits, and I can't remember any, are quickly forgotten.

AGROUND IN
THE HIGH ARCTIC

HW Tilman
Triumph and Tribulation
Nautical Publishing Co 1977

HW Tilman was truly the last of a breed. Born in 1898, a monument to the best of old-fashioned values and a soldier by trade, he fought with distinction in two world wars. Between hostilities, he became famous by pioneering Himalayan mountaineering with Eric Shipton. When the 1950s brought increasing numbers of climbers and even tourism to the mountains, he looked elsewhere for adventure, accepting the fact that, despite his being unusually fit, the inevitable advance of age would soon place the extreme altitudes of Nepal and Tibet beyond his powers. Instead, he followed his fortune into the ice and unclimbed peaks of high latitudes, both north and south, in a series of ancient pilot cutters. Fortunately for us, this man so impervious to hardship became a literary figure whose

books of the sea rank among the finest. They also delight the reader with the wryest of understated humour. The work of this well-read man abounds with the sort of quote that begins this extract from Triumph and Tribulation. *We find him, his crew and the 50ft cutter* Baroque *near the end of a circumnavigation of Spitzbergen at 80°N. It is August 1974.*

There is nothing so distressing as running ashore – unless there is also a doubt as to which continent the shore belongs. –Lecky's Wrinkles.

THE breeze having died we were again under engine when at 0400 I took over the watch from Alan. What followed is not easy to explain and still less easy to excuse. Perhaps, having spent the last three days mostly on deck and enjoyed only disturbed nights, I was not as bright as I should have been. West of Cape Heuglin along the north coast of Edge Island the water was shoal and we intended passing north of the Zeiloyane islets which, with the engine and the tide, we must have been approaching at 7 or 8 knots. Before I had really hoisted in what was happening we were heading between two islets a mile or so apart. To attempt to pass between unknown islets however wide apart they may be is always a hazardous proceeding. A shoal joined the two and the rate we were going ensured our being carried right up on the back of it before we ground to a stop.

If the crew thought the old man had taken leave of his senses, they studiously refrained from comment. As soon as the tide slackened we ran out a kedge astern bringing the warp forward to the winch. The engine had no power in reverse and the winch alone failed to budge her. Circumstances had combined to make things as difficult as they could be. We must have gone on at or near high water and the tides were taking off. The range proved to be only around 2ft, which in one way was a good thing because the boat remained more or less upright.

We had no choice but to jettison half the ballast, all of which *Baroque* carried inside. The nearest islet was half a mile away and in the absence of any appreciable slack water there was no question of rowing a heavily laden dinghy across to put it ashore. In spite of a strong westerly wind blowing out of the strait the sea remained calm and the boat motionless. There was thus no fear of damage from pounding, but when the west-going stream started again it brought with it numerous ice-floes, large and small. The big ones grounded on the edge of the shoal about fifty yards away where they furnished a kind of protective barrier. There were, however, gaps through which anything drawing less than 7ft found its way at several knots to threaten disaster to our rudder or propeller. Even at only half a ton or so, these bits of ice could neither be stopped nor diverted with boat-hooks. Watching a small floe apparently on a collision course we could only hold our breath and hope. Twice the rudder sustained a savage blow. Nor were we much better off when the tide turned, for those that had already passed came back with the flood. We had only to stay there long enough for the worst to happen.

It was clear that until we could get her pointing the way she had come and so make full use of the engine we should never get off. Having got us into this mess I at least should have had 'skilly' for supper; instead we finished up with one of David's increasingly majestic duffs. Care weighing heavy upon me, I could only toy with this, notwithstanding the advice of that strong-minded gastronome Dr Oppimian – 'Whatever happens in this world, never let it spoil your dinner.' No doubt the reverend doctor had never assisted at a stranding that might well become a shipwreck if a piece of ice with *Baroque*'s name on it hit her in a vital spot.

Having disposed of the duff, we turned with renewed vigour to taking out the remainder of the ballast and emptying the water tanks but for a few gallons for immediate use. The crew worked like heroes, Paul groping in the bilge prizing out the slimy chunks of pig-iron – some weighing 80 to 90 lbs. – from the filthy bed where for years they had lain undisturbed. Besides all the ballast and most of the water, we threw overboard an old flax mainsail. When wet, as the sails stowed on a rack in the peak always were, it must have weighed about four hundredweight. Normally I take harmless pleasure from throwing overboard superfluous gear. The mainsail might be included in that category, but certainly not the ballast.

We had already lost a kedge and now Andrew went off in the dinghy with the big Fisherman anchor hanging over the stern ready to drop in the selected spot. We were reconciled to losing this too, for if she came off we were not going to risk going aground again trying to retrieve it. The boat was now a lot lighter and in the course of the night, we pulled her head round until at last she pointed in the right direction. The westerly wind seemed to be a permanent local feature and later when we were trying to make headway through the strait we had good reason to curse it. As they say in Africa, 'cross the river before you start reviling the crocodile's mother', and at this juncture, twenty-four hours after the first stranding, we wanted a west wind, the more the better. So with the whole mainsail and staysail set and drawing, the flood tide making, the engine flat out, the kedge warp quivering under the strain of the winch, and a subdued cheer from the crew, she began to move.

The big anchor had played its part and, having got in all the warp we could, we cut it. A moment later we came to a shuddering stop alongside a large floe grounded on the edge of the shoal. We lost no time in playing our last card, a kedge of only about 25 lbs. Surprisingly enough this diminutive anchor took good hold, and as we winched in on it – the sails, the engine, and the tide all working hard to assist – the boat reluctantly bumped off. We were too anxious to be clear of this baleful shoal to bother with the little anchor. This, too, became a sacrifice together with two other anchors, all the ballast, and the old mainsail.

Giving the northernmost Zeiloyane islet the widest possible berth we headed for Freemansund. We managed to make good some five miles inside the strait against the westerly wind before the turn of the tide obliged us to anchor with our last hook on the north shore behind a little cape where we found less wind and less current. Before beginning the long haul homewards we needed ballast and water and I had intended to look for these at some anchorage in Storfjord. On going ashore that evening, however, I found a trickle of water as well as an assortment of reasonably sized stones. Like the plums in a poor man's duff they were not that plentiful and would need gathering, but we might go further and fare worse, so I decided to stock up here. The plain that extended inland looked as barren as the beach, yet on it I counted eighteen reindeer busily grazing on gravel slightly flavoured with moss.

The evil day had at last come when, our bread finished, we had to go on to biscuit, and since the supply of that was not abundant we agreed on a remarkably small daily ration. After a large dose of stiff porridge most of us went without the breakfast allotment, saving it for lunch when it could be used to convey to the mouth cheese, sardine or peanut butter, all more interesting than marmalade. We were lying a good 400 yards out and I had assumed we could bring the boat much closer to the beach, but when we found the water started to shoal almost under the bows I had half a mind to push on. Nevertheless, we blew up the inflatable and set to work with that and the pram dinghy.

Since the amount of stone that would fill the space occupied by the estimated 3 tons of jettisoned pig-iron would not weigh nearly so much, we made additional space by emptying the food lockers under the bunks on either side of the cabin. Even when stones had been shoved into every available hole the pessimists reckoned that we should not be carrying more than 2 tons. Others put it as high as 2½ tons, while Andrew, despising guesswork, invoked the aid of Archimedes and his well-known Principles. Weighing on our spring balance a piece of iron and a piece of stone, he then measured the volume of water that each displaced and in due course, all calculations made and checked, announced smugly that our stone ballast would weigh exactly a quarter of the original pig-iron. So much for what Goethe called the charnel house of science. Nothing has an uglier look than reason when it is not on our side and we hastened to tell Andrew what he could do with Archimedes and his bathwater.

By 0200 we brought the dinghies on board. Ever since the stranding the crew had cheerfully given all they had in back-breaking, wet, and grimy toil to retrieve a bad situation. On the morning of 10 August we completed the passage of Freemansund, homeward bound at last. Sorkapp would have been a useful point from which to take our departure, but fog hid everything. On a long voyage taking one's departure is a navigational luxury rather than a necessity and, according to Scoresby, whalers homeward bound from the Greenland Sea had only the vaguest notion of where they were starting from. As he writes:

'It is not unusual for a ship to bear away without the navigators having first obtained any certain knowledge as to their longitude, not having perhaps seen any land for some weeks or even months; having neither a chronometer on board, nor the means of taking a lunar observation; they set out ignorant of the meridian and sensible to being liable to an error of five or six degrees of longitude. If they steer too far to the eastward they make the coast of Norway, and if too far to the westward they probably make the Faeroes.'

In other words, you can't go wrong, and although we started off on a rather better footing than the whalers, we too were not fussy about our next landfall. We would take the wind as it served and if we got pushed too far to the west would call at the Faeroes for bread and water, otherwise we would make for Lerwick in the Shetlands. Having been there before I had a slight preference for the Faeroes, but as it happened we made neither…

In fact, Baroque *arrived in Stornoway on 6 September after a grim passage. On the 21st, the last gasp of the ancient engine, which had served her so well in Freemansund, powered her into the Lymington River where the yacht club greeted her with her traditional finishing gun. The adventure was one of Tilman's happiest and most successful. He made three further voyages before being lost at sea in 1977.*

ON THE ROCKS

Desmond Holdridge
Arctic Lights
Robert Hale 1940

Desmond Holdridge was a writer in the late 1930s. He was also a seaman, in both small craft, which he mainly skippered, and merchant vessels, which he did not. Like many men of his era, his interests spread widely, but he had never considered himself an explorer of note until one day he received a letter from the American Geographical Society asking for further details of a voyage he had made in the mid 1920s. He had then been a mere 18 years old. Taken with a lust for adventure, he had purchased a tiny half-decked fishing boat for a ridiculously small sum, had her converted into a more-or-less fully decked schooner for $75, then sailed her to the unexplored extremities of Labrador from Nova Scotia. He and his youthful shipmates lived in what are best described as seagoing slum conditions. They were seasick, their navigation was out by as much as 150 miles on occasion, and near the end Holdridge and the third hand, a taciturn Scandinavian, came very close to murdering each other. Despite numerous setbacks, however, they achieved their goal. Seamanship was lacking through sheer inexperience, but any shortfall in this department was compensated by their passing one test of character after another.

Holdridge's book Arctic Lights *is illustrated after the fashion of the day with atmospheric Edward Shenton engravings, which seem to capture the essence of their experience so much more effectively than a hundred pin-sharp electronic photographs. The trip ends in disaster as the good ship* Dolphin *is abandoned after almost completing her final passage, but the extract here, anchored in virgin territory just south of Cape Chidley across the Davis Strait from Cape Farewell in Southern Greenland, speaks volumes for her bold crew. No GPS, no lifejackets, no survival equipment of any sort. These were different times.*

O n the fifth morning of our stay in the fiord, I awoke at dawn a trifle disturbed about something, although I did not know what.

The wind's voice was as loud as ever – or was it? It seemed that perhaps its truculence had become slightly less and the motion a trifle easier. We had, the day before, lowered the centerboard, thinking it might stop something of the schooner's unchecked rolls. But, just as I made up my mind that the wind must be moderating, a squall struck and I realized that it had not. Quickly I dozed off again.

It cannot have been a minute later that a frightful blow was struck our schooner and we rushed out on deck like rabbits.

The *Dolphin* was in the breakers under a frowning eminence of broken boulders and ice-rounded rock. With every sea she lifted and fell, hard and terrifyingly, on the unyielding sand and rocks, drifting nearer to the shore, now only ten feet off, with every blow. I ran forward to retrieve the anchor, which we thought had dragged, but in came twenty feet of cable and then a frayed end; it had parted. The pounding seas bore down on the schooner, heeled over at forty-five degrees from the vertical and, laying her stern against the jagged shore, went to work at the destroying of her.

I dived below and stood in the cabin for a full minute, but in that place it was impossible not to believe the schooner was falling apart, so I came out again and with the other two stepped onto the boulders to watch; for there, at least, you could think, and desperately did we need to. If we had had a small boat and a spare anchor, we might conceivably have launched it, planted the anchor as a kedge, and dragged ourselves off. But we had neither boat nor anchor, so we did an ineffectual-seeming thing. The tide was low and, ripping up the cabin floor, we got out a pig-iron block weighing about a hundred pounds. Around it we secured a wire bridle and to that we made fast the remaining anchor cable. Then, all three together, we flung that contrivance into the deep water on the exposed port side. We pulled it. It dragged.

So, for two hours, we carried rocks on board and threw them on top of the piece of pig iron in order to hold it in place; it made quite a respectable heap. We shifted a large quantity of ballast up into the bows in order to lighten her aft and then we sat on the shore watching; until the tide came up there was nothing else to do. And during those two hours of constant battering on the rocks the *Dolphin* did not fall apart, simply because she was light and strong and cunningly fastened. Nonetheless, I expected momentarily to see that the sides had at last been beaten in, for as the water dropped away in the hollow of a wave it

could be seen that part of the side, normally curved, was flattening out; had those frames been of the heavy sawn variety, they would have been fractured and the planks would have given way.

With nothing to do but wait and see if the tide would rise before the *Dolphin* was pounded to pieces, I walked alone to a spur of barren hillside from where I hoped to see how bad the sea was. As I walked, I thought out as carefully as I could what must be done if, instead of coming off, the schooner was driven higher up on the land and left there a wreck. The nearest settlement, the only one in the world so far as we were concerned, was Port Burwell, twenty-five miles away, air-line. But between us and it there were the boiling waters of McClellan Strait, and possibly another such passage, for the chart indicated that Joksut Fiord went through to Ungava Bay. Without a boat we could never cross; therefore, the sails must be saved first and every bit of wood, rope, and wire; from these fragments we would make a canoe and then, using what food we could save, we would win our way to Port Burwell. Or we would try.

From the spur I could see out across the Atlantic and to my dumbfounded amazement, its face was serene, touched only by the breath of a moderate westerly wind. The outer bay of our fiord was churned by a moderate gale. The inner bay, where we were stranded, was still being tormented by a violent storm. At once it became clear that this thing was a local condition. The westerly wind from Ungava Bay was compressed by the mountains and then, as though from a gun, discharged over the fiord; during the five days we had lain there, the Atlantic had been smooth and splendid. I also had a view across a narrow sandy spit into Ekortiarsuk, another unexplored fiord. It was calm.

I ran back and told Robbie and Niels; if we could get her off now, we would be safe. At least, safe is the word I used for our situation aboard an anchorless, rock-pounded schooner, should she float. As the tide rose – and it was the six-foot tide of the true Labrador, not the thirty-footer of Hudson Strait – she began to drag farther ashore, but between the pig-iron kedge and desperate poling with our sweep, we held her for half an hour and she floated forward, although the shocks as the sea raised her and dropped her on the rocks were as bad as ever.

As Niels poled and Robbie hauled on the pig iron, I hoisted the reefed mainsail, sheeted in flat, and at that moment one of those great squalls struck us, driving layers of spindrift with it and, using the sail as a lever, hurled the *Dolphin* over on her side.

Something had to give. The sail had to burst, the schooner had to collapse, crushed between the upper stone of the wind-filled canvas and the nether stone of the boulders on which she lay, or she had to drag herself off.

Robbie hoisted the jib and she dragged herself off.

She made a lunge forward and struck the submerged cairn we had built over the pig iron. She glanced off it and crashed against a boulder. She glanced off that and then, with a tremendous wrench, urged by sail and pole, she hove herself free and shot out into the deep water, almost capsizing with the thrust of the mainsail.

Swiftly we dropped the main and jib and replaced it with the reefed foresail, its gaff dropped and lashed to the mast, leaving the sail scandalized, a minute three-cornered piece of canvas that drove us swiftly out of the fiord.

We shifted the ballast back to its normal position. We swore and shouted and thanked God; we were without an anchor, we were not even sure how long the schooner would float, it was September 1, and we were still far north of the tree line, but we were jubilant; the *Dolphin* was free and homeward bound.

As it seemed from the high spur, the outer bay was smooth and, when we reached the far sea, we had to set the whole foresail, the jib, and the main, in order to move, for the wind was light to moderate. That fiord had harbored a treacherous and unusual meteorological phenomenon and, had I not since heard of several others like it, I would now doubt having seen what I did indeed see. I tried out my homemade log and, as we passed Cape Kakkiviak, got a result of five knots.

'Just the same,' Niels muttered, 'there's something wrong. She don't steer like she used to; look at that.' He pointed at the tiller; it was slightly down, that is, with the booms broad off, she needed a little lee helm to keep her on her course. For the experiment's sake, we put her on the other tack and then she needed the helm nearly hard up to maintain her.

I went below, took hold of the centerboard chain, and pulled. Nothing happened. We had tried to pull it up back there on the boulders where we had been, for a while, a wreck, and it had been jammed. It was still jammed. I went out on deck.

'The centerboard's squashed up on one side,' I announced. 'We'll have to steer her this way until we can beach her somewhere and bend it back into place.' And that is the reason I do not like a centerboard.

The schooner leaked, but not nearly so badly as we had expected; though the water she took in was considerable, it constituted a nuisance rather than a menace. As for the spot on her side pounded flat by the awful beating she had received, in a few days this sprang back into its original shape. It seemed to me, then, that there was much to be said for resilience in ships and people; it seemed that, as an abstract virtue, it was preferable to brute strength. The time when I would decide that resilience alone is of small avail without inherent strength to boot was still weeks away. Our food supply was low, in fact almost exhausted, and for the first time we were unable to catch more than a few fish. We had little firewood left and saved it for meals, which each day were scantier. A series of calms made our passage along the coast slow and often we lay idle on the oily water, a lowering gray sky overhead, and inshore the jagged heap of the frost-split Torngat Mountains. Fresh snow covered their dark peaks and flanks and every day there was more of it. Once it fell on us, but lightly.

We had to put into Hebron in order to buy a new anchor and fresh provisions, but it took us five days to make it and twelve hours before arriving we ate every scrap of food aboard. For the last meal I cooked a kind of oatmeal pancake; it was wonderfully good and, try as I will, I have never been able to make one like it since.

THE LAST UNKNOWN

Alvah Simon
North to the Night
International Marine 1999

In 1994 the adventurer Alvah Simon sailed to extreme north-west Greenland in his 35ft steel yacht, Roger Henry, *with his wife, Diana, and the cat, Halifax. He was following a lifetime dream of wintering in the High Arctic. Simon had already worked his way around the globe under sail. Now he set himself the greatest challenge of his life. Like many Arctic sailors, he is a true philosopher, a free-thinking man whose appreciation of his place in nature is as subtle as his understanding of the chasm between us and the last indigenous folk of the North. The following extract from his book* North to the Night *reveals both these remarkable qualities in full measure.*

We join Roger Henry *shortly after she has left the US Greenland military base at Thule opposite the entrance to the Northwest Passage. Here she meets with a depressingly unfriendly reception and Simon is determined to press on further north, little realising that he and his wife are about to be tested as never before.*

As we sailed away, I sadly looked over my shoulder at the exact spot that Rasmussen and Freuchen first called *Ultima Thule*. The Last Unknown is no longer. With radars and radios and airplanes and rockets, those manning the Thule air base were defending freedom as they understand it. By pushing on north and out of this region entirely, I was defending freedom as I understand it.

Much to Diana's dismay, we set a course offshore direct for the Kane Basin, 150 difficult miles to the north. This long body of water lying between Ellesmere Island and Greenland is constricted like an hourglass at the entrance. To the north, in the ever-rotating Arctic Ocean, ice floes break off in epic scale and drift down the Kane Basin toward these narrows where they compress into a grinding congestion. But just fifteen meager miles beyond that danger lies Etah.

Not a living human soul is there, yet this is the spot where English officers Ross and Parry contacted the first 'Polar Eskimo' in 1818. Until their ship with its giant white wings had appeared from over the horizon, the secluded Inughuit, two-hundred strong, had thought themselves the only human beings on earth – a philosophical perspective almost too profound to imagine today. The English officers presented a ludicrous sight, standing in full dress regalia with polished and pointed shoes punching through the soft snow. Dandy feather plumes swept back from pointed hats that would neither stay on in a wind nor warm heads and ears. The mystified Inughuit asked, 'Are you from the Sun or the Moon?'

The closer we crept through the thickening floes, the more excited I became, knowing we had achieved the same latitude that William Baffin had in 1616. Diana had read all the books and remembered the details too well. 'Our intention was never to set a record for the farthest point north,' she argued. 'We used too much fuel getting here. The great explorers had enormous boats and huge crews, and there are only the two of us. Kane's boat was trapped for two years, then crushed. Peary's was violently pushed ashore. MacMillan was dropped off and told he would be relieved the next season. It was *four years* before a ship could break through!'

I climbed the mast as much to escape from logic as to see ahead. The last thing I wanted was to be confused with the facts. I looked out on a heady view of that which so few have dared – true wilderness. Ellesmere Island lay large on the western horizon. That name rings synonymous with adventure, and I ached to walk its shores. The horizon was solid white; we could make no straight progress. Between the old floes, new ice was forming like congealing fat. I tried to dismiss the weather reports in spite of a fast-falling barometer. Cape Alexander, the sentinel to the Kane Basin, was disappearing in dense fog. We might round it, but if the wind strengthened before we reached the protection of Etah, the grinding polar pack ice would trap us. I looked back at the miles of dense ice through which we had wound our way. A wind shift would compress it quickly, blocking any retreat. *Should we make for the village of Qaanaaq, refuel, and wait?* I had to decide. Ahead, only half a day's travel after half a lifetime's dreaming, there at my fingertips was all the history, all the glory of the North, but that too is the story of the North. You cannot be too timid, nor too bold. You must simply be *right*, exactly and every time. I tried to make all the factors add up to what I wanted them to say: *Press on!*

My head was spinning. I clung to the mast. *Think! What have you learned? Remember the lesson of Kane's unchecked ambition: 'Prudence and foolhardiness lie within sight of each other up here.' But what about 'Fortune favours the brave?' If you hesitate out of fear, then you must move directly toward that fear.*

That thought was based on the silly notion that all fear is unfounded. Still, I might have made the mistake of rushing headlong forward had I not looked down just then from the high masthead. We were butted up against an ice wall. The boat was lost in the brash of ice chips and dwarfed into insignificance by giant floes. Diana stood on the bow. I looked up and out on this tumbled ice and terrible land, and then down again. She looked so small, so vulnerable. And then it hit me – hard. *My God, what am I doing? I've pushed myself this far north, but I have pulled that poor woman. I'm up here blathering about the virtues of bravery. What about trust? What about responsibility? No, we are not just at the edge of the ice – we are at the edge of our experience and endurance.*

I shouted down to Diana, 'Please enter in the log 77 degrees, 45 minutes, our farthest point north. You're right; we cannot go farther safely.' She exhaled a long-held breath and rolled her eyes skyward as if a prayer had been answered. That she wasn't already in open mutiny was a testament to her toughness. We turned to the southeast and steamed for Qaanaaq. Diana had seen the accumulating signs of approaching trouble, and she knew that nature always speaks the truth. An hour after we altered course the *Piteraq* struck.

Sixty knot winds howled off the ice cap. The sea boiled. Ice boulders heaved and rolled on its surface. It is that rumbling noise, as if the ice is calling out your name, that is most terrifying. We made a run for Herbert Island, looking for protection in its lee, but there was no lee. The wind blasted us from port, then starboard, then astern, then from above. Currents rammed the ice in behind the island. Waves pounded the shores. Clouds hurtled across the sky in confusion. Tying off to floes that were fifty to five hundred feet long, we trailed along behind, letting them clear out the smaller brash in their path, but then they would spin and press us toward another danger. At one point, caught in the fork of a Y closing with the point of a wedge, we frantically cast off. We pulled clear just as the ice vise slammed shut. We tucked in behind another. I jumped onto the slippery floes and, one after another, frantically pounded ice screws into each one's hard surface, shouting above the din for Diana to throw me a line so I could pull the boat up tight to its edge. For a while we would remain safe; then the pan would rotate and we'd be squeezed out. Onto another, then another, always being pushed down toward Qaanaaq.

After twenty-four hours of this, we passed into the real maelstrom. The winds rolled off the smooth ice cap, then funneled into steep valleys that turbocharged them into screeching williwaws seemingly bent on our destruction. Two more days of battle left us exhausted. Too spiritless to fight it any longer, we moved in closer to shore and tried to anchor. We dragged anchor and re-anchored a dozen times. My arms ached. I did not think I could haul on the heavy chain again when, finally, the anchor held. But then, to windward, three building-sized blocks of ice pressed down on us. I did not want to weigh anchor again – anything but that. I considered risking that the shallow icebergs would narrowly miss us. These are the dangerous moments, when body and will weaken, when one is tempted to do something less than the right thing.

I hauled away until my arms screamed in protest. I grabbed the handle of the windlass and, with furious strokes, started to ratchet in the rope attached to the long anchor chain. Just as I threw all my weight into it, the windlass jammed. I heard a snap in my back and fell down in white-light pain. The berg bore down on us steadily. I screamed to Diana at the helm for help. Hand over hand, with me on my knees sweating in pain, we pulled the rope until we could run it aft to a halyard winch on the mast. We ground away, our bodies aching and hearts thumping. The anchor clanged into its rollers just as an ice wall towered over the *Roger Henry*. There was a shudder, then the protest of twisting steel. I watched in horror as a steel stanchion collapsed in slow motion. I rammed the boathook into the berg, planted my feet, and spun us off, paying dearly for that exertion.

Diana ran back to the helm, slapped the gear lever forward, and swung away to avoid the next threat. The engine screeched and belched black smoke. Above the roar of the engine and the howl of those winds, we shouted to each other the location of approaching dangers like a bomber under fighter attack: 'Two o'clock, two o'clock!' When the wind stripped the words out of our mouths we resorted to a series of hand signals developed over our years together. And when we said to each other that it simply could not blow much longer, it did, with even more fury.

After three days the storm vented its rage, and conditions abated a little. Relieved, I thought our ordeal would soon be over. By chance I looked back and, heading out over the last ice pan, skipped a happy Halifax. Our thoughts were of survival, hers of freedom. Philosophically, she outranked us, but I was plenty mad just the same. We raced back. I scrambled onto the treacherous ice while Diana fought to control the vessel. The more frantic I became, the louder I shouted, the farther Halifax fled. Finally, I sat on the ice as if it was a quiet day in the park. Halifax ran back to me, enticing me back into the chase. I pounced on her and pressed her back into onboard service.

I lay on the bow, trying to relax the torn muscles in my lower back and sneak some sleep between intermittent dramas. In spite of the pain, fatigue, wind, waves, and ice, I realized I was thoroughly enjoying myself. This was true adventure, life in the North, as it was, as it still can be. We were privileged to be able to share in its harsh reality. That privilege, however, lasted four full days, stretching us to our limits.

When the storm was over, Diana tended the boat while I managed to get ashore at Qaanaaq (the Far North), a ramshackle town of five hundred Inuit scattered across an open slope. There is no natural harbor and no apparent reason for placing a town in that forlorn wind tunnel when the entire hamlet was moved there from Thule. Fortunately, the Inuit are accustomed to shifting fortunes. The presence of that jumbo landing strip broke the seal that held the far North in impenetrable remoteness. Change crept in like water on a floodplain, its tendrils probing in different directions. Their lives now span the Stone Age to the space age. High antennae and satellite dishes make useful landmarks for homebound kayaking harpoonists. Grocery stores, with frozen-food sections full of fish caught in Greenland, shipped to Denmark, and re-imported to Greenland, do a brisk trade in expensive colas and chips. Racks at the checkout counter conveniently display last-minute necessities – bread, milk, matches, pornographic movies.

A people whose minds conceive in circles now live in square, modern houses. Now there need not be darkness, for when the sun goes off the generators go on, powering the VCRs that fill their heads with images of the Rambo culture to the south and the feeling that their lives pale in comparison. But from those lit doorways still emerge thick-chested men with flat, wise faces framed in bangs of straight, ebony hair. They walk with the shuffling gate of slick-surface dwellers into a world they know well. They are clad in sealskin boots, polar bear-fur pants, and long parkas fringed in wolf or wolverine, and they carry draped over their shoulders rifles, nets, and spears.

Printed with the kind permission of the author, Alvah Simon.

LONG-DISTANCE CRUISING AND RACING

Ghosts in the night Val Howells

Singing through the storm Uffa Fox

An impromptu ocean race Richard Maury

A girl in each hull James Wharram

Stowaway Edward Allcard

Ripped off in the Red Sea Dwight Long

Drama and farce in the far Pacific Ben Pester

GHOSTS IN THE NIGHT

Val Howells
Sailing into Solitude
Temple Press 1966

In the summer of 1960, Sir Francis Chichester, Blondie Hasler, Val Howells and Dr David Lewis set out from Plymouth towards New York on the first-ever single-handed transatlantic race. The prize was a wagered barrel of beer. By today's standards, even Chichester's 40ft Gypsy Moth would be considered marginal for the job. Two of the other three were delicate 26ft Folkboats. The fourth, a slightly heavier Laurent Giles Vertue of similar length. Of the numerous books that have been written about this and subsequent similar events, Val Howells' Sailing into Solitude stands unique in its self-deprecatory humour, coupled with an almost unbelievable honesty. Howells – seaman, farmer, restaurateur and a man larger than life in every way – completes the voyage after a sojourn in Bermuda, but it is a slog that seems never-ending. He chooses the southern route where the heat of the sun and the often dreamy conditions work on his mind in a way he bravely elects to share with his readers. He talks of Iron Mike, his self-steering gear, as a sort of shipmate, but there is a darker presence aboard too – an alter ego who appears unannounced from time to time to deliver a cutting commentary on his boss's performance. We join Howells and his strange crew 800 miles east of Bermuda with the ghostly companion doing the talking.

'THAT evening I just couldn't stand his company any more. I thought that if I didn't get away, even for just an hour, he would drive me mad. I made him a decent meal, but all the time I slaved over the stove he stood moodily watching me, then he picked it over, so fastidiously, and I had to put up with his grumbles. It even put me off my own meal. A person can only stand so much of that sort of thing, can't they? Then they're off. I left him. I tell you straight. I couldn't stand it for another minute.

It wasn't only the grumbling you know – Oh no! It's that hulking great body of his.

It's laughable really. There he is – prancing about near enough nude. Nature boy indeed, but what riles me most is his language. I just can't stand profanity, and he really has a foul mouth. I don't like that in a man, do you? There's no need for it. I can express my thoughts without those filthy words, and it isn't as if he was being completely honest. Look at him now – lying on the starboard bunk on top of our sleeping bag. See how he's sweating? And to think that I have to go back, and lie alongside that. And he dreams you know. Not those amusing little things we used to have together. No – he doesn't seem satisfied with that. Now it's all got to be on a gigantic scale, and in full colour. Sometimes he wakes me up by the absolute frenzy that he works himself into. Nothing I can say seems to do any good. What's the use when you have a man like that? There are other things too. Nasty dirty beast that he is. Just lately his dreams have been taking on a queer twist. Yes – they're becoming very erotic. In the beginning they worried him. But now he seems to be enjoying them – and it's me who is getting worried.'

It was a fine night, the breeze had veered a point and fallen away to little more than a light air. We went before it as lightly as a thistledown, not keeping a very good course, just wandering away to the Westward. I felt that I could hardly complain to Mike, I was finding it difficult enough to concentrate on the essential tasks. Sometimes I felt quite incapable of movement, as if some essential cog were missing. Then, whatever it was would return, and once more I would be capable of action.

At five-thirty, another blood-quickening sunrise; the forerunner of another scorching day. We were reaching now as close to West as Mike could hold her. It was just too hot on deck and I had to be content with his performance. This morning, when I was filling the kettle from the daily-use can, I discovered that I had used three-quarters of a gallon of fresh water during the previous twenty-four hours; much above my normal rate, and it was all used for drinking purposes. I also drank a can of beer.

And the answer to that, mate ... 'Stay out of the sun.'

Sleep – deep, refreshing, dreamless. Re-stitching the corners of a poorly seamed mind, worn threadbare by the passage of the numberless days and the endless nights. An altering perspective, foreshortening the task.

The barometer still high, had even climbed during the night, and now stood at 1048mb, betrayed by its own extravagance, but another fine day. We are making progress. Still being surprised by the sudden appearance of flying fish which leave the startled ocean as a flight of starlings might leave a quiet wood. One has flown aboard, perhaps when I was below, and it was dead when I found it, lying on the port side-deck, robbed of life by this incalculable chance.

Another minor tragedy. I lost my yellow plastic bucket.

It cuts me as the passing of a friend, the more so because it was entirely my own fault. Who else? I was leaning outboard, dipping up some of the bright blue water that changes amazingly as it is encompassed by the yellow pail. As the lip of the bucket caught the water, its weight increased so rapidly that it was snatched out of my grasp before I had time to curl my fingers.

I was fond of that bucket. I had bathed in it, spewed up into it, washed the crocks in it, swilled the decks with it, sluiced away sulphuric acid with it. It had been a purposeful bucket, and now it was gone. All that remained was its red partner. This was the bucket of the toilet, which would now have to be used for every task. A disturbing thought.

During the afternoon a dark round object appears ahead. No need to alter course, we pass close-to, twenty yards to the South'ard. It is rusty, trails long weed, is four feet in diameter. It is almost certainly a mine.

'I just have to laugh. There he goes again, vainly trying to rationalise. Almost certainly a mine! I ask you? How can he possibly tell? Of course, he *thinks* it's a mine. He saw it when it was three miles distant. It stood out well on the top of a swell. He is very proud of his eye-sight, you know. That's another of those little things that I find so irritating. His boastful attitude, to what is, after all, just average performance. Now he's worrying about the number of similar objects he has passed during the night. I can tell him. Dozens! From where I am now, I can see a large baulk of timber a few miles to the South'ard. And only the night before last she sailed within a few feet of a water-logged lifeboat that's been drifting around for years; I just sit back and wait for the crash. What fun it will be. See him scramble madly out of the cabin. He will have been sleeping, of course. I keep telling him that he's getting much too blasé about this look-out of his. He will only have a few seconds to get up on deck, barking his shins on the companionway steps and howling like a dog in his despair. If he is lucky, he will be able to cut away the liferaft before she sinks. If he manages to get the thing blown up, he'll scramble in, and sit like a Buddha, week after week, while he drifts helplessly. I don't mind telling you – I don't fancy going with him on that job. About half a mile from where we are now there are several sharks – big ones. Poor Howells. I've told him. They'll soon know there's something amiss and they'll be along to join in the fun before he can say a round of prayers to that funny God of his. Didn't you know that he prayed? It just goes to show what I've been saying. You can't trust him. But all his prayers won't do him any good. Oh no. The sharks come just the same.

Many's the time I've told him that pride comes before a fall. There's a lot in these old sayings, y'know. Isn't there?'

As I watched the mysterious object drop astern I wondered vaguely how long it had been wandering the ocean.

While filling in the evening journal I noticed that the log had stopped once more, and while I was pulling it in to clear the weed I slipped and cut the sole of my foot on one of the brass wing-nuts that held fast the hatch of the after locker. It didn't seem serious and I just cleaned it out with a little disinfectant and stuck an Elastoplast over the wound.

'That's a laugh, it illustrates what I mean when I say that you can't trust him. That's the very subject he keeps bothering me about most – his great ugly body. He's always on about it, looking at it, feeling it and relating its present to its previous performance. It's quite obvious to me that he's afraid that something will happen to it. Once, when he had fallen while he was doing some silly job up on the foredeck, he thought he had broken his leg, the left one I think it was. You should have heard the language! It must have been quite agonising for him, the way he tried to work himself down the companionway steps into the cabin. Even I felt a twinge of pity for the brute. He had fallen awkwardly and his leg was broken above the knee, which must be more awkward than one below. Anyway, he was crying like a baby by the time he had managed to ease himself into the cabin. He fell down the last two steps, and the jagged end of the bone stuck through the skin. It gave me quite a turn to see it, I can tell you. And then he couldn't reach the First-Aid box. I was very tempted to help him, but what could I do under the circumstances? He made it eventually. And then almost cried when he found there wasn't any morphine. The fool had forgotten David Lewis saying it was illegal to carry the stuff. Anyway, he used some of the alternative tablets that David had given him. But he said they weren't very effective.

The wound soon turned septic, as I told him it would. I told him all the time. Straight up, I told him. And all he did was to heap abuse on my head. I ask you, how can you help a man like that? After a few days he became delirious, and I found it quite impossible to stay with him. That's why I'm up here now, waiting for him to get back to normal. It's a frightful bore.'

I was glad to see the dawn that Thursday morning. It had not been an easy night…

SINGING THROUGH
THE STORM

Uffa Fox
The Crest of the Wave
Peter Davies 1939

Uffa Fox (1898–1972) was not only a fine seaman and boatbuilder, he was also a philosopher, writer and commentator. After he'd set up his first boatyard in a pensioned-off Cowes chain ferry, a typical early exploit was a Channel crossing in an open whaleboat with his troop of Sea Scouts. He swore the lads to secrecy lest their fathers forbid the enterprise, as they certainly would have done. Setting his sights on Paris he returned home to be charged with 'placing young lives in jeopardy'. The parents declared him the Devil incarnate, but the boys loved him.

Uffa pioneered planing dinghies, and in 1928 his International 14 Avenger won 52 'firsts' in 58 starts, including the Prince of Wales Cup. He was always fond of a glass, and his more apocryphal exploits include riding a horse into his bedroom after a session with his cronies. During the Second World War he is said to have liberated the guns from a shot-down German aircraft, setting them up on his roof to blaze away at incoming bombers until the ammunition ran out.

Uffa Fox's inaugural deep-sea experience came in 1920 when he signed on as crew from Cowes to New York on the last day of August. Readers who have studied the North Atlantic crossing will agree that this was not the favoured season for such a trip with the Typhoon, *a gaff ketch of 35ft waterline and 6ft draught. Uffa's father declared her 'unbalanced', with a 'hollow, weak bow and a broad stern'. When his son pointed out that she had recently sailed over from Nova Scotia without incident, the old man responded unarguably that 'if you threw a box overboard in North America it would cross the Atlantic and be unable to help itself coming to England'.*

Uffa signed on regardless for what was to prove a nightmare passage. One gale led to another with matters going really to the bad in early November, close to their destination. In his book The Crest of the Wave, *Fox describes a ferocious battering, but his sheer delight in living shines through like a sunbeam. Great seaman he surely was, but his comments transcend the mere lessons to be learned from his acute analysis of what happened. He always lets us in on the funny side.*

We join Typhoon *on 16 November 1920, about 350 miles south-east of New York, just as her main gaff lacing carries away. Uffa is at the mast struggling to lower the mainsail.*

0610. Blowing and raining like old Nick. WWN (skipper) woke as Jim was casually dressing. He heard the wind whistling and the mainsail flapping and got wild (we all do when hungry). He chewed Jim up and rushed forward to me and banged me on the nose with his elbow. Good job I was there or he might have gone overboard (motion of ship pretty bad) but my nose brought him up. Asked if he'd hurt his elbow, he said 'a bit' and thought it was the mast he'd hit until I explained afterwards…

1030. Jim, Charles and I got out and half hoisted trysail to blanket jib, which then stowed. Jim asked me once if I'd hurt myself as a sea banged me against the bowsprit. I replied, 'No, but I've given myself a hell of a twist,' as I noticed my oilskins were on the wrong way round…

WWN at the wheel getting impatient, so take time hoisting trysail; would like a penny for every time I've answered his anxious enquiry with, 'Nothing broken, only a wheel come off,' a bad habit rubbing people up the wrong way. It is rotten of me for WWN owns the ship and is responsible for kids like Jim and myself…

By afternoon the weather had deteriorated further.

1510. Charles relieved me at the wheel. Seas worse, which seemed impossible five hours ago: everything can be worse, but it is not very comforting when after losing thirty bob *[£1.50]*, a friend tells you it is better than sixty *[£3.00]*.

We got knocked down with our masts in the water. I'd just taken off my oilies when with a bang we went over to port. I grabbed the table and Dillaway's bunk, he just managed to stay in it. Jim dropped from his bunk on to WWN, who was lying on the port seat. Jim had an amazed expression as he cleared the ditty box on the dresser. I wanted to laugh, hadn't time to get frightened before she came up. Suddenly thought of Charles (at the helm) and looking through the port was relieved to see him sitting at the wheel with a very worried and puzzled expression on his face. There was the cockpit full of water, and our empty kegs floating about with the last of our salt beef. Charles looked exactly like Robinson Crusoe on his raft just leaving the wreck. He looked so funny that I laughed, which made WWN wild as he had just discovered his pyjamas covered with fuel oil.

By now it was dusk, and to make steering easier we trailed two long lines astern, which steadied her as she was on top of the seas. The difference in steering was so great, that we decided to run on through the night rather than heave to…

From 0700 till 1300 the wind had increased, and was still increasing; the new sea making up over the old was heavier and more confused than the sea we had before encountered. The wind blew harder than ever in a succession of vicious squalls. The tops of the seas were blown off, and the valleys were streaked with spume and spray flying across like snow before a gale. The sting of the spray could be felt under oilskins, and we had already streamed our second rope astern, this time bent on to a heavy iron pail, otherwise no helmsman on earth could have steered *Typhoon* for five minutes.

The skipper now decided to heave to, and we prepared the Voss type sea anchor below, as it was easier to work there than on deck, and then took it to the cockpit to rig, with Charles sitting and lying on it as the wind tried to lift it out of the boat, when it would have blown away to leeward and perhaps turned into a kite. The sea anchor warp was already rove through a fairlead on the bowsprit end to the cockpit, so we had only to drop it over from aft and all would be well.

So we were all ready: Dillaway was to pump bilge water and oil out with the bilge pump, Jim and I were to lower and stow the trysail then make our way aft and help Charles stream the sea anchor, while the skipper steered. And Jim and I were to put lifelines on, but although we said 'Yes' to the skipper, we foolishly disobeyed orders, feeling that they would hamper our movements. I went first to the mainmast to gather in the trysail halyard before Jim left the cockpit to join me for the actual hauling down of the sail, which we thought would stick in that wind; for all our halyards and ropes were trailing overboard and astern like the arms and legs of an octopus.

As soon as I had coiled the halyard, I signalled to Jim to come forward. He had just climbed out when one heavy sea came, but he held on to the mizzen and I to the mainmast for that one, which was the forerunner of another with tons and tons of water, which broke aboard us from an enormous height. That sea towered above us like a church; in moments like that the size cannot be judged accurately, for the brain is too excited, but to me it looked to have a face that was practically vertical, but with the top like an overhanging cliff thirty feet above us, and we had already climbed about fifteen feet from its base. So there *Typhoon* seemed to me to be climbing the face of a plumb cliff, and when she had climbed fifteen feet the other thirty feet crashed down on her. It was pretty grim. Jim, who was half–way between the two masts on his way forward to me, with only the handrail to hold on to, had no chance at all and was swept off. I had my legs wrapped round the mainmast and held on for a fraction of a second. Then I seemed to be swept miles and miles, and the mainmast came down and hit me, so clutching it grimly, I hung on, and slowly at first, *Typhoon* righted (for she had been knocked on her beam ends and past). I was lifted out of the water, and found myself right up the mast clinging to the hounds. Sliding to the deck I gave a heave at the trysail, and it came down as easily as though there had been no wind at all.

I then rushed aft to help with Jim who meantime had caught one of the ropes we had trailed astern, and had been hauled alongside as *Typhoon*'s way slackened. Our struggle to hoist him aboard will always live in my memory. It seemed hours before we three could hoist him over the rail, and it was not until the skipper had put a heavy boathook under him and prised down on it, using it as a handspike, which raised Jim to the level of the rail, that we slid him in to safety.

Jim was pushed below, and the sea anchor streamed. But first of all it burst its spreaders, and then the warp carried away, and we fell away again broadside to the seas. Making things snug on deck, we went below and left *Typhoon* to her own ways; it was the best thing we could have done for she seemed quite happy…

We made ourselves as comfortable as we could, spreading towels over the floorboards to keep the broken glass underneath, and then opened the last tin of soup, the last tin of beef, and the last tin of mixed vegetables; we thought how close we had been to missing that last meal altogether, and that we might take it inside us wherever we went. We also opened a bottle of cognac, after which we sang our best songs, and then to bed, with the seas crashing down at regular intervals.

And we none of us woke till it was broad daylight. The wind had eased and Charles lit the coal stove; we found some porridge, which had fallen into Dillaway's bunk, and fried it for breakfast, and with a tiny drop of soup felt braced up and cheerful.

'Joy cometh in the morning,' I used to sing without realising how true it was, for how can a boy of twelve know the full meaning of words? Those who have spent a night of doubts and fears at the bedside of someone dear to them, will understand when they remember the hope the bright gleams of sunshine brought, how joyful we were and how our joy was increased by finding the porridge in Dillaway's bunk.

The sea anchor mentioned by Uffa is of the type made famous by Captain Voss, a pioneering voyager in canoe yachts. Voss put his survival down to this heavy piece of gear, the forerunner of the modern para-anchor.

It was deployed to keep the yacht head-to-sea rather than presenting her shoulder to the elements as recommended by L & L Pardey in their excellent book Storm Tactics. *It is small wonder that the canvas-and-timber contraption – very likely past its best after prolonged stowage in airless conditions below decks – carried away. For an old-fashioned, heavy displacement gaff-rigger to survive subsequently by lying a'hull was by no means unusual. Many, including my own, did so successfully with far less risk of being rolled than would attend a lighter, beamier craft.*

Reproduced with permission of Tony Dixon.

AN IMPROMPTU
OCEAN RACE

Richard Maury
The Saga of Cimba
George G Harrap & Co 1939

Yachts cruising the South Seas were a rarity in the 1930s. As a result, their exploits are filled with a colour and richness that's hard to find 80 years later. In 1933, Richard Maury set sail from Connecticut in the 35ft 'Bluenose' Nova Scotian schooner Cimba *with commendably little money in order to discover the Pacific for himself. The voyage is documented in his book* The Saga of Cimba, *first published in 1939, and now available in reprint. The prose is expansive in a way nobody could emulate in the literary world of the 21st century, yet Maury keeps his sentiments in check with a pre-war stiff upper lip which those who seek modern, 'in-your-face' emotional description simply fail to understand. The work remains*

controversial, but is acknowledged by some to be a classic of nautical writing.

Aged 23 when he left, Maury was joined by two companions on this leg of his voyage; they had all served in square-riggers. In the extract below, the young men rise to the challenge of an impromptu yacht race while carrying a group of locals from Bora Bora to reef-strewn Maupiti, 30 miles away. The race is great fun, the locals grand value, and the running of the then-unmarked pass through the reef is memorable to say the least.

Tragically, Maury subsequently lost his ship, not to the sea despite a stranding on the reefs of Fiji, but to local bureaucrats demanding taxes, bonds and all the other officially sanctioned robberies which have subsequently multiplied on a global scale. Once again, he has been criticised for his actions by people who were not there. A more positive point of view of this clearly resourceful man might be that in the sorry end to his tale he was, as in so much else, a true pioneer.

R ETURNING to Vaitape, we found a yacht, the *Potii Farani*, the only craft of the lonely island of Maupiti, riding at anchors. A good six feet longer than the *Cimba*, she was of an able model, sweet of line, amply masted – all in all a worthy rival for the Bluenoser. And this she was to be, as we, also bound for Maupiti, accepted a challenge from her crew.

At 7 a.m. on May 17 both craft got under way, the *Potii Farani* with a native crew of six and one Gerlac, a young German wanderer, while the *Cimba* had eight passengers aboard – Tira, an ancient Maupitian, stranded on Bora Bora for more than a year; Tu, a large, happy native, who could never save a franc for the fare home; his wife, Clotira, their grown daughter, and four little girls, all of whom had been marooned from Maupiti for over three years. When the sails were set the womenfolk, refusing to go below, prepared for sea in the manner of all Polynesian women, binding cloths tightly about their middles before lying on deck, prostrate, covered head to foot in white sheets, neither to stir nor speak until Maupiti was gained.

Side by side, schooner and yawl ran for Te-ava-nui Pass, neither one able to lead the other to sea. Reaching open ocean, they drew fair, light winds, in which the handsome yawl pulled away, heading for Maupiti, thirty miles due west. With Gerlac, the German, playing a harmonica on her deck, she crept out ahead, lifting neatly to a sea just making up, until finally Tu, standing on our deck ridiculing the other crew, grew comparatively quiet, and old Tira, with a lure of pearl-shell wagered on the schooner, subsided into philosophical silence.

Running wing and wing, we attempted to pull under the yawl's stern, blanketing her sails with our smaller ones. We failed. When a wingsail was set to aid the foresail and mainsail the crew of the yawl broke out a big spinnaker, ran a smaller one up the jigger, and to catch draughts between main and spinnaker hoisted a fifth sail, a catch-all jib, filling over the bowsprit. At that point, however, a series of gusts favoured our quarter; the *Cimba* hurried, closed the lead, ran under the yawl's counter, came alongside, carried way, and took a full length lead amid loud shouting, led by Tu, who, leaning overside, hurled insult upon insult at the men of Maupiti. As the deck began to cant we secured lanyards about the immovable women, only one of whom stirred, and then only to give Tu an inscrutable look. The lead was held, the shouting turned to laughter, and as we swayed over the sea the natives of both craft began to sing, while Gerlac, the wanderer, struck up an Island song.

Ten minutes passed, the variables withdrew before the steadier, lighter trade wind, and the yacht-like *Potii Farani* drew abeam, and despite the jeers of our vociferous passenger swept ahead. The heretofore unbeaten Bluenoser, her bow spooning water, fell farther and farther astern, to taste defeat, which, like despair, like hope, like victory itself, must, in the blind acceptance of all revelations, also be known first-hand. And now one thing became certain: the trade wind would grow no bolder. It had set in for the day, a wide wind not to fluke, increase, or diminish, to favour neither craft over the remaining twenty-odd miles. Old Tira steered, Tu amused himself with a harpoon; we held the after-deck, meditating in the sun, while gently the sea rocked the freight of shrouded women.

An hour and a half went by, and then, with Maupiti rising quickly in the west, and the yawl running in miniature quarter of a mile out in front, Dombey suggested that we were holding our own. All hands watched, gauging the separating space. Finally there could be no doubt but that the *Cimba* had begun to hang on, and at the end of another fifteen minutes' work we knew that she had taken in a little of the lead. Rolling her fisherman's shear, setting astern a noisy flow of white drift, working with her cut-water, she began to march out to her rival with the half-drunk, half-graceful movements of a scudding craft. We could make nothing of it, nothing at all. The wind, favouring neither vessel, had not altered direction or velocity. The yawl appeared to be moving as unconcernedly as ever, to be aided by every ounce of her canvas as the *Cimba* closed in, a slug of broken water under her foot; and we knew that as crews we were not outsailing the Maupitians, who were managing their craft as adroitly as ever our schooner was being handled.

The two craft came together, lunging over a skeleton-work of spume, diving, swinging in the trade-wind chop, rolling their cloth over vast, shadowless space, tense with movement, restrained, dancing rather than racing, leaving their crews to the calculation of results.

With old Tira at the helm, we moved out in front and reached for the black hills of Maupiti, rising into the sky. Now the turn-about was explained. It had been calm at the outset, but the trades, returning after a night of rest, had not been long in forcing up a short, steep sea, causing the yawl to labour more and more, the schooner to begin planing on rough capped water. Hull-lines, not sail-power, had brought about the unexpected. The *Potii Farani*, for all her good looks, had a bow that was inclined to be walled, a type found occasionally in yachts insufficiently 'appled' to run down-sea; a bow designed primarily for slicing to windward, not for all-round work, and certainly not for bolstering a press of sail before sharpened wave formations. And she had one last defect. As in many yawls and ketches, the mainmast was stepped, without rake, so far forward that while running the bows became overburdened and staggered, rolling the wind out of the sails.

As the *Cimba* went by, the natives of the yawl cheered, answered Tu's catcalls, and appeared quite pleased that the schooner was to show them home. For there was no catching her. The breaking sea pleased her, she planed crest to crest, forged through the troughs, and drew up off Maupiti Pass half a mile ahead of the yawl.

The race was over, and now something of a more serious nature lay ahead, that of shooting the pass, a dangerous inlet holding the island of Maupiti and its immense lagoon in eternal isolation. Even while laying-to quarter of a mile in the offing we could see a great play of water rushing the coral barrier, and hear the boom of heavy surf above the wind. The yawl drew up, the lower edges of her sails wet with spray, her crew shouting for us to precede them – etiquette of the Islands, no doubt. Rolling wildly, they brought up into the eye of the wind and stopped to watch us enter.

We did not hurry. The women and girls were untied, and after much persuasion, aided by the energetic and jubilant Tu, were sent below. The wingsail was carefully stowed, the boom unshipped and secured between the shrouds, the mainsail and jib were brought down, the foresail was close-sheeted to act as a steadying sail, and the engine, primed for the occasion, was set going, to be vigilantly tended by Dombey. The noisy Tu was brought to silence. With decks cleared and the motor running smoothly we headed for the passage. I kept forward to con from the bow, Taggart stationed himself beside Tira, our pilot, whose eyesight we had yet to learn was failing, while Tu, his lips pressed tightly together, crouched in the waterways.

Twenty yards off the entrance a languid swell moved in, glided for the stern, elevated us, paused. The inclining top of glass moved slowly, curved, mounted, acquired an edge, a thin line of agitated water that arose, trembled, grew higher, whiter, broke, exploded, and flung us headlong at a narrow coral mouth. Down into a mill-stream, green and foaming, barred with eddies and wild currents, we ran, at ten or eleven knots. The bows swerved, uncontrolled; the engine coughed, missed a stroke, continued. A woman screamed; then the noise of the pass drowned out all sound. A triangular wave caught us, half submerged us, ricocheted us into the coral to starboard; the helm was jammed over, the masts jumped, the entire rigging quivered. The bow cut past the coral, missing it by yards, angled down-water, headed for mid-channel, into an island of bright submerged coral, then, forced over by propeller, by rudder, drew away just in time, curving in a quick arc into the slash of a whirlpool. The hull trembled. A mass of water lifted over the bows, hiding the island ahead. Some one shouted, 'She's through!' The water fell away and we were shooting between two walls of palm-trees, running downhill into a large and placid lagoon.

With a sigh I turned aft. Tu was still in a crouching position, but the runaway schooner had been too much for the amiable Tira, and I saw that Taggart, a smile on his face, had taken the helm in a crucial moment. Over their heads the flying *Potii Farani* was running the pass, with coral close aboard to either side, her bows in foam, her masts lurching wildly. In another moment she had swept through, to join us off the two islands at the edge of the lagoon. Someone laughed, flung open the companion, and ordered the women on deck. Dombey appeared from the after-hatch, the hero of the occasion, having struggled successfully to bring the failing engine back to action within the dark and rolling storeroom. Every one was happy. Tu, himself once more, kissed the women and children, who turned on reaching deck, looked at their home island, and cried!

The two vessels left the uninhabited islets astern, crossed the lagoon where a wide spit of sand stretched far to the eastward, and tied up at the landing-place beneath the cliffs of Maupiti. Never before had two vessels reached Maupiti together, and the people, perhaps three hundred in all, swarmed excitedly about the craft. Tu, brimming over, exuberant, threw his arms about old friends, kissed the women, while Tira tried to explain a year's absence to an ancient wife, who, though apparently deaf, was certainly by no means mute. There was much laughter, some weeping. The crew of the yawl cheered the *Cimba*; the crew of the *Cimba* cheered the yawl…

A GIRL IN EACH HULL

James Wharram

Two Girls, Two Catamarans

Abelard-Schuman 1969

A great pioneer of multihull voyaging, James Wharram sailed from Las Palmas towards Trinidad two days before Christmas, 1955. His crew consisted of two girls, Ruth and Jutta, and Pepe the dog. His boat was the 23ft catamaran Tangaroa, *which he had designed and built himself. Against advice from most of the pundits of the day, he held true to beliefs which he still holds to this day (2015), after putting them well and truly on the line across the oceans of the world. His work has opened long-range*

voyaging to many who would never have made the leap into the unknown without his inspiring example.

Following the philosophies of the traditional seafarers of the Pacific, Tangaroa's *tiny plywood hulls were connected by flexibly mounted beams and an open slatted platform. It is impossible to conceive of a vessel further removed from today's high-tech race boats. Wharram's first book,* Two Girls, Two Catamarans, *has a charm that has stood the test of time.*

'THE Polynesians did it, and so will I,' went the refrain through my head, but an echo came: 'They had catamarans 60 to 90 feet long, with many experienced men.' Only the desperate, fleeing from war would have ventured three thousand miles across the ocean in a twenty-three and a half foot catamaran. 'It will be all right,' I assured myself. 'Once in the trade winds, it will be all right.'

The longed-for easterlies arrived on Christmas Day. Despite unexpected cold, hard winds and big seas, Wharram and the girls set up a modest pair of twin spinnakers and led the sheets to the tiller in an effective self-steering arrangement. All went well until the New Year.

Tangaroa's deck was littered with boxes of vegetables, spare sails, oars, but finding a spot by the mast, I braced myself against it, and as I ate my breakfast, watched *Tangaroa* rise endlessly over the steep seas.

A cliff face of water would advance, crested white with foam. It seemed impossible to rise over it, but at the last minute, *Tangaroa's* stern would lift. Leaning my head back, I looked up at the wind-filled spinnakers bending the mast. My eyes followed the controlling ropes from the boom ends leading to the rudders, which constantly moved, correcting *Tangaroa's* course. The knot of anxiety and discomfort, because of the weather of the previous days, began to dissolve in the sun and beauty of the scene; then, suddenly, it was all over. The port spinnaker and boom shot forward, flapping wildly as it lost the wind. The full starboard spinnaker dragged the rudder over, and *Tangaroa* was beam on to the waves.

Whoomph! The first crest slammed in and sprayed like a fire hose across the deck. Then another came and another. The shocked girls scrambled out of the cabins. My first thought was that the sheet had snapped, but when I crawled to the stern, I saw the port rudder at right angles to the boat 'fishtailing' through the water. The 6ft deep rudders, constantly moving under the strain, had caused the long rod to crystallize and to snap.

Stripping my wet clothes off, I crawled to the stern. Jutta steered with the remaining rudder as Ruth passed the loose one forward over my head and then gave me the four-foot long spare rod to slide into position. Lining up the rudder hinge holes with the hinge holes fitted to the stern was a back-breaking struggle. The stern, weighed down by Ruth and me, was swept by the seas. In between, I could get it lined up and have the rod ready to drop in, but the next wave would wrench the rudder out of my hands.

Fortunately, we had tied the rudder on a safety line. Gulping for air in between the body-submerging waves, I actually had the rudder rod half in position, when a wave battered the whole boat.

'Your hands!' Ruth shouted above the wind. They were streaming with blood where they had got pinched between the fittings.

'Give up, Jimmy! Give up till the sea goes down. I can steer,' cried Jutta.

Dragging the rudder and the long rod, I crawled back into the security of the deck, then dropped into the cabin utterly exhausted. Pepe nuzzled up to me, giving my face a lick, as if to say: 'It will be all right.' But I could not rest. My whole body lay aware of the movement of the boat and the sea. In the late afternoon, I felt a lull.

This time, I sat on the stern, my feet dangling in the sea. I slid the rudder blade down between them, getting a firm hold over the lower end.

'The bolt, quickly, Ruth.'

Over my shoulder it came. In between the sweeping waves, I guided it in. I had succeeded. *Tangaroa* had two rudders again.

It was too rough to hoist both spinnakers for self-steering. Throughout the night, each one of us would sit damp and shivering on the steering position at the stern for one-and-a-half to two hours before stripping off our wet clothes and dropping naked into the cabins. At least we kept our bunks moderately dry and warm. Pepe made a splendid hot-water bottle. He, of the whole crew, seemed the least affected by the hardships, but then, he came from a long line of Spanish seadogs.

By the morning of the second day of January, we had enough confidence to hoist the twin spinnakers again. Relieved of steering, I slumped in my position at the foot of the mainmast watching the clouds overhead sailing by.

In a half exhausted doze, I had my eyes fixed on the head of the mizzen mast, which was swaying, not in time with the boat, but in some dizzy dance of its own. I leapt up and pushed my shoulder against it to hold it up before it crashed on to the deck. Once more, it was 'all hands on deck'. Struggling and cursing, we lowered it.

The mizzen mast was held up by wires which ran up one side of it, looped round the head, and ran down the other side to the deck. The loop was held together by a rope lashing – a time honoured method of rigging. In Las Palmas, just as I had replaced the rudder rods for safety, I had renewed the lashing holding the loop together. But I had left the actual lashing to another yachtsman. I vowed that never again would I trust someone else to do a vital job for me. It took little time to fix a new lashing, but half an hour of muscle tearing work to heave the mast into position.

Tangaroa's progress was now dogged by steering failure. Three nights later, one rudder gave way again and the crew kept short watches as she limped towards dawn.

Ruth was next on watch. I was awakened out of my sleep with the waves hammering on the hulls, and spray lashing across the decks. Poking my head out of the hatch, I bawled:

'Can't you keep her on course, woman?'

'Jimmy,' Ruth's voice shouted back against the wind. 'Jimmy, the other rudder's gone, too.'

'Jutta, Jutta, come and help.' In the dark we toiled to haul in the second broken rudder. 'We must put out a sea anchor and drogues,' I explained.

Jutta and I lashed a small raft of oars to the sea anchor, ballasted it with the anchor, then paid it out over the stern. This drogue helped *Tangaroa's* stern to turn into the seas. We slipped off our wet clothes and climbed into the same cabin, huddled together for comfort and warmth.

Next morning, the wind and seas had eased a little. I had no more long rods for the rudder, just bits of galvanized rod. Instead of one big rod, I would have to make short bolts for each individual fitting. But how, without a machine-shop and work bench? The girls had incredible faith in my ability. A man with the confidence of a loyal woman can achieve almost anything. I had two.

Instead of threading a nut on to the end of the bolt to stop it dropping through the fitting, a process which would have required a machine-shop, I hacksawed notches in the end of the rod. Then I heated the notched end of the rod over the primus stove and with a cold chisel splayed the ends out. Reheating it, I hammered at the notched end to 'burr' it over. The end of the rod looked a little like a well-bashed wooden tent peg, but it served instead of a thread and nut to work as a rudder bolt.

To add to my torn muscles and cut fingers, I got a few burns on that job, but with the aid of those two magnificent women, I succeeded in re-hanging the rudders and we sailed into the third week of the voyage with 1180 miles behind us, and slightly less than two thousand miles to go.

Soon, fixing broken rudder hangings became almost a routine task. Finally, one of the blades fractured. This was cobbled up in suitably workaday fashion, but a jellyfish entered the fray and laid Wharram low with stings. The girls maintained his morale and he notes a preference for 'soft kisses' over 'vinegar' for treating jellyfish stings. Even worse problems arose when Ruth reported a leak resulting from a teredo worm infestation in one hull.

As the leak was not in my cabin I said: 'Bale it out,' and went back to my *Country Life* magazines. A little later there was a 'crew delegation' and Ruth and Jutta insisted:

'Repair the leak or else – no food!'

Faced with this unarguable opposition, the skipper turned to and prepared a tingle out of plywood, putty and an old blanket.

The girls baled fast until the bottom was almost dry. I slammed the ply-blanket-putty sandwich, putty down, over the affected area, hammered nails all around the edges and to my relief I could feel the nails bite into solid wood. I dried the wood around the patch, and mopped up the last puddle with what Jutta reported to be her best blouse. What did it matter, I thought, as I sagged against the cabin side.

After this crisis, the boat sails ever onward with food growing short and nocturnal hallucinations beginning, until finally Trinidad approaches. Wharram has already noted that his team are not like 'ocean heroes', but rather more parallel with early settlers discovering new worlds for themselves. His comments on his first ocean landfall tend to confirm this.

On Wednesday, I was convinced I could see, with the old Polynesian method of looking for a stationary cloud at sunset, the position of land. Next day there were many seabirds, frigate birds, according to Jutta, wheeling around us.

Land was near, by Atlantic crossing standards, but we were not sure precisely where it was. Ruth had been unable to pick up the B.B.C. time pips for several days. For weeks I had wanted land at any cost, and was prepared to sail the boat at the shore, crash-land it and walk off. Now I was demanding of Ruth a precise position to within five miles after nearly six weeks at sea.

Working from her dead reckoning, she gave me a position that Trinidad was sixty miles ahead. My spirits soared. Then, she picked up Radio Trinidad. The time given was not the precise detail of a B.B.C. time pip, but at least accurate enough to estimate that we were 120 miles away. I was bitterly disappointed, and quarreled with Ruth over her conflicting positions. Jutta stopped that unfairness on my part. With two women on board, I never had a chance. One always protected the other.

When Ruth finally said that tonight we should see the lights of Galera Point at about four in the morning, I only half believed her. Jutta did. From about three in the morning, instead of sleeping, she was standing on the cabin roof. She suddenly jumped down, leapt at me at the steering position, and flung her arms around me.

'Jimmy, I've seen it, the lights, land, land!' I left her at the tiller, and called Ruth. Sure enough, there was a light blinking away.

Later that day they were safely anchored.

It was like paradise, great pelicans dropping into the sea, green hills and smooth water. Sitting on the deck, eating the evening meal, drinking wine and watching the sunset, we began to talk of the last weeks. I summed up our attitude:

'Our lives can never be the same again. We have been near death. We must always be gentle. Nothing can hurt us, for we are now strong!'

And strong they were. Almost fifty years on, James Wharram and his team still design and build catamarans. James remains a free spirit whose refusal to compromise with increasing bureaucracy has made many a modern sailor ponder more deeply on what really matters.

STOWAWAY

Edward Allcard
Temptress Returns
Putnam & Co 1952

In 1949 Edward Allcard became famous for a solo voyage in his 34ft 1910 yawl Temptress *from Gibraltar to New York. He recorded this most ably in his book* Single-handed Passage. *Less well known but perhaps even more interesting is the homeward-bound leg, described in* Temptress Returns. *After surviving a hurricane, he stopped off in Horta, Azores, to repair storm damage. Taking his departure one midwinter's night for São Miguel, Madeira and Gibraltar, single-handed as usual, he hadn't been at sea 24 hours before events took a surprising turn…*

A grey dawn showed the islands well astern, surrounded by massive lumps of drab cloud.

I was in need of a hot cup of coffee to warm me after the cold and cramped hours at the helm, when a movement at the hatch caught my attention. My heart rolled over in momentary fear at the sight of a clutching hand, followed by a frightened white face half-hidden by straggling black hair. Unbelievingly I stared; open-mouthed; speechless.

It was a girl.

A wave splashed on deck. The boat was right off course; it broke the spell. I spoke quietly to her in Spanish; she climbed awkwardly out of the hatch and sat beside me in the cockpit. Frightened. Silent. She gave me a fleeting smile.

'What is your name?' I asked.

'Otilia Frayão.'

An extraordinary discussion followed, complicated by the language set-up.

'Why did you come?'

'To go England.'

'I am not going to England.' No reply.

'I take you San Miguel?'

A flood of Portuguese followed this statement, with a hint of tears in her eyes. I felt I had been an awful cad and hastily changed the subject.

Conversation followed for about half an hour, the main decision being whether to call in at San Miguel or Madeira; at either place she would presumably be taken ashore and sent back to Horta, where life would become so unbearable that she would probably commit suicide...

A gentleman should not take advantage of a girl, nor should a gentleman refuse any request from a lady. Therefore, strictly speaking, I could not refuse to take her to Europe...

Although feeling sick and apprehensive, the girl not only offered to take the tiller, but did so. I altered course to the south, explaining that the large S on the compass card must be kept near the lubber line. I stole a look at my stowaway through a gap in the hatch. Her black hair was swept loosely back and was being blown about with the wind. She had large brown eyes accentuated by a small nose. Her full lips were pressed together in concentration. Her rounded chin hinted at determination, but of no aggressive quality. My luck had evidently changed – but which way? She was steering well. The blood of the old Portuguese navigators must run in her veins. Sleep had seemed out of the question, but a minute later I was deep in slumber.

After several hours below, I rejoined Otilia in the cockpit, with the intention of trying to dissuade her from continuing, but after her tremendous decision to leave home and trust herself to a total stranger, there was no other alternative but to go on. Nature loves rough wooing, and who was I to ruin someone else's life?

So adaptable is the mind that even after only a day it seemed quite normal to me to have a girl on board. It was just our own business and the rest of the world became exceedingly remote. During the afternoon the weather broke out into a rash of squalls. Two turns were rolled up in the boom – child's play with somebody else steering. At dusk I took the helm, ready for a long night's trick. Otilia went below, leaving me alone with a jumble of thoughts. My mind, freed from the fretful bonds of indecision, ventured on a disturbing variety of possibilities. What difference was a stowaway, and a female one at that, going to make to me? Could her warm presence spoil my single-handed future?

Those thoughts marched, counter-marched, jostled in confused, increasing circles, both sublime and ridiculous, but mostly my thoughts were of Otilia herself. She had acted, in a most original and courageous manner, to further her ambition. My admiration for her was great, even though her scheme had interfered with my own plans. Nonetheless, I commended her to the special department of Guardian Angels who must surely look with benevolence on such a fearless soul.

At the first chill light of dawn I banged energetically on the deck, and after a time Otilia took over the helm, with scarcely a word. I went below to snatch a few hours' sleep. Cold and weary I turned into my bunk to find it warm. Otilia evidently had forsaken the damp focsle and retired into my bunk. To come down from a cold watch to a warm bunk was by far the best arrangement. The matter was not mentioned between us; but what would they have said at Horta, I wondered.

It was Otilia's second day at sea, and her diary recorded:

I have a feeling of non-existence in mid-ocean in a boat only a hand and a half long, which is taking me to a faraway land with an unknown man. I must say that in spite of his most unattractive beard I feel far more reassured when he is by my side...

A quiet night followed. *Temptress* slipped through the pale darkness under the first light of a new moon. With the tracery of rigging swinging gently past the stars we sat in the cockpit talking until late. Indeed the romantic setting was conducive to confidences, but by noon the next day we had only managed a run of forty-two miles. All during the night the swell had been rising from the south-east; the barometer dropped. Darkness faded. A streak of red sandwiched between clouds and sea indicated a sunrise stillborn. Bad weather was imminent, and soon a strong southerly wind forced us to heave to.

Two days passed, with *Temptress* drifting away to the north-east. Water breaking over the foredeck flooded the focsle. Otilia moved her belongings into the saloon. She was sea-sick, but after a while recovered sufficiently to cope with the cooking. On the third day she said, with a little nod of conviction, 'If I had known it was going to be like this I would still have come.'

Thank God, she had a sense of humour too.

Alas, for my hopes for a fair wind, this was one of the very rare depressions that pass well south of the Azores. We had completed no less than ninety-six hours of being hove to, and still the wind blew viciously from the east. A large sea caught the boat unawares, knocking the bow round up to windward, causing a thunderous flogging of the mainsail and boom as they lashed furiously from side to side. The boat rolled in great sweeps to port and starboard. Otilia was chucked off the saloon settee on to the floor, and hung on with an expression on her face as if she thought the end of the world was at hand.

At night the wind finally diminished, but was still from ahead and *Temptress* was left hove to overnight. The following day the colours were so brilliant that they almost hurt. The wind still blew keen but finally it veered to the south and freed us. Otilia's diary translates as follows:

The sun at last, and not so much water falling on deck. Special lunch to celebrate. A good wash with buckets of water, in the cockpit. After his wash, Eduardo put on his best flannels and told me he would take me as far as England if I wish. I am beginning to realise that his beard is not altogether lacking in interest.

The more days that we were together, the more my girl pleased me. Explain it in terms of proximity, lack of competition or what you will. I did not care or bother to search for any other explanation than that she was a woman and a good companion.

Otilia could steer quite well during the day, but found it too confusing to do so in the darkness, even with the stars to guide her, or a light in the binnacle. However, it was now a night so brilliant with moonlight, with only a gentle breeze blowing from before the beam, that I thought she could manage. Well muffled up, she took the helm. Three hours later I returned to the deck to find her half perished with the cold. 'So beautiful!' she shivered, 'Very good to make poetry, but – ' she turned as she descended the hatchway, '– too (Portuguese adjective) cold.'

It was six o'clock when the moon set behind clouds low down in the west. *Temptress* was cutting along with a 'chop, chop' of wavelets on the bow. The sky gradually lightened over the eastern horizon, with me yawning ungracefully at the fugitive stars. Another half-hour passed before the familiar outlines of the rigging could be picked out, and the compass card clearly read. Colour strengthened. Little by little it spread across the sky. Marble-shaped clouds merged from red to orange, then yellow. Lo! it was daylight. One more night was over; a beautiful day at sea had commenced.

Later, I pointed out a Portuguese man-of-war to the lightly clad Otilia, who was sunning herself, sitting on the sidedeck, with her back against the cabin-top coaming, then I relapsed into silence, admiring the excellent example of the female form in front of me.

She looked up, with questioning eyes.

'What is?' (I knew that 'What is?' in Otilia language meant 'What are you thinking about?')

'Oh. Thinking that your waist is pinched in just enough to make room for a man's arm.'

'What ees peenched?'

I gave up the unequal struggle and frowned into the bowl of the compass instead.

Night came once again, and conditions were tricky for steering but I went below, leaving Otilia at the helm.

At dawn the yawl was going like a rater and the sea was making up every moment. After reducing canvas to the equivalent of close-reef, I lashed the helm. The boat crashed on and soon one hundred more miles lay astern.

By late afternoon I wrote: *Moderate Gale Force with no signs of improvement.*

Once again, the time had come to heave to. I played the old game, rolling up the jib and backing the staysail. The boat lay stopped; safe from the breaking seas, and after the turmoil on deck it was miraculously quiet below. During all my hectic activities Otilia had been reading, reclining gracefully on the lee settee.

The moon rose that night, big and orange, flooding the swiftly moving surface with an uncanny light. After nearly twenty-four hours hove to, we were under way again.

Otilia writes: *27th January. Eduardo spent the day at the helm. Rough sea. Huge waves, impregnated with wind, falling on* Temptress.

I feel genuinely, overwhelmingly happy, but how 1 would like a piece of bread and island cheese!

30 January. What a wonderful life! Less than a month ago I was living quietly in Fayal without the remotest chance of travelling. Today here I am in mid-Atlantic. Eduardo says we are 116 miles from Casablanca. If the wind does not behave naughty we could be there tomorrow.

31st January. The wind did not change. Eduardo makes himself ridiculous: up and down all day with the sextant: and doing sums in the saloon. We expect to sight land at any moment, but the sky is laden with heavy clouds. There is an occasional shower and a steady breeze.

Afternoon. The smell of land is in the air. Africa! It seems a dream.

Nightfall swiftly came and before it was properly dark there was a faint and regular flash of light reflected in the clouds. The lighthouse on Cape Dar el Beida. Half an hour later there was a great glow in the sky – the lights of fabulous Casablanca.

By midnight many lights were in sight all along the shore, and the beams of the lighthouse swept extravagantly through the night – three sharp flashes every fifteen seconds.

Now the great wind that had borne us on became hushed. We were finished with the breezes of the ocean and it was the land which had control. Switching on the masthead light and pinning in the mainsheet we left *Temptress* rolling to the incessant north-west swell, waiting for the daylight. In the bright morning sun, the white houses of Casablanca could be clearly seen. We had been twenty-four days at sea, but the sighting of land had swamped our minds and in a flash the whole voyage was forgotten. By the time we had finished breakfast and the engine had been started, fog blotted out the land, but I had already taken bearings and headed confidently for the end of the long breakwater.

Inside, a motor-boat arrived with harbour officials and police; details; passports; embarrassing questions; ship's papers; signing forms. But all was in order. We gave sighs of relief as the Frenchmen queued up to ascend our ladder to the deck. They went. We were free.

Otilia recovered her poise instantly.

She jumped up and impulsively threw her arms round my neck. I kissed her, and said, ' Come on! Let's visit Africa.'

After what sounds like a very pleasant few days' run ashore, Otilia flew to London from Casablanca where she sold her story to a Sunday newspaper. She paid off her flight with the proceeds and was thus an independent woman. The two did not meet again until the remarkable occasion of Allcard's 95th birthday. The reunion was reported a great success. Edward Allcard, 105 years old in 2015, now lives ashore in Andorra, a monument to the health-giving properties of a life at sea. His yacht Temptress *has spent many years in the ownership of the sailor–author Mark Fishwick. Like Mark's famous predecessor, the boat is still in good trim.*

After moving on from Temptress, *Edward Allcard and his wife Clare became the long-term owners of a 90-ton Baltic trading ketch,* Johanne. *As it happens, I was sailing aboard this very vessel when I met my wife, Ros, in 1969.* Johanne *served the Allcards well and was instrumental in shaping my life. And so the whirligig of time swirls ever onwards.*

Many thanks to Edward Allcard for permission to print this article.

RIPPED OFF IN THE RED SEA

Dwight Long
Sailing All Seas in the Idle Hour
Rupert Hart-Davis 1950

Like others on both sides of the Atlantic, young American Dwight Long made a break for freedom in the decades leading up to the Second World War. At age 22, he bought Idle Hour, *a 32ft gaff ketch, for £500, emptied his bank account of the remaining £600 and set sail for England, west-about via the Pacific. His book* Sailing All Seas *makes a rollicking read. Dwight Long turns out to be a young man of exceptional ingenuity, and after his Tahitian shipmate dies tragically in Colombo, he takes on crew who pay their way. He lectures, writes, offers guided tours of his 'ship', and generally turns his hand to anything to boost his tiny budget. He succeeds magnificently and goes on to run successful businesses, which is no surprise after what he went through in these, his formative years.*

Dwight Long's tribulations in the notorious Red Sea and the way he tackles them are typical. All cruising sailors will warm to him as he rails against grabbing harbourmasters ripping off his funds after he has just evaded jail, the lash and armed guards chasing him across the dunes. We join him at Jeddah with a dodgy chronometer. Ripping yarns don't come much better.

I decided to take advantage of the kind offer of the captain of one of the pilgrims' ships to check my chronometer. The steamer was anchored half a mile to windward, and I embarked on a small dhow to run out to her. Unfortunately the wind and seas were so high that the tiny shallow-draught boat could make no headway, and as the gale was increasing, seas began to break completely over us and fill the little craft. As we were close in to the shore, I motioned my boatman to beach his craft; for if my deck watch should get wet it would be ruined and there wasn't a watchmaker within 500 miles of Jidda.

I landed in the nick of time, for the next wave capsized the boat; but no sooner had I waded up the beach than four armed Arabs appeared from nowhere and surrounded me.

I tried to recall the few words of Arabic I had picked up to explain to them why I had landed, but they refused to let me proceed back to the city. I was over a mile from the walls, and night was coming on.

After a lengthy consultation between themselves, three of the men made off into the darkness, leaving me in the charge of the remaining one. I waited some minutes to make sure that the others were not returning, and then started to walk towards Jidda. My guard immediately followed me and grabbed me by the arm to bring me to a stop, but with a quick movement I wrenched free of his grip and made a bolt for it.

I could hear his feet thudding on the ground behind me as he ran, but he was hampered by the yards of drapery he wore and I was in shorts, and I soon outdistanced him.

I was expecting a shot in the back at any moment, but it didn't come, and when I had gained a sufficient lead to be comfortably sure that I was out of range of his revolver, I looked back and saw that he had given up the chase.

He probably thought I would not be able to enter the city anyway, as the gates all close at sundown, and as I approached the wall, the same thought occurred to me. However, as I neared the gate I recognised in the gatekeeper an Arab to whom I had given five piastres only the day before for posing for a photograph at this very gate. To my relief he let me in without the slightest hesitation, and I thankfully proceeded to the house of my fellow American, Mr. Twitchell, from the Saudi Mining Company.

Mr. Twitchell told me how fortunate I had been in entering the city by the Medina Gate. Had I attempted to enter the Mecca Gate, I would probably have been shot, for no non-Moslem has ever entered that holy portal. I stayed at his house that night.

The following morning, one of Mr. Twitchell's boys came in with the news that Milton, one of my crew, had been arrested and was being held at the customs gate of the city. He had been mistaken for me! He was to be taken to gaol, where my boatman was already languishing on a charge of having landed a stranger on the coast, and not at the regular customs gate. Mr. Twitchell hurried to the Khan and explained the situation, relating how I had made a forced landing to save my watch from being ruined. The Khan was under the impression that I had sneaked ashore with the intention of going to the forbidden city of Mecca! When the situation had been cleared up we were given an order of release for Milton, and made our way to the gaol as fast as we could go. We were only just in time, for when we arrived the unfortunate boatman had already received thirty lashes, and my hefty shipmate was only waiting his turn.

The wind had veered round to the north-west again – a dead headwind for us. If we went out we would be blown south and lose the valuable northing we had made, but we had been given a day to leave or suffer the consequences. We sailed.

The wind was heartbreaking. We would sail for twelve hours on one tack, beating hard against the short, steep seas. Then for another twelve hours we would pitch and buck on the other tack, to discover that we had actually made three miles! At this rate, it would take us seven months to make Suez. The wind freshened steadily from the north, and the seas got bigger and bigger. The gale blew off the foam-caps of the seas, reducing our visibility to nil, and our decks were awash from morning till night.

It was a miserable business. The bilge overflowed with the water we were taking aboard, and the bilge-pump jammed. Oil from the engine slopped over, covering our bunks with a slimy film – and still we bucked into the north-west gale, struggling for a wretched mile or two of northing each day.

We finally got the bilge-pump working again and cleared things up in the cabin, but all day and every day the roaring, baffling wind continued out of a cloudless sky and fought us bitterly for every inch we made. Each night we had to anchor in the lee of some reef in order not to lose the precious northing we had gained: and each day the mirage mocked us with land ahead where we knew no land could be.

With mirages confusing me – my chronometer too far out to be of any use, head winds baffling us and the constant fear of reefs as we made the coast at the end of each tack – I was rapidly becoming a nervous wreck myself, and seriously beginning to wonder if I should ever get out of the treacherous Red Sea alive and in my right mind.

To make matters worse, I had tried to get the engine overhauled in Jidda. A native mechanic had taken the clutch to pieces, as a thrust-bearing had broken, and had then devoutly departed for Mecca, leaving me with the engine in bits! I had not seen him take it apart, but as we had to sail in twenty-four hours, I had to put it together again as best I could. As might be expected, I hadn't done it very well, and now the clutch was dancing about with a stream of water pouring in through the stuffing-box, which had been loosened by the excessive vibration.

I was expecting something to break, as the engine could not stand treatment like this for very long; and finally I got up courage to try to alter the bearing beds. If I should break anything during the process, we should have no way of repairing it and would have to proceed without an auxiliary.

I managed it somehow, and with gum patching the leaky petrol tank, and broken files propping up the main bearing, *Idle Hour* proceeded northward slowly. We were almost out of petrol now, and I decided to make for Yenbo to refill our tanks.

Yenbo is a snug little harbour, and thus far superior to Jidda. The walls of the city border one side of the anchorage, and as it is surrounded by reefs on the other sides, it is protected in all weathers. A tiny island crowned by the tomb of some old sheikh is just opposite the city wall.

It was the last day of a three-days' celebration when we arrived, and scores of dhows were racing in the harbour. Everybody seemed to be very happy, and it reminded me of the South Seas, as the drums were beating and the crews of the dhows were all clapping in unison. We were not allowed to roam about freely in the streets, but had to have an armed soldier accompany each one of us. Petrol was very dear, but I had to get fuel, and there was not another port between Yenbo and Suez where it was available.

I was also taxed heavily for harbour dues. I showed them the receipt for the heavy fees in Jidda and pointed out that those were sufficient for the whole of Arabia. But that was where I put my foot right into it, for they now raised their dues and charged me exactly what I had paid in Jidda! I was then informed that in every Arabian port I touched at, the fees would be the same. Then and there I definitely decided that this would be the last time I would set my foot ashore in Arabia, for a couple more stops and I would be bankrupt.

That evening it was full moon. Against a cloudless sky were silhouetted in the east the towering mountains of Rudhwau. To the south was the domed tomb of the sheikh, glistening whitely in the moonlight, and with a light showing in one of the niches of the stonework. To the north was Yenbo, with its white houses and towering minarets. The massive walls and turrets made it look unreal – a magic city, half compounded of the moonlight itself.

I awoke my companions to see it. As I had spent over £20 in the port on fuel, tax and dues, I wanted my friends to enjoy the expensive scenes.

We left Yenbo and started the long beat once again. Each night we would anchor in the lee of some reef, and each day we zig-zagged backwards and forwards across the width of the Red Sea from Asia over to Africa and back to Asia again, hoarding each scanty mile as a miser hoards gold. We seemed to have been months at sea when at last we sighted Mount Sinai towering over the barren, red volcanic hills. Soon, from the masthead, I spotted the date-palms lying just to the south of the Egyptian village of Tor. They were the first trees I had seen since leaving Aden.

In Tor, they can accommodate ten thousand pilgrims at a time as they return from Mecca. Lying in port was a pilgrim ship full of Moroccans who had been granted a free trip to Mecca, sponsored by General Franco, on the condition that they would fight for him in Spain when they returned from their pilgrimage.

As we sailed up the Gulf of Suez after sunset, the western sky was lit by the radiance of the planet Venus as if by moonlight. So brilliant and dazzling was it that I could well believe it was the Guiding Star which led the Wise Men of the East to that manger in Bethlehem nearly two thousand years ago.

As we were entering the harbour at Suez, a giant passenger liner was just emerging from the canal. She had stopped for a few moments in order to drop the canal pilot.

This palatial steamer, with its cinemas, cocktail bars, dance pavilion and dining-rooms, was about to traverse the Red Sea – a two-and-a-half days' journey! Hundreds of passengers lining the decks took their last glimpse of Suez. As the liner gained momentum and headed south, I thought of the out-lying reefs, the barren desert wastes, and slave-trading dhows plying in and out among the reef-infested waters. Little would the passengers of this floating hotel see of the real Red Sea and its treacherous shores.

DRAMA AND FARCE
IN THE FAR PACIFIC

Ben Pester
Just Sea and Sky
Bloomsbury Publishing 2010

It is always charming to read accounts of long cruises made 50 years or more ago. I am aware of only one book, however, that refers directly to that Golden Age, written by the man who was there, but not until half a century had passed. Ben Pester (1924–2010) came to England in 1943 from his homeland of New Zealand to join the Royal Navy. Ten years later, now a lieutenant, he was posted back home and asked for unpaid leave to sail there. This was duly granted by a service that saw the benefits of young officers learning from their own decisions, and Pester set sail from Plymouth in the old 40ft Claud Worth gaff cutter, Tern II. *The boat was entirely innocent of technology. Even the navigation lights were oil, while the minuscule engine, such as it was, ran (occasionally) on paraffin. Together with his redoubtable crew, Peter Fox, Ben Pester made a successful voyage on time and on budget. The marvel of his account in* Just Sea and Sky *is his commentary on how things were, how the same issues are dealt with today, and his judgements on whether our lot has really improved.*

The extract below is taken from Tern's *passage from the Galapagos to the Marquesas. She has just escaped the doldrums and is rollicking downwind in the trades under squaresail and raffee when one unexpected crisis follows another.*

AT the end of the week there occurred another memorable day. I fell overboard.

Peter was soundly asleep below and I was having an easy time on the tiller. The wind being broad on the quarter, the boat's motion running before these south-east trades was relatively easy and life was altogether congenial. Responding to the call of nature, and lashing the tiller, I

went forward. Leaning my shoulder against the after lee shroud left both hands free for the operation but, for once, my shoulder slipped and I found myself in slow motion pitching head first into the water sluicing along the topsides. I tried to catch hold of the gunwale, but it was just out of reach and moving fast past my outstretched hands. Now, left swimming off *Tern*'s rapidly receding stern, the gap widening fast between me and my sole life support system, the realisation flooded over me, pragmatically and quite matter of fact, that I was going to drown. It was as if I were just a witness to a scene of which I was not part. I was calling out to Peter but I knew that, deeply asleep in his sleeping bag, he would not hear me over the sound of wind and rushing water. It was at that moment I remembered the 'fish'.

Trailing astern of the boat was the thin plaited line that towed a metal, finned rotator, the fish, which in turn rotated the line to give a reading on a dial mounted on the boat's stern, the whole device being known as Walker's Patent Log. Its function was the determination of distance run. It was to save my life. My only hope now was to get across to where the log line was trailing and hang on to it. I thought the line might possibly take my weight but I was not sure if the mounting on the deck would accommodate the sudden shock. I also had to be quick to catch the line running out to the fish before the whole lot went past and disappeared ahead, taking my only hope of survival with it. I made it. Letting it slip through my hands, I slowly tightened my grip on the twisting line to avoid any sudden load as my weight came on it. Everything held, and I was now safe and once more connected with my sanctuary. *Tern* had been doing the best part of 6 knots when I went over the side, and although her speed had slowed with me in tow, the line was cutting into my hands and my head frequently dragged under water. The question was, how long could I hold on until the boat wandered off course and stopped by bringing the squaresail and raffee flat aback, or until such time as Peter woke up? By great good fortune I did not have long to wait. Peter appeared in the cockpit. I was saved. He said afterwards he did not know why he had woken. Perhaps it was a change in the boat's motion as she had slowed with my load on her, or was it something else? He knew not what, he said, but I suspect he had a private conviction. He was a believer, possessing a strong faith. Unlashing the tiller, he brought the boat to the wind and laid the sails to the mast.

Slowly hauling me in, hand over hand, he got me under the counter and lowered a bight of rope over the side such that, with his help, I was able to drag myself onto the afterdeck. Neither of us said anything. Peter got *Tern* sailing again and whilst I climbed out of my dripping gear he broke out the rum bottle. It was only some time later that Peter spoke of his shock when he emerged into the cockpit and, looking round, saw no one.

Next day we belatedly rigged waist-high lifelines along the side decks and agreed that in future, when alone on deck, we would not leave the cockpit without tying a line around our waists with the tail secured to a nearby fitting on deck. We were two chastened men, but to this day I remain unconvinced about the merits of the present-day practice of religiously 'hooking on' whenever one sets foot on deck in the open air. Safety first in the modern world is all pervading, with lifejackets, lifelines and deck jackstays integral with going to sea in small boats. There is, however, a downside to this philosophy. In *Tern*, as we were not in possession of any of this gear, we would usually make sure we were following the old sea rule of 'one hand for the ship and one for oneself'. We watched our step, literally. The danger is a feeling of false security fostered by the wearing of safety gear. An element of overconfidence can be engendered. However, in our real-life man-overboard situation I had certainly been too relaxed and paid the price accordingly.

It is food for thought that if I had been wearing a harness and lifeline, the chances are I would have still ended up in the sea before the lifeline had taken up its slack as I pitched over the low guardrail. I probably would then have drowned by being dragged under because of the high speed of the boat. In this hypothetical situation, assuming I had been able to release the lifeline or myself from it, I would still have drowned, the boat sailing on without me. The moral, of course, is not to become overconfident by putting too much reliance on safety aids. This includes lifejackets. We did not carry these in *Tern*, so there was no debate about whether or not to wear one. The latest designs for the leisure market are light and unobstructive, so much so that in recent times there have been campaigns by the RNLI and others, pushing for them to be worn at all times when afloat and, heaven forbid, this could even become law. It could be argued that this is a dubious practice to foster. It is reactive rather than proactive, in that it is a safety measure applicable to the wearer who has fallen over the side rather than focussing on the need not to fall over in the first place. The dangerous inference is that one has only to wear a lifejacket and all will be well. On the contrary, the emphasis should be 'prevention is better than cure' as the guiding principle. Even if we had had lifejackets on board, I doubt if we would ever have worn them. That was not the way we saw things in those days. Safety was not the god it has now become.

If I had, in fact, been lost overboard, Peter would have been presented with a major dilemma. Initially there was the psychological hurdle to overcome of coming to grips with the situation. He would then have to think calmly through the recovery steps he should take. First he had to get the boat in a state able to be sailed back up to windward again. This would have involved dropping the raffee and brailing up the squaresail. Then he had to get the engine started to begin heading back whilst he set the fore and aft sails so he could beat back against the trade wind, progress under engine alone being severely limited. To get the mainsail hoisted it would first be necessary to get the sail cover off, this having been put on to protect the sail from the weather while under square rig. Next would be the task of resetting the working jib, which had been taken off and stowed down below.

The decision now would be whether to attempt a reciprocal course tactic or to undertake a 'square search'. A crucial decision, bearing in mind that Peter was having, entirely on his own, to do everything: sail the boat, navigate and concentrate on the visual search. Because it was not possible to proceed directly back into the wind along the reciprocal course, Peter would have to follow a zigzag path, beating to and fro across the target mean track. To have done this whilst keeping a check with any accuracy on his changing position would have been almost impossible. The alternative, and more precise, approach was to embark on the square search. In the end, this would have been more likely to be successful, but correspondingly more difficult to execute, even for a fully crewed craft, let alone a single-hander. What would be entailed was first to make a best guess where the victim might be, then, having assessed one's maximum range of vision, establish a search area in the shape of a square box around this possible position. Along the sides of this box the boat is sailed in ever increasing parallel legs, covering a wider and wider area, until hopefully the person in the water is sighted. The difficulties for Peter in achieving any degree of precision with this method would have been formidable. Apart from anything else, a head in the water, even with only the slightest of seas running, is a very tiny object indeed, especially from the deck level of a small boat.

Whatever practice Peter had followed, in the end, with fading hope of success, the ultimate decision would be how long to keep searching. Eventually he would have had to decide when to give up. For the rest of his life he would have been beset by nagging, dreadful doubt. Had he failed me by abandoning the search too soon? Should he have continued just that little longer? All hypothetical, perhaps, but it could well have happened. Furthermore, on arrival at the next port with no corroborative evidence to hand, Peter would have come under close scrutiny and, in the face of inevitable suspicion, be unable to prove his innocence of wrongdoing. All of this would have added immeasurably to his distress.

Life moved on. We were, as it was soon to turn out, about to have another crisis. We ran out of toilet paper. I took this somewhat personally, as it could have been construed as a reflection on my stores planning, but in fact it was easy to flush out the reason for the shortage and to get to the bottom of it. So why had it happened? We had restocked in Cristobal at the commissary, and the toilet tissue on the shelves there was of American manufacture. Tissue was the right description, being appreciably less robust than the British dreadnought variety. Americans, it would appear, preferred the softer touch. Knowing how many rolls we had consumed during the Atlantic passages, I had restocked accordingly for the next legs. After changing over to American stocks the usage rate rose dramatically, so that whilst we were still some way out at sea our stock was wiped out, so to speak.

What to do? We were to find there was more to a book than just reading it. *Tern*, being an easy boat to steer, enabled us to develop the practice of reading while on watch. When the toilet tissue issue came upon us we were reading Compton MacKenzie's *The East Wind of Love*. MacKenzie's work was ideal, with the pages of the right size, soft but strong and easily removed, the book getting progressively thinner as we sailed on. The covers being hardback they were discounted as 'not fit for the purpose'. I am sure the author would have been gratified that his creation was being so widely distributed across the Pacific.

Tern II *remained in the South Pacific, living various lives, until she was found in Vava'u. When last heard of, she was undergoing a full restoration in Auckland.*

SMALL CRAFT

The true test of friendship Stanley Smith and Charles Violet

On the mud Portsmouth Sea Scouts

The unforgettable race Keith Shackleton

Bilged by the launch Henry Plummer

THE TRUE TEST
OF FRIENDSHIP

Stanley Smith and Charles Violet
The Wind Calls the Tune
Robert Ross 1953

More than half a century ago, a boatbuilder from Yarmouth, Isle of Wight, created a series of diminutive cruisers called 'West Wight Potters'. These unusual little craft with their whaleback sheer and tucked-up transom developed a remarkable following that spread as far from home as the United States. Anybody with an eye for a boat who sails the Solent will have seen a potter, perhaps without realising quite what some of them have achieved. I was among them until I read an account by Mr Smith about the delivery of an early one to Scandinavia in October. The trip was dogged by the sort of weather I suppose Stanley should have expected, and a catalogue of troubles came his way, but I was left mightily impressed by his seamanship. I knew of no further exploits on the water, so it came as a special joy to discover The Wind Calls the Tune, *a book written by the irrepressible Stanley and his shipmate Charles Violet. The story is not about a potter. It concerns a 20ft clinker yacht he'd built in the basement of a church in Canada in 1949. He called her* Nova Espero *and her first passage was home from Nova Scotia.*

We join Messrs Smith and Violet in June 1951 on Nova Espero's *second transatlantic voyage. This time, she is outward bound from England towards New York. Her crew are lying to a sea anchor in an unseasonal storm 400 miles east of the Azores, resolute to remain friends despite appalling conditions and a major rudder problem.*

WE had started off on our journey filled with a strong determination to give the lie to those who told us we would be the fiercest enemies long before we reached New York. One of the stricter rules we laid down was that on no occasion were we actually to swear at each other, even in a jocular manner. Also, neither of us must ever swear at the boat. This sounds silly, but proved very wise. A resentful, exasperated man turns viciously upon any unlikely excuse for offence. We each, therefore, had a companion and an area twenty feet long by six feet wide, at which we were not to direct strong language, but around us lay the boundless expanse of sea and sky. On the elements we had complete freedom to express our feelings to the limit of our resources. We proceeded to exercise that freedom.

As the day progressed the seas got bigger until, during the afternoon, they towered considerably higher than our mast. We think we are being conservative when we say about thirty-five feet, and that some of the peaks were possibly more than forty. To us they looked simply stupendous, for each represented a heap of ocean, millions of tons weight moving at about 25 knots.

Towards dawn after the second night we noticed, after a blow from a somewhat more severe breaker, a peculiarly ominous thumping in the bottom of the cockpit. Then we became aware that the boat had turned broadside on to the advancing seas, and the motion became so violent and uncontrolled that we knew something was seriously wrong.

We struggled out to the cockpit to investigate. Our first thought was that we might have carried away the sea anchor but a tug on the warp showed that all was well, except that the warp fell off to port far more than usual, so the cause of the trouble lay elsewhere.

While this was going on, we tried to bring the boat back head to sea. It was then that we discovered the catastrophe. The steering gear was damaged. The tiller moved too freely and was evidently useless. One of us scrambled out of the way into the cabin to give the other room to curl down into the bottom of the cockpit to investigate the trouble.

We at first thought a small bolt holding the tiller fitting to the rudder shaft had sheared off. If so, it was something we could easily fix. Closer examination proved us wrong. With alarm we began to realize the appalling situation. Something had carried away underneath the boat, where it might be irreparable. If so, we were in a terrible fix. The nearest land was at the Azores, nearly 400 miles dead to windward, and we had no rudder. However, there was a more urgent problem. If we continued to wallow disabled in these huge seas more damage must quickly follow. The mainmast would soon be snatched off the deck, for the stays could not long sustain the violent motion from side to side. Also, the danger of being smashed in by a heavy breaker and swamped was imminent.

The desperate need was to get the boat head-on to the waves. We hastened to get a spare length of warp, and bent it on the end of the sea anchor line to increase the drag. Then we had to get the mizzen as flat as possible to make it more efficient as a 'weather cocking' influence. The mizzen mast had no forestay, so we let go the halyard and made it fast forward, before 'bowsing' down on the mizzen sheet for all we were worth. This helped and the little boat rode closer to the seas.

When it was light enough to see properly, we hung over the side to see what damage had been done to the rudder. All we could see, however, was that its trailing edge was jammed athwartships against the bottom of the boat. We endeavoured to get it amidships by passing lines under the hull, but without success.

We were lying on our bunks below trying to decide on our course of action when the wind seemed, if anything, to have increased and had backed a little to the south-west. The seas now tumbled more heavily and heaped up in stupendous confusion. When we looked out of the little portholes, we saw only the blue sky above or a foaming valley stretching away below us, as we pitched for a moment across the backbone of some huge monster of a sea. But there was nothing we could do so we turned back to continue a shouted conversation above the noise.

Suddenly, in a weird hush, we heard a slight warning hiss high above the boat. The cabin darkened. We remember only a fantastic roar and a deafening, stunning bang.

Charles was hurled out of his bunk on the port side into the cabin roof opposite, together with the radio and a mass of loose clothing, cans, and bedding.

Everything went dark as night, and water seemed to fill the cabin.

We remember thinking only, 'This must be the end,' when we found ourselves in a heap in the starboard berth.

A second later, with a loud sucking noise and another tremendous bang, we saw light again. We watched the water fall down from the cabin roof drenching everything. We heard it swilling about heavily from side to side. The little boat had righted and resumed the old familiar dance. Slowly we sorted ourselves out and in stupefied amazement, shaking violently with shock, scrambled out into the open cockpit. We could hardly believe our eyes when we saw everything dripping, but in place.

It is not easy to reconstruct exactly what happened. This is what we think: … the wave … must have formed an arch over us, shutting out the light. A moment later, swept along under the curl of the breaker, we were turned almost over. That we were flung into the cabin roof bears out our belief that we were capsized to such an extent that the masthead was carried down beneath us to within a few degrees of vertical.

There she must have paused until the weight of the keel restored equilibrium, and she suddenly snapped back the way she went over. The

Nova Espero has narrowly escaped destruction several times in her short life, but how she survived this punishment and came through unscathed we cannot imagine. Nevertheless, after that great wave the worst was over. It still blew a gale and the seas were high, but they did not seem quite so dangerous.

To our intense chagrin the direction of the wind held in the west, driving us steadily back. The sun smiled benignly out of a clear soft blue sky and, when yet another night came, the stars swung serenely over our heads while we glowered with frustration, for we could do nothing toward repairing the rudder until the seas subsided.

The morning of the 13th June showed signs of improvement. The wind lowered its voice and the seas began to moderate. By one o'clock we began work on a new rudder, as it was clear that we could do nothing with the old one, which seemed to be loose on its shaft and wobbling under the hull.

If we could get sailing again, the forward motion would release the rudder, bringing it back with its trailing edge aft, though, loose as it was, it would swing from side to side with every pitch or roll of the boat. Drifting slowly stern first, while lying to the sea anchor, the rudder jammed hard over athwartships, and it was this that put the boat in the dangerous position of beam to the seas.

We needed two strong eyes to screw into the transom and two hooks to go into them, so that the new rudder (if we could manufacture one) could hinge on them. The only screw eyes were on the canvas bunk lee-boards in the cabin. We took these off, but came up against an unexpected difficulty when we tried to screw them in. One of us hung head and shoulders over the stern and bored the holes in the transom, while the other hung on to his legs to prevent him being washed or thrown overboard by the still highly unstable seas. This seemingly simple little job took an hour to accomplish. Most of the time the work lay under water. All the while the boat rolled and pitched wildly.

When this part of the operation was complete we turned our attention to the making of the rudder itself. We lifted up the bunk mattresses and took out the two for'ard locker hatches. These were about thirty-three inches long by nine inches wide, and were made of bonded plywood. We looked at them dubiously, but we had nothing better, so we cast about for some other more solid length of timber to form the equivalent of a rudder-post to which to fasten the locker boards. Beneath the great pile of gear at the fore end of the cabin we knew there was a piece of pitch-pine which Stanley's father had cut out to form a compression strut beneath the mast in case of exceptional stress manifesting itself here. We blessed him now for his anxiety. It took us a long time to dig down to it, but when it was brought up we saw some hope of success, for it was about three feet long by three inches wide by two inches thick.

We then rummaged under the cockpit for some small blocks of wood we had aboard for no particular reason, except that they might come in useful for something sometime. When all these odd pieces were assembled we had to laugh, for they looked unlikely material for steering a boat hundreds of miles through fair and foul Atlantic weather. By the end of the afternoon, however, our hacking and banging had produced a satisfactory parody of a rudder.

We rigged it over the stern with various shackles and nails for pintles to go through the screw eyes. Then, lo and behold! when we got sail on the boat, and trimmed them a little freer than usual to give us more speed, we were delighted and relieved to find that our new creation took some effect on the course of the boat. We were no longer rudderless.

The boys made it to the Azores where they hauled out to sort their rudder before sailing on to a landfall in Nova Scotia on 6 August. They arrived at New York in good order a few weeks later…

ON THE MUD

Portsmouth Sea Scouts
Log of the Portsmouth Sea Scouts
1948

The year 2007 marked the centenary of the Boy Scout movement. The Sea Scout branch was founded in 1908. Many sailors who have never been involved are unaware of what it has meant to so many. The watchword has always been self-reliance, and this extract from the log of the '38th Portsmouth' for 1948 brings us a typical example. Never written for wider publication, it describes a weekend cruise made by a group of scouts aboard the Benbow, *an ex-naval cutter. These heavy, open vessels were propelled solely by oars and an awkward dipping lug rig that demanded blistering physical effort as well as a high level of seamanship. Despite the mishaps described so colourfully, 'Swampy', 'Nobby', 'Dinger' and the crew cope admirably.*

The level of freedom granted to these boys is a sobering commentary on changing times. One of them, now very much a senior sailor, loaned me the book and pointed out succinctly that he and his chums never seemed to come to irreversible grief. When I first saw the beautifully written log, complete with sketches, charts and 'Box Brownie' photographs, my reaction was simply, 'Can you imagine youngsters being allowed to do that sort of thing today!'

I think that says it all.

S*UNDAY 9th May 1948*
10 a.m. – First we had to clear two floats and a rowing skiff off the slip. Then we got the boat completely cleared out and began to move her! We had a lever at the bow, with Dinger, Tony and Swampy on it, and the rest pulling on the sides. We levered and pulled it as far as the spot where the concrete meets the wooden slip. Here we stuck. For ages we tried every way of moving it we could think of – and broke the lever in the process. Eventually after getting five of us under another huge lever we raised the stern enough to slip a roller under – a good heave and she went with a rush, entering the water just on 11.45 a.m.

Friday 14th May
About 7 p.m. this evening Dinger, complete in new peaked cap, Swampy, John – the new quartermaster – the two Colins, Peter Lenton, Smythe, Junior, Stoo, Mike, Ken and Nobby boarded the cutter for the beginning of 'THE CRUISE'. The *Benbow* was piled with gear, personal, three casks of water and primuses, and a lot of other heterogeneous stuff including a wireless set. There was little wind so we hoisted all sail. Main, mizzen, jib and a foresail made of a large Bermudan mainsail supplied by Swamp. We rowed and sailed all down the harbour and then, waving farewell to friends at Sally Port, we set our course for the open sea, as so many have done before us.

At 8.30 we anchored about 300 yards offshore in Stokes Bay and turned in where we could. It was not a very restful night. Smythe moved from the stern benches to amidships where he got wet in the bilge. At 1 a.m. Swamp got up and took in the sails. In the early hours all were awakened when a liner's wash rocked the boat violently.

Saturday
At 5.30 we rose and as soon as possible weighed anchor and set sail. With no prickers and a strong wind it was found that the primuses

wouldn't function properly. The water refused to boil, so tepid cocoa was made and the breakfast was a cold one. There was a good wind for sailing and we bowled along on a broad reach – course South 80 degrees West – to Cowes.

At Cowes we wore round towards the Hamble River. After a while we were excited to find that we were rapidly overhauling a smaller cutter-rigged yacht. Although the wind was increasing in strength we hung on to every stitch. Slowly we crept up and past them. Actually, although we were sailing faster, we made more leeway so as we passed we had to go on their lee side. They were also driving hard and their lee deck was awash right up to the cabin side. We drew ahead of them and pressed on for the Hamble. Swamp, at the helm, took us out of the channel across the Brambles. Our plate touched twice and raised mud. We arrived at the Hamble at about 10 a.m. and lay off a pier to try lighting the primuses. A load of Merchant Navy types came along to do boat drill and turned us off, so once again it was a sandwich lunch and water with it.

At 2 p.m. we rowed up to Warsash where Colin and John went ashore for prickers and stores. The boat was tidied up and then we watched the traffic on the river. One boat trying to come alongside missed five times; a second missed her moorings and collided with another yacht. One man caught his leg halfway up the mast and hung upside down for ten minutes. Tony went in for a swim and soon came out. Later the Rover Scouts rowed past in our whaler on their way to Botley campsite.

At about 4 p.m. we set our mizzen and headsails. The wind was strong and we were soon very literally 'shaken'. Eventually we decided to try the old mainsail as a foresail. We put three reefs in it before hoisting. What a queer sight it made – a tiny triangle of canvas with a huge rolled up bag below. Still, it had the desired effect and we sailed faster and therefore steadier. On our way down Southampton Water the *Queen Mary* passed us. Beating into Cowes proved impossible as we had the tide against us. Rowing was equally futile, so eventually we headed away for Beaulieu River. On the way a school of porpoises swam past the stern.

Beaulieu River is not easy to distinguish from seaward. Besides our charts, however, we had a detailed account of the shore in a book by a yachtsman *[None other than K Adlard Coles himself! – Ed.]* called *Creeks and Harbours of the Solent*. Due to a misunderstanding at the helm, we almost sailed across the spit (it was low water but the eastern end was not showing); we just went about in time.

We were soon in the river sailing between spit and shore. Eventually the channel turned north and we were in the real river where we were forced to anchor through sheer weariness. The spot was just mud flats with stubbly grass growing in it. It was cold and dispiriting, so the first thing we did was to rig up an awning. The sails were lowered and a rope stretched between main and mizzen. Then out came the two old wartime rubber dinghy covers. They had been circular in shape. Cutting down a seam in each made long pieces which were buttoned together – the buttons or clips being already on them. This we slung over the rope and lashed it like a tent to the side of the boat with codline. It gave us cover from the wind and enough headroom for us to sit on the thwarts.

At last we got a primus going for tea and cake. At 10 p.m. we turned in dead tired. In the raised sternsheets slept Colin J, Pete Lenton, John Lee and Ken. On the stern bench, with a ridiculous lashing which he imagined would save him falling off, Pete Smith. Nobby curled up in the bottom with canvas and a raincoat between him and the bilge. Above him was an old plank with Stoo and Junior. On the port side were Dinger and Swamp on the oars, all laid together longways across the thwarts. Tony slept in a dip of the mainsail which was stretched from side to side. Mike and Colin H lay longways across the thwarts with boxes to fill up the gaps. AND SO TO BED.

We arose next morning at about 7.20 and set sail under fore and mizzen whilst the cooks got breakfast ready. At 8 a.m. we went aground. Ken allowed her to get too near the lee shore. He put her about but she missed stays and drifted down onto the mud – with the tide ebbing! We tried pushing her off with the oars but it was no use. Everyone but the cooks hopped out and tried shoving her off, but we were firmly stuck.

There we remained for the next seven hours, but at least the cooks finished getting breakfast. This consisted of cornflakes, sausage, bacon and scrambled egg plus the usual bread and tea. It was the first good meal since Friday and we were heartily glad of it. After breakfast we cleared up the boat and sat down to await events. Not for long. Colin decided to wade ashore through the mud to see a man about a dog. For this purpose he borrowed Swampy's gumboots, but he hadn't gone far when he sank right up to the top of the boots. After we had had our fill of laughter at his expense we sent Swampy out to help him and together they staggered ashore. Undaunted by this episode, Smythe decided to go too. Even more unwisely he also borrowed Swampy's boots – and his socks as well because the boots were too big. At his first step his foot stuck while his second one came out of the boot completely and he strode forward steeping Swampy's socks deep in the mud. Lastly, John made a pair of splashers, flat boards tied to his feet. He had wisely refrained from wearing socks, for at his first stride the strings broke and he also stepped into the mud.

Lunch was salad, fish, greens and bread. John threw away all the green stuff off the onions, curses be on his head.

At three o'clock a pull on the anchor warp showed us to be moving and within five minutes we were rowing downstream. We were dubious of what we should find outside, because hardly any yachts had gone out whilst a lot had come in seeking shelter, but the green of the Isle of Wight and the clear sparkling sea was beautiful beneath a blue, sunny sky.

With the flood under us we tacked up the Solent, making good way. Off Cowes, the tide changed, the wind increased, the sky assumed a dull heaviness purporting rain, and we were not gaining much on our tacks. To crown it all the sea became very choppy and began to shake the boat considerably. Steering was difficult because the rudder was almost out of the water. Just about this time we saw some madman paddling a canoe. After finally rounding Castle Point we made good way as the land there sheers away into a bay and we could lay Wootton Creek on our gaining tack. At the entrance we didn't bother to look at a chart and, all unsuspecting, sailed across a rocky reef, but fortunately there was no rending of timbers and in-pouring of the sea.

As we were looking for a mooring, some of Tony's friends who were crewing a yacht of Mr Brown's invited us alongside for tea. Once ensconced in a very comfortable cabin we decided to pool our supper. What a feast it was! Cold meat, cheese and pickle. We ate until we could eat no more while our genial host told us how to convert the cutter into a cabin cruiser. We rolled into bed at 1030 on full stomachs.

Sunday
At 0715 the slackers unlashed the edges of the awning to watch Colin J, Pete L, Rex Chase and Swampy disporting themselves in the cold water. Breakfast of porridge, hard-boiled eggs, PRUNES and FIGS. Trips to the 'heads' were numerous before we left at 0930.

With Colin and Peter at the helm we tacked across Spithead passing a Dutch Liner and the *Aurora*, which had just been given to the Chinese Navy. Speeding through Portsmouth harbour mouth we reached our berth 40 minutes later after sailing gloriously at maximum speed surrounded by a sea of foam and heeling so much that everyone was on the high side.

After a meal of soup, Ryvita biscuits with butter, tea and cake, we cleaned ourselves up, brylcreaming the hair. Unloading the kit we were met by one of the Rovers who was moaning because they had to row all the way to Botley. There was hearty and derisive laughter at the poor wretches' fate. What did we care about rowing? We had only done 15 minutes all weekend!

Many thanks to Bill 'Swampy' Marsh for permission to print this article.

THE UNFORGETTABLE RACE

Keith Shackleton
Yachting World Annual
1956

The Prince of Wales Cup for International 14ft dinghies has always been an event of the highest prestige. For almost eight decades, the '14's have been noted for technical innovation and their crews for 'going for broke'. Great names such as Uffa Fox shine down the years of their history, but in the 1955 event at Seaview on the Isle of Wight, it was Bruce Banks the sailmaker who carried a remarkable day. The account below was written a year later by his crew, the late Keith Shackleton MBE, *for* The Yachting World Annual *of 1956 – a publication that, to put its time into perspective, also features a trailblazing article on the benefits of plastics over wood in boat construction. Reading Shackleton's account underlines the high standard of literature that sailing has produced, by no means*

always from professional writers. This rollercoaster of a report is more than mere penmanship. It exemplifies that splendid, ironic humour that characterises the best of British. Shackleton, by this time in his life, was already making a name for himself as a painter of marine wildlife. He went on to become one of the world's greats in this discipline.

Read on, and rejoice!

ALL this happened over a year ago, so it is not news; but at the same time so much was packed into those few hours that I feel determined to recall them in the same sort of way that the Victorians, in a more generous era, had time for embroidering slippers and pressing ferns in their Bibles for a keepsake. I have read through the bulletins, which are detailed and accurate, but they have done little to revive the facts in my mind, because however accurate an official account of a race may be, it never seems to tally with the participant's jumbled memory of the jammed winch, the broken sheet, and the small human crises within the boat herself. It is for this reason that he is the first to read the onlooker's views with interest, having seen less than nothing of what really counted and sometimes not even having been aware of his finishing order.

I shall remember the 1955 Prince of Wales Cup because it had everything condensed within it that I had ever known before and much I had never seen. If there were the chance of having one race over again, this would be the one; and I wish sincerely I had written down its every detail the night it happened; but because of its outcome there were more important celebrations. Final victory is by no means all, but it is a risk one has to take when crewing for Bruce Banks, and it happened to be the joyful conclusion to my race of a lifetime.

The beginnings followed the pattern of the week, an intensity of colour and heat with a sea wearing the dusty bloom of an untouched damson. The whole morning had been one of those sit-around affairs, screwing the tongue into ice-cream cornets. The start of the race was in much the same vein, making concentration well nigh impossible.

I think that concentration fails at the point where one becomes aware that Fortune is playing the upper hand. Much has been uttered on the sinfulness of lotteries by the sanctimonious; do they really believe it possible to escape them in their lives? I believe this feeling was with everyone, and the knowledge that it was the big race of the year did little to allay it, because at that time Nemesis seemed to be entirely in control. The expressions on the faces all round suggested people who had just been asked to open a tin of beans with their bare hands.

The confetti of slow-moving and stationary boats congealed itself into a purposeless coagulation of colour and conversation which rested like a rash on the sea and waited. The only semblance of order in the mass was that nearly all the boats were more or less bows-on to the weather mark, showing at least uniformity of intent. By this time, and admitting the presence of an all but imperceptible movement of air, the 'weather' mark, the first mark of course, was in fact straight to leeward.

During the next hour, we sat without moving and the sun rose high. In some way that could hardly be identified with the airs, we found ourselves nearest to the first buoy with the rash of boats still little changed but stretched away in the carelessly splayed-out shape of an amoeba. Around the weather mark were camped the watchers' boats, filled with men in sun-hats and women beneath umbrellas, while some swam about and others lay in the sun. Their voices came clearly to us as we hung over the gunwales spitting into the water to discover whether we were moving, and seeing from time to time in the boat's shadow the pattern of a sandy bottom four fathoms down.

It seemed an interminable age since the start before the buoy came alongside, and the chance to move was as good as a long drink of cool beer. With the movement came the breeze, and with the breeze that exultant feeling of progress after the doldrums. Even at this stage I would never have credited that so much could happen before this contest was to end. We had watched the great bastions of cloud that grew over the mainland and lay heavy on the Downs, their tops towering and white. Gulls that took off in the heat of the day found strong thermals and rode effortlessly higher and higher until practically lost from sight.

In my memory this race consists of three main parts – the doldrums, the storm, and the aftermath. This made it like the perfect play, introduced with an overture which paved the way to the excitement that was to follow, ending with a passage of respite which gave time for contemplation before the final completion.

Storms can break with surprising swiftness; and though we had for minutes listened to the roll of thunder and watched lightning stab from the darkness into the vanishing mainland, it somehow seemed that the storm would follow the coast and never reach us. A look away for a moment or two sorting something out in the boat, and then everything seemed to have changed. In the main shipping channel a tugboat was making its way to Southampton; she carried her smoke in a high column, the air from the south-east being just the speed of the tug herself; and together they went slowly along, the tug and her smoke, bright in the sunshine against the slate grey beyond. But the grey was rapidly becoming black and now close enough for the turbulence in the cloud itself to appear like a seething cauldron, and the lightning cracked closer with a sort of brittle ferocity. Then, as we watched the tugboat, her smoke was all at once caught by an unseen hand and laid on to the water with incredible swiftness and certainty like the falling of a dry-fly cast. An instant more and the vessel had vanished.

It was then that we heard the wind, and at the same time we saw its effect which crossed the sea to us not in the form of cat's-paws, but rather like shoals of berserk fish tearing the surface into foam, fast coming closer and yet lacking any semblance of direction, and as it came the grey sea was being turned to white. We were still in front, but Stewart Morris was close behind and I could see him looking and wondering too. There was just time to swim into a sweater and put in a fine big reef, the type of reef Bruce Banks calls 'comfortable'. With everything slack we waited, not knowing from which direction the first blow would fall, and trying to memorize where the next mark lay before it was obscured by the elements.

Then the wind arrived, a wild side-swipe that seemed to sweep the boat up bodily and send her skimming along like a flat stone. The reef was by no means comfortable enough, and the jib had to go as well. The rain came solid and icy cold and beat from the sea a kind of strange mist about gunwale height that made it hard to see the water's surface. The effect was much like those films of warders searching Dartmoor with dogs, where the set is flooded with a sort of volatile Scott's Emulsion in which the warders vanish to the knees and from which the tails of the dogs emerge, or their heads when they have lost the scent.

We planed through this strange phenomenon at what seemed a reckless pace, with one small piece of mainsail left, flat out for all we were worth to hold the boat up and watching the rain swamp her with an unbelievable swiftness. For some minutes around this time it was only just possible to keep her down to a fairly buoyant weight by incessant baling, so we toiled away, secretly wishing we had the new and cunning devices for emptying boats while you watch; and all the time over the boom the water came in as a gigantic ribbon and the Scott's Emulsion enveloped us. But the buoy stood out ahead and just astern came Stewart Morris, and occasionally between the two of us lightning came down to the sea, a searing violet flash together with its thunder, leaving behind it that strange smell one sometimes notices in power houses.

It is at such times as these, when hard pressed from astern or chancing to pass another boat, that one is tempted with the 'damn-the-expense-give-the-cat-another-goldfish' attitude, and round the buoy we set a spinnaker. The memory of that run is quite the sharpest of the whole race. The rain still as strong as ever flattened the top of the spinnaker's curve like a heavy hand, and one could actually notice water coating the whole sail and pouring from its foot, so that it was no longer possible to see clearly ahead. Then lightning struck the sea again to either side of the boat, seeming to mushroom out into the water, and as it came I felt a strange vibration in the sheet which gave the feeling of having my fingers closed around it and being unable to let it go; the sensation lasted for a second or two, but Bruce felt nothing from the main sheet at all – which would add strength to my secret belief that he is probably impervious to pain.

And so we sailed out of the storm, but it had left behind it a sort of elemental chaos that took hours to sort out. Several times we came upon surface mackerel shoals moving nowhere, which took fright when the boat was upon them and fled in a flurry driving themselves against her bottom. People said afterwards they had come upon fish lying stunned in the water belly uppermost after lightning had struck, and that gulls were looting among them. We saw razorbills flying despondently in circles, as if the heavily charged air had damaged their sense of locality.

The sea, not knowing which force of wind to obey, gave the impression of upheaving from beneath and breaking outwards; and sailing through this was a comic affair. Curtains of rain swept across the sea as the wind went round.

Before the race was over we had run with a spinnaker and beat to windward on every leg of the course. Slowly order returned and a light breeze carried us in for the finish over confused grey water, while the sky, spent of its fury, became soft and pale again and seemed to draw back from the sea into its appointed place. In the reaction which followed we found we were very cold and could not have been wetter. As the wind quietly died on the last reach home Stewart Morris was still close behind, and it seemed as likely as not that the original calm would return, leaving us kedged on the lumpy sea to finish as we had begun.

One has strange thoughts at this point of a race, conjuring up in the mind morbid possibilities that could snatch victory away. The mast, having been through so much, might fall overboard under some last straw of burden; a shroud or forestay or jib halyard could so easily part without warning. The plate or rudder could fail and float away, and the loss would be an embarrassment hard to overcome. But from the side of the Committee boat came the happy doughnut of blue smoke and a second later the bang of the gun, a feeling of much exultation and a vision of a welcome friend waving a rum bottle.

How quiet and content a dinghy looks tied up behind a motor-boat, her boom and sails resting in her lap, loose halyards slapping the mast to the movements of the waves, and the quiet slap of sea water under her lightened hull. I felt, with the help of the rum, that she had seen more in the last few hours than in her four years under sail, and much of it she would never see again in a hundred. For me it would always be the race of a lifetime.

BILGED BY THE LAUNCH

Henry Plummer
The Boy, Me and the Cat
Cyrus Chandler Co 1961

Henry M Plummer was a New England yachtsman of the Edwardian period who, over the winter of 1912/13, made what seems to have been the first ever sailing yacht passage southward down the United States Intracoastal Waterway. His yacht was a classic, shoal-draught, 24ft cat-boat. His crew were his son, Henry M Plummer Junior, and Scotty the cat. In his own words, 'This cruise was undertaken on my part as rest for a set of frazzled nerves and tired eyes and to limber up a back slowly recovering from an old-time injury. Henry and Scotty went just naturally, 'cause they had to.'

Plummer's book The Boy, Me and the Cat *was originally published in a 'Subscription Edition' of 700 copies. Sixty years later, one of these came to light and was recognised for the remarkable work of quintessentially American literature that it is. It has subsequently been republished several times. Enough photographs have survived to give us a picture of the dramatis personae and the boat, while Mrs Plummer's sketches drawn after the events enliven the works with a charming naivety.*

As to the voyage itself, those making the passage to Florida today would consider it so commonplace as to be unworthy of recounting, but in 1912 things were very different. This is a pioneering effort of the first order, pushed through with indefatigable guts, considerable skill and a steadfast refusal to complain about misfortune. The pithy, Yankee humour of Henry Plummer is a seaman's delight. Join him now to seaward of the Outer Banks of Carolina just south of Cape Hatteras as he comes within an ace of losing his yacht and the 16ft launch which, with its tiny inboard petrol engine, was his only auxiliary as well as his tender. This man was one of life's originals. His writing style is inimitable. Read on, and in a page or two you'll have joined the exclusive Henry Plummer Fan Club.

*D*ECEMBER *11th, 1912*
The wind not being friendly, hauled out south, and we took up the job of making it tack for tack along the shore. The afternoon brought thickening clouds and my glass still standing high with the southerly air began to make me mighty uneasy as to what was coming next, for I felt there was a change in store, and soon. The situation was not a good one. Before dark I could not reach the slew inside Frying Pan Shoals off Cape Fear. To run 19 miles to sea and round the shoals meant risking a gale on one of our worst bits of coast and I had decided that we were soon to have a shift either northwest or northeast. The sea was comparatively smooth and I thought that now was the time to take a chance at an inlet.

On the chart the New Inlet with 4 feet at low water looked good. We reached it at 3:30 p.m. at low tide, and sailed back and forth outside the line of breakers to study the water and best place to tackle. There was a middle ground and the seas seemed less spiteful on the southerly side so we put storm hatches on cockpit, shut cabin doors, took out scupper plugs and lashed everything down. Gave the launch a 10 fathom tow line and started at it. For genuine excitement give me the next 12 to 18 hours. We took bottom on the first breaker and broached to, bilging to seaward on about the third. The fourth came roaring over cockpit rail, and flooded us knee deep with lanterns, oil cans, etc., etc. swashing about promiscuously. Fortunately the next sea pushed us along and threw us over onto the other bilge so that we escaped being flooded again very badly. The launch came whooping along on her own hook. Just missed hitting us. Brought up on bottom and rolled over and over with the next breaker and sank.

We got sail off and with the hope of turning her head towards a little deeper water which we saw some 50 yards to starboard, Henry waded out and placed the kedge anchor. Might as well have put out a sweet potato. We were bound for that middle ground and nothing would stop us. We were pounding mighty hard, but didn't jump our fire so thought we better mug up while there was a chance. Went below after sounding pump and finding boat tight. Had mess beans and all you had to do was open your mouth and get beans at every crash she made, and she made 'em about once a minute. Centreboard box was weaving all over the cabin and bunks twisting horridly. Just before dark we tried to get launch up under our lee in effort to bail her out, for it ain't so pleasant to look forward to a long, black 12-hour night, pounding the heart out of your boat and nix to get ashore with in case of breaking up. After hard work we dragged old 'helpmeet' close aboard and, then came a big comber to which we rose, and crunch-o, the nose of the launch went through our bilge for a 6-inch hole. Up she went again, and bang-o, there was another hole. My eye! we would soon be a pepperbox at that rate. Before another surge caught us we twisted her bow round with the spinnaker pole and a sea catching her, rolled her over and away. Things were getting interesting. I ran below for hammer, tacks and canvas. Water already over cabin floor. Lanterns all filled with salt water, but with the last of daylight and using his hammer under water, Henry cleverly put on a canvas patch. We sounded pumps and after half an hour they sucked. Some relief to that sound. Believe me.

Could do nothing more, so went below, cleaned out a lantern, dried wick and got some light. Waited until 8:30 when I began to fear that full tide would not carry me over that lump of a middle ground. It was busy bees then and half a ton of iron ballast went over pretty quick. With a heavy lurch and crunch she slid into a little deeper water and floated once more. We counted on a strong flood tide to carry us up the inlet, but push with poles all we could we couldn't get her anywhere, and finally dropped big anchor in only 6 feet water and just inside of breakers. Not a quiet or particularly safe anchorage, but mighty sight better than pounding in the surf. Sounded pumps and they sucked. What a noble piece of boat building it is. It was 11 o'clock, pitch dark and raining, with wind still soaking drearily from southward. We were soaking, too, but not dreary, you bet. Went to work and made a new anchor stock for little anchor.

It broke short off early in the circus. The kedge was still on the bar with a bit of furring on end of warp for a buoy. Am going to take a picture of that anchor stock, for under conditions it was shipshape and Bristol fashion. Then we shipped all weight over to starboard and got holes in bilge out of water, threw over little anchor to keep company with big one, and after a mug up turned in at 1 o'clock. Since leaving Beaufort some 42 hours before I had had only one or two 1-hour naps, but felt all right and ready for what next which I still felt would come soon.

December 12th

Had to turn Henry out at 3 a.m. in drizzling cold rain for tide was out, we were over on our bilge, and now was chance to bail out launch if ever. His report was soon made that you could as easily bail out the ocean for her stern was split wide open, likewise her bottom and several planks. Now what do you make of that? Just after fixing her all up tight two days before at Beaufort. Nothing more to be done about it, however, so turned in again clinging to my bunk like a bat to a rafter. Went to sleep in a minute, but H. was a bit nervous at the roar of the breakers close aboard and couldn't do much in way of sleep. About 5 o'clock the black night ripped wide open in northwest and down came a sizzling norther. Gee whiz! how it blew for a few hours. With flooding tide our anchors held all right. Day came, and in the early light we could see the bow of the launch come out of water like a white shark, turn and plunge again to the bottom. Kind of consoling sight with half a gale blowing off shore and no chance to work further into inlet, for with ballast gone I hardly dared to put cloth on her. Had good breakfast and Scotty was mighty companionable and seemed perfectly content with the way everything was going. About 8 o'clock a man turned up in a skiff and came on board. I surely was glad to see that skiff and that man, too. He remarked that it was some blustering day and I admitted to a little ozone in the air. He said he thought our launch was sunk. He was a very truthful man. I gave him eggs on toast and coffee at once. While he was eating, tide turned ebb and along came our ground tackle and we for the bar once more.

'My man,' says I, 'cut out the egg and coffee habit, jump right into your skiff, under-run that anchor and carry it up stream.' He was a sailor all right and with no back talk, he was away on the job.

First one anchor and then the other. I kept him at it and soon had her kedged all snug and comfy out of harm's way. Then we hauled the bric-a-brac of a launch to the beach. 'Good,' says I, 'now you can walk the beach home for I need your skiff in my business.' He was all right that man and he lived in the 'piney woods'. We talked politics and he allowed that rather than be a politician, he would live in the 'sticks' with the coons and wildcats where a man could get 'hisself' a little sleep and quiet. Bye and bye we put him ashore and he started away for his shanty somewhere, a lonely looking figure trudging through the sand, head down against the gale. So I read the signs right after all, and I felt justified in taking the chance I did, for this blowing to sea in a December norther is no joke. Where all my trouble came was not understanding the difference between a skiff such as I am used to and a launch which sinks and holds onto bottom like a rock. You watch me next time.

When tide dropped I sent down my throat halliard tackle and after rigging up some sand anchors with oars, poles, &c, we greased some slide boards, and to Henry's surprise and joy hauled the launch up high and dry. It was all nuts to me. Everything smashed up, but time, tackle and tools, to fix it all up again. I turned in early for some good few hours' sleep but had to roust out at slack water to place anchors one up and the other downstream, for tide ran some 3 knots or better and only a narrow gut to swing in.

Guess charts are of little use in these places, for my piney woods man said it had been ten years since there was any water in this inlet and my chart gave me 4 feet on the bar at low tide.

Printed with the kind permission of the Catboat Association, Connecticut, USA.

VOYAGES
UNDER DURESS

Tempest tossed Voldemar Veedam and Carl B Wall

On the run Oluf Reed Olsen

Atheism renounced John Caldwell

TEMPEST TOSSED

Voldemar Veedam and Carl B Wall
Sailing to Freedom
Phoenix House 1953

Although written only 70 years ago, Sailing to Freedom *is a book that begins in a world few in the West can truly comprehend. A group of freedom-loving Estonians exiled in Sweden at the end of the Second World War find themselves in an impossible situation. Having originally fled the horrors of their Nazi conquerors, they are now required by the Swedish government to return to a native land groaning under the yoke of Stalin's Russia.*

These realists know that repatriation will mean one-way tickets to Siberia for many of them. One of these is Harry Paalborg. His wife, children and mother are at risk because his sea-captain father defected to America, ship and all, when the Russians ordered him to return. The author, Val Veedam, was sentenced to death in his absence by the Nazis and has already been described by the Soviets as 'unsuitable'.

In the end, they become desperate and decide to sail to Captain Paalborg in America. More refugees join them and together they acquire a 37ft semi-derelict ex-working boat. The double-ended Erma *carries no ballast, but achieves a degree of stability by virtue of extreme beam. Seriously lacking in headroom, she is over 50 years old and has just survived a major conflict. By 21st-century standards, she represents a very shaky prospect.*

Sixteen men, women and children cram on board with what water and stores they can cobble together. They fool the coast patrols with the unlikely claim that they are off for a weekend cruise, and avoid the English Channel because rumour has it that the French are forcibly repatriating refugees from the Baltic States. Leaking chronically, they make it across the North Sea to the Caledonian Canal where the free air of a democratic Great Britain astounds them. Next they thrash out into the Western Ocean and down to Madeira, leaving at the end of October, bound direct for east-coast United States.

Even with a standard crew of four adults, Erma *would have been ill-equipped to tackle a full ocean gale. Critically overloaded as she was, heavy weather was a fearsome prospect. A late-season North Atlantic storm might be viciously cold, and the seas would build to 40ft or more, yet they had no viable alternative.*

We join the Erma *about 500 miles south-east of Cape Hatteras on 28 November 1945. It has been blowing a gale for 24 hours.*

THE gale did not grow worse during the night but neither did it ease. In a wordless, gloomy mood we sat, slept, and fought through it. The pump was manned much of the time. It clogged once, and Heino fingered another potato from the inlet. Lembit said that at this rate the bilge might keep us provided with food, but nobody thought him funny.

At midnight, we spotted a steamer's lights. They kept disappearing, which meant that the waves were higher than her mast lights. In the early morning the wind increased slowly but steadily, and during the forenoon watch reached full gale strength. The spume-filled wind rushed over us, angrily howling, and the *Erma*'s steel rigging trembled and cried. Enormous seas rolled by, their crests wrapped in froth and thunder. Above them dark clouds raced with spout-cold showers; jagged fragments from their lower edges, torn by the gale, hung down like ugly rags trying to sweep the seas.

I stooped over the pump handle, straining to keep my balance. Warm water flowed over my bare feet; the *Erma* was taking water through the bottom, the deck, and the cabins. Up and down went the pump.

'How many strokes?' Harry asked.

I leaned against the roof of the after cabin and inhaled deeply a couple of times before answering.

'Five hundred and fifty.'

This had been the second pumping during the watch and there was at least one more long one to come.

The next sea looked more than a quarter of a mile away, but it approached very fast. We were carried higher and higher along its long forward slope, then, suddenly, were flung ahead on its top where, the horizon widening, we could see endless rows of similar ridges. Before we knew it we were sliding down into the next deep valley. All in all, the time of getting from one trough to another might have been not more than half a minute.

As I gave another stroke of the pump our two captains Arvid and Harry came up from the cabin.

'North-east', Harry was saying.

'We've been blowing away from the land about thirty hours now,' Arvid said. 'And it looks like only the beginning.'

A roar split our ears. Then something gripped us and the *Erma* shot forward amidst a cloud of spray. Then we slid down and I resumed pumping.

'Our provisions won't last much more than a week, even eating only once a day', Arvid continued. 'And you know the water…'

'Yes, it's bad.'

'And it looks like it's going to blow a couple more days. That means it'll be six or seven hundred miles to shore instead of the four or five hundred that we are now. To try to come back from so far, in this late season – and without supplies!'

Harry shook the rain from his face and looked at Arvid balancing beside him.

'How about trying the sea anchor? It's too small and it won't check her drift much, but it's better than nothing.'

Astern, Heino loomed up to relieve me at the pump. He had rolled his pants to his knees and wrapped his blue bandana tightly about his hair. As he slid over the shining wet deck and landed in the cockpit he looked almost like an Arab pirate. At that moment Paul appeared carrying a bundle in his right armpit. 'Here', he said, giving it to Harry. Together, they rolled out what seemed to be a green canvas bag.

Our sea anchor resembled a funnel whose wider end was fastened around an iron hoop about eighteen inches in diameter. The opening on its narrow end measured only an inch. On the wider end was a three-branched bridle. Lembit was already in the after cockpit lifting the ninety-foot coil of rope that had been presented to us in Fraserburgh. Harry tied one end of it to the bridle; Paul took hold of the coil and walked forward, Harry following with the sea anchor. At the same time Arvid put the wheel up.

'Go to the halyard,' he said to Heino, 'and when she swings into the wind, lower the jib.'

As the next sea hit us, the crest did not break and the *Erma*'s bows pointed upward. She was hurled astern as the big sea rushed by, then wrenched violently to starboard, but by that time she had topped the hump and was slipping down the back slope. As soon as the jib started to slat, Harry cast the sea anchor overboard. Like an elongated serpent with an evil green head, the canvas bag dashed away with its long, yellow line trailing. The line yanked taut, jerking the *Erma*'s bows down so that a gurgling thin layer rushed over her decks. However small, the sea anchor was strong enough to make itself felt.

Arvid left the cockpit and joined the others around the mast. 'Not so bad, after all,' he said.

Another sea snapped the line taut. The *Erma* tore at it like a frenzied animal and ducked her bow, but she kept level with the water.

'If she only stays hove-to,' Harry said. 'With her shallo…' He did not get farther. A vicious sea, a bubbling part of an overhanging breaker, hit the *Erma* on her port bow with a high, almost metallic sound, hurling us broadside. Instead of swinging back into the wind, she immediately started to veer away in a wide circle around the sea anchor until she floated lengthwise in the trough.

We fell into frantic action.

'Hoist the jib,' Arvid shouted, as he leaped to the helm. Harry and Paul were up in the bow, working hand over hand on the stubborn sea anchor. We knew well enough that getting broadside-to meant danger, but in it came as another huge hill arrived, dark as night, streaked with a creamy net of froth, thundering and swishing.

'Watch out,' Arvid cried. Harry and Paul gripped the windlass. Frightened, I cast a quick glance at the crest above and noticed that it was not toppling over us. But anyway … We sidled up its steep side, the spray flew about us, the *Erma* heeled to starboard, whirled herself this way and that, and I hung on to the cabin top. Then it was gone, and we coasted down the slope.

'It didn't break', Lembit said with a sigh that sounded almost like a prayer. 'We're lucky.'

'I wonder how it would work from the stern', Harry mused. 'Her stern is not as shallow as her bow, but the swamping might be more disastrous.' Both men were silent.

Finally Arvid concluded, 'We might as well try it.'

Harry tied the painter to the middle of the main traveller, Arvid steered the *Erma* before the wind, then Heino lowered the jib and Harry launched the sea anchor. The sack went dancing off over the wash of the waters. The line straightened out, the seas rushed by but did not come aboard, nor did she go off broadside with every sideways push.

For some time we watched the tug and tear between the boat and the sea anchor. After a while Harry said, 'Seems all right.' He sounded rather surprised.

Arvid nodded. He turned slowly away from the port railing. 'I think I'll go below.'

No sooner had we left the *Erma* unattended, than a huge sea hit us. Although both the slide and the doors of the companionway were shut, the cabin at once half filled with water which spurted in through the cracks. In a flash we were out of our bunks, stooping, soaking wet, under the low ceiling, Rommy eyeing the wet book in his hand and I still clutching the diary in which I had been trying to write. The next moment we had torn open the slide and were scrambling out. From below came the wails of the children. Ellen thrust a frightened face out of the companionway.

'We all fell on to the floor,' she said. 'Stoves, shoes, clothes, everything is awash.' Behind her Grandma Paalborg was peering about grimly trying to assess the damage.

Harry bent over the traveller and grasped the end of the line. 'Lend a hand, will you?' he called.

Rommy and Paul jumped to the slippery stern. There, on the narrow segment of bare deck, flush with the sea and in a cloud of spray, the three men hauled in the sea anchor.

As we stood in a puzzled, discouraged group, trying to think what to do next, the main hatch opened and Grandma P stood in the companionway, her hair flying in the wind and spray. She viewed the seas with a determined face, her usually calm eyes flickering.

'There must be some way we can use the sea anchor,' she said, looking at Harry. 'How about streaming it from one corner of the traveller so that she'll ride before quartering seas?'

'Hell, she wouldn't stay that way,' Arvid said.

'Why not, if you hoist the jib and steer her on the right course?'

'Yes, you're right,' Arvid acknowledged slowly, 'but we'd still make fast headway.'

'It would be slower, though, than now,' Grandma P persisted.

Arvid suddenly looked up. 'What your mother says makes sense, Harry. But we'd still run at three or four knots. We'll have to make the sea anchor heavier, too. The only question is, how.'

Harry suggested the heavy 6ft oak log that was lashed to the port rail.

'You want to put it between the sea anchor and the line?' Paul asked. Arvid nodded.

'Crosswise, in between. It'll offer more resistance.'

The finished rig resembled an outstretched cross with the sea anchor as its head and the log its arms. As the *Erma* was moving ahead, the anchor took away fast and the beam bounced and wriggled along the cascading slopes, sometimes standing upright. The line yanked taut and slackened according to the run of the seas. With the anchor pointing directly into the eye of the wind, the boat pulled from one corner, inclined away from it, and sailed with the wind about 20° on the quarter. Arvid looked satisfied.

'She stays that way almost of her own accord. She doesn't need too much helm.'

Scarcely had he spoken when a savagely howling sea cracked against the *Erma,* sending spray and sheets of water over her stern. When it pulled the anchor line taut, the *Erma* canted deeply to port and quivered all over. Harry immediately came aft again; he sat on the after-cabin top and watched the traveller. Every time the line was pulled taut, the boat jerked violently, and the heavy iron vibrated with a rumbling pizzicato.

'The tension is terrific,' he said. 'Something will give.'

Arvid cast a quick look towards the next comber, a good quarter of a mile away, then said to Harry, 'I'll try to reef the jib.' He reached the mast in three leaps. With one motion he freed the halyard from the pin and sent the jib slatting down. He caught the falling canvas in mid-air and in scarcely more than a moment had unhanked the sail and detached the halyard block. Trapping the wildly shaking halyard under his left armpit, he wound the head of the jib into a huge knot, fastened it back on to the block and in a few heaves had hoisted the much-reduced sail.

In what seemed less than a minute Arvid resumed his position at the helm. The rest of us looked at him with awe; never had we seen such seamanship.

The drift was cut down by about a knot, but the strain on the traveller was still too great.

'We have to lengthen the line,' Harry said. 'We can use half the anchor cable. That'll give us sixty feet of heavy chain.'

Harry fastened one end of the chain around the traveller, then directed us to pull in the line for a couple of feet so he could untie it and connect it with the chain. We fell on it, all five of us, and slowly it began to come in. Suddenly Harry called, 'Let it back. You can't hold it. I'll douse the jib.'

He ran to the mast and let the canvas down. Before that Arvid had held her stern-to in the wind. As the *Erma* floated free, the tension eased considerably. Harry loosened the line from the traveller and tied it to the last link of the free end of the chain. While we still held the end of the line inboard, Harry and Arvid let out the chain, slowly and carefully, hand over hand. We eyed the ocean warily. Seas did sweep over us, soaking us, but no killers came along. Heino hoisted the jib, Arvid took the helm and the *Erma* resumed her course.

'Well, at last that's the job.' Arvid watched the slowly heaving chain. Intermittently it rapped at the traveller which clanged with a gong-like ring, but the pulls were not so strong.

'We're making only two knots now,' Harry estimated.

The *Erma*'s deck resounded under the barrage of the sweeping seas, and every blow sounded as though it were the last the boat could take. We had gone below, when a noise like a shell burst fell on her exposed side, pouring a cascade of water over her. Possibly she would have capsized but for the pull of the sea anchor, but out on deck everything was in order except both cockpits were flooded. Heino was pumping. Harry's face was expressionless as usual, but Arvid looked annoyed.

'I don't like it. It alarms the women and children.'

'If we had an oil bag we could try oiling the surface.'

Grandma P, who was standing in the main companionway, suggested some sugar bags we had bought in Madeira. She dived down, to reappear with a small linen sack. Paul filled it with the old Swedish 'tar'. It dripped like a sieve.

Arvid hung it out from the same port corner of the traveller to which the sea anchor was attached. The effect was instant; the water behind took on soft, curved lines, and even the wildest seas were not so sharp.

'It's magic,' said Lembit. But Arvid was not entirely satisfied.

'The oiled area won't be large enough to keep occasional seas from hitting us.'

At that Grandma P smiled.

'Better half an egg than an empty shell.'

And so it was. The storm blew itself out after three and a half days and the Erma *reached Norfolk, Virginia, on 17 December 1945. The complications of the US immigration service were surmounted and all hands ultimately settled in America which, though passive, must be one of the heroes of this tale. Perhaps therefore the final words should be those of Emma Lazarus from the Statue of Liberty…*

> *Give me your tired, your poor,*
> *Your huddled masses yearning to breathe free,*
> *The wretched refuse of your teeming shore.*
> *Send these the homeless, tempest-tossed, to me…*

ON THE RUN

Oluf Reed Olsen
Two Eggs on My Plate
Allen & Unwin 1952

One rainy Sunday in Harwich, I picked up a battered, salt-stained volume in a used-book shop. I'd never heard of the title or the author, but when I began to read it that night on board I knew I'd struck gold. The book was Two Eggs on My Plate *by Oluf Reed Olsen. It tells the tale of a group of young Norwegians escaping the Nazi occupation in September 1940 in an ancient 18ft yacht called* Haabet *(Hope). They had been resistance fighters, saboteurs and spies, and were now well and truly on the run. Hidden in a deck beam were all manner of secret documents, with photographs of German coastal installations. The Nazis had only one punishment for spying. It was Blighty or bust – literally.*

Their adventures are too many for a single catch-all sketch, so I have chosen four anecdotes from what proved an epic voyage. We all suffer privations when we go to sea, but nowadays these are served up by the weather. As well as storms, Olsen and his shipmates had to contend with machine guns, naval ordnance and the certainty of a terminal interview with the Gestapo if they were caught. We join them first as they slip out from home between the islands that fringe the Norwegian coast.

A T 1 a.m. *Haabet* stood out from Kristiansand through Vestergabet, with a light night breeze from the north. The sky was overcast and it was dark, but not too dark for us to see clearly the outlines of islets and rocks. We passed out slowly between the various German fortifications. To us who sat there working and did not even dare whisper to each other, our pace seemed still slower. We ran a risk by keeping to the middle of the waterway, as we didn't know the various submerged rocks in the channel and could not use too much light in consulting the chart. But all went well. We did not hear a sound from anywhere, and after about two hours we left behind the last rocks of the skerries.

In the morning our luck changed when the wind dropped quickly. When it grew light the coastline appeared on the horizon; we had not come as far out as we had hoped. The boom swung in time with the boat's movements in the swell. Not a breath of wind! It was a long way to England...

Then Kaare started up, stared and pointed. 'Look there!' I turned round, weary and worn after twenty-four hours without sleep. But what we both saw had more effect than a bucket of ice-cold water. A German destroyer! Out with the fishing-lines!

There was no doubt about the destroyer's intention; she was making straight for us at full speed. Next moment two shots rang out in quick succession, followed by two explosions in the water straight ahead of us. Kaare and I continued to haul on lines as if nothing had happened. A man shouted to us in German from the destroyer's bridge and ordered us to prepare for boarding. We continued to haul on lines. A boat came across with a lieutenant and two ratings. There were no polite phrases this time! The lieutenant ordered curtly that *Haabet* should be thoroughly searched, and then turned to us. We both feared the worst. First papers. Then an explanation as to why we were so far out. We who had fishermen's passes ought to know quite well that we might not go farther than one sea mile from the coast, etc.

Curiously enough, the lieutenant believed our explanation, and when one of the two ratings found a whisky bottle, three parts full, there seemed to be no doubt in the lieutenant's mind. Till then we had been in great anxiety lest the Germans should discover the cache in the deck beam. But the whisky bottle seemed to have saved the situation! I utilised the interest momentarily aroused to ask for a tow in towards the coast again. The lieutenant stayed aboard alone and the episode which followed was too comic to be ever forgotten. We went coastwards in tow of the destroyer so fast that the water spurted up at our bows. On board *Haabet* we sat with the lieutenant swallowing one grog after another. The bottle was soon nearly empty. Kaare and I pretended to be drunk, and the lieutenant actually was as drunk as a lord! And the best part of it was an admirable musical contribution from all hands: *Denn wir fahren gegen Engeland.*

Following this episode, the boys set sail once more. This time they are visited by the Luftwaffe.

The jagged mountains of Norway were just vanishing below the horizon. How long would it be before we again saw that land which we loved so much?

Suddenly Kaare yelled 'Look!' We followed the direction of his outstretched hand. Two planes coming towards us! 'Out with the lines! Back the sail!'

Over the side went the line, and a minute later when two Heinkel 115s reached us, we were busy hauling on it. For a few breathless minutes they circled round *Haabet*, which was now flying the German swastika flag together with the Norwegian. They grazed the masthead three times, then finally dropped two red flares to seaward. To emphasize their meaning, one fired a salvo of machine-gun bullets hardly ten yards from us – between us and England. They bore away again while we stood literally gasping for breath.

Was that all? Or was it only the beginning? It seemed, however, that they were satisfied. Soon afterwards, an unbroken cover of mist and rain moved in towards the coast and we ourselves could not see for more than a few yards, so our mad career continued.

Three days and 300 miles later, the yacht sights distant land south of Aberdeen. However, a violent gale springs up and drives them back to sea. Olsen takes up the story again eight days later with their victuals virtually exhausted.

The following night, there was a sudden shout of, 'Light ahead!' It could only be a lighthouse on the Danish coast. Should we continue straight in and give up now while we had 'safety' in sight? But what would happen if we landed in Denmark, occupied by the Germans? Undoubtedly we should all three be captured and sent back to Norway for trial. The result of that trial could hardly be in doubt. Was all we had gone through since we had left Norway to be of no avail? On the other hand, how long could we continue this nightmare, without water, food or sleep?

Summing up, we found that the choice lay between two different kinds of death – either being put up against a wall and shot, or finding a common grave in the depths of the North Sea. Despite toil, thirst, cold and everything else, there was complete agreement. We continued our wild chase before wind and ocean.

When we rejoin the ship for the final time, the Norwegians have been at sea for two weeks. Food and water are gone save a pound of butter and

*two cans of sardines. Their position is uncertain. Morale is low, but not in
a state of collapse. Somehow, they keep on going.*

September 29 dragged by. I was steering west. Kaare was sitting by me in
an attitude of prostration; Rolf was lying inside the cabin and the water
was already half-way up his pillow. It was 2.35 p.m. I was just going to
wake Rolf to pump when I heard a sound – not from the sea, not from
the rigging, nor from Kaare's laboured breathing. It grew louder. I slowly
looked up...

'*Plane*!' I yelled as loud as I could.

Kaare took over the helm while I rigged up a soaking wet Union Jack
befouled with oil. The Norwegian flag, which was now ragged and filthy,
but which we had hauled down before the worst weather came, went to
the masthead.

As the plane came closer I set light to our last rocket with a cigarette-
lighter; it hissed up and burst. The red light sank down slowly and went
out. At the same moment the plane swung sharply and came roaring
down over. Rolf danced round the mast like a madman. Kaare sat aft
holding tight to the tiller, while the tears ran down his face. I myself
could hardly see for tears.

An hour later we had three planes flying over *Haabet* mast-high. This
time there could be no doubt. They signalled to follow their direction,
and I acknowledged: 'Have escaped from Norway. Thank you.'

We suddenly took courage, and in a few minutes *Haabet* was under
full sail. It was not the thing for a boat like *Haabet* to sail into port close-
reefed! We went so that the foam flew.

Now Rolf standing on the forecastle, shouted, 'Smoke ahead! Ship!'

Each time *Haabet* cut over a wave-top we could see the masts of a
ship coming straight towards us. At 1645 we were about a quarter of a
mile from the British destroyer. What a sight! I had all the time a feeling
that I was dreaming, and every time I tried to share my joy with Kaare
and Rolf it was as if I had something firmly lodged in my throat, and I
could not say what I wanted to.

We were told by a megaphone on the destroyer's bridge to come up
on the lee side, and soon afterwards we got hawsers aboard fore and aft,
while the crew, who at that moment lined the ship's rail, gave us three
ringing hurrahs.

Without a thought of military restrictions, my first question was: 'What is our position?' Five minutes later the answer came: 'You are twenty miles off the English coast where the Thames comes out into the Channel.'

After we had had a keg of water lowered to us and had quenched our thirst, the commander told us he had received orders to pick us up, but, he was sorry to say, not *Haabet*. We exchanged long looks. Let *Haabet* go to the bottom now? No, thank you. The food and water we had taken on board, with the medicine we had been given, which had already had its effect, made us all three shake our heads. If *Haabet* had crossed and re-crossed the North Sea and kept us safe, surely we could manage the forty miles which remained! We felt big in our shoes. Moreover, *Haabet* was all that we possessed!

The last words we had through the megaphone from the skipper were these:

'I've heard many stories about you crazy Norwegian Vikings, but it seems to me you beat them all! Good luck to you!'

Yes, there was no doubt that we ourselves did not really know what we were doing just then, but our pride in being Norwegians, our pride in having won, was too great.

Two hours later we were hailed by another destroyer. This time there was no question about it: the skipper told us his orders were to pick us up, and *Haabet* too. We did not have to be asked twice! One after another we clambered up H.M.S. *Bedouin*'s rope ladder with the map and lists and more than a thousand films of German defence works in our arms. Now we were carried below, each to a luxurious officer's cabin. With hot-water bottles above and beneath and beside me, and after an injection of something or other by the ship's doctor, I fell asleep... This was England!

After landing in Britain, Oluf and Kaare went to Canada where they trained as pilots. Kaare lost his life in an accident. Oluf returned to Norway in 1943 to fight directly again for the freedom of the land he loved.

ATHEISM RENOUNCED

John Caldwell
Desperate Voyage
Victor Gollancz 1952

John Caldwell was born in Fort Worth, Texas, in 1919. He signed on with the American Merchant Marine during the Second World War and in 1944 he married Mary in Australia, only to sail back to the United States two days later. Desperate to rejoin his bride after the war, he travelled to Panama in May 1946 searching for a ship. Not a berth was to be found, so he bought the 29ft cutter Pagan *and, with zero sailing or navigation experience, set sail across 9,000 miles of the Pacific. The voyage began with predictable minor disasters, but it was not until he was dismasted in the eye of a hurricane between the Caroline Islands and Samoa that things really deteriorated.*

Pagan *was left a waterlogged wreck, but he contrived a jury rig and sailed to safety. It took him a further 36 days, 22 of them with no recognisable food and little more in the way of water.*

We join Caldwell shortly after a second dismasting. He has just eaten his last pair of boots and his favourite belt. The ship's rat has escaped by being washed overboard, but any bird unlucky enough to land has been eaten alive, bones and all. Frantic for nourishment, he is contemplating a bottle of aftershave that has somehow survived the tempest.

In two further exhausted tries to step the mast I failed miserably, missing the hole by a foot. Then I saw the shave lotion. I opened it, sniffed it – it was unbearable, but throwing my head back, I downed a hearty portion. As I capped it, I felt an electric sort of surge through my body. Before I realized what I had done, I had jerked the mast off the deck, had pointed it up like a broom handle, and it was stepped. Everything I did in the next hour was effortless. I lashed the mast in place at the heel; set the shrouds and stays; hoisted all sail; lashed the helm alee. I felt boundless; I even felt like diving over and giving one of the sharks a bad time!

Under even shorter sail *Pagan* took more time to move. She was sluggish, but she tilted slightly before the southern wind and soon I was plodding along at something less than a knot.

Each day I read the Bible more assiduously. I learned the Twenty-third Psalm by heart, and spoke it every rising and sleeping, and often in the night as I heaved at the pump. My Bible – a gift of my grandpa when I was a boy – I had never read a chapter of. Aboard *Pagan* I read it cover to cover twice, devouring its words, searching out its comforts. Men who sail small boats know the verity of the Good Captain who piloted my boat. Atheism with me had been an old story. I picked up a good background at college and in the War. Aboard *Pagan* the petty arguments of 'college' atheism dissolved under the touchstone of vital need and vital want. The test proves; the argument only conjectures. I smile when I meet atheists.

That afternoon I heard a heavy thud on the starboard hull. I hurried feebly out on deck and looked around. Near the bow ploughed the fin of a new arrival to the school of sharks that loafed constantly in the wake. He glided amidships and swung his ponderous body gruffly against the planking. *Pagan* shivered. He wandered gracefully off abeam, then came again. There we were, eyeing each other, wondering how to eat the other.

The trouble was I had no harpoon, but I was full of ideas. I knew that if I could get something big enough into a vital spot, he was mine. There was at the very least a quart of fresh blood I could draw out of him – enough to last five days. I relished the strength it would give me. I could dry his half a ton of meat, and with plenty to eat I could make out with a quarter pint of water daily. It would be a tight squeeze: but it might see me through to land.

In the bilge, I found an old file; under the forepeak was my hacksaw, rusty now; beneath my bunk lay an eight-inch strip of steel, one inch wide, a quarter thick. From it, I envisaged a wicked killing spear. The work, as I cut it out in my mind, could be done the next afternoon if my endurance could hold. As for the shark, if he were like the others, he would be hovering close astern for days. The material was comparatively soft, but fashioning it would wear down my last reserves. The whole venture was a vast gamble.

I marked the rough outline on the section of steel, then commenced the long task of driving the saw along each mark. I watched the ceiling as I worked so I couldn't see the slow progress of the cutting. Each time

I looked down I tried to be surprised at the few hair widths I had bitten away. My thoughts turned to the kill I would soon be making and the heavy feasts to follow. The devils of appetite returned and I drank a half pint of my water, but I felt it a worthy risk with a feast of meat and blood in the offing.

I was too worn and weak to begin the filing of the spear point; that would start the next morning. I went to bed early but it wasn't easy to sleep. My stomach needed food, but every last edible was gone. I thought of pages from my books, but I had tried that before and it had created unbearable problems of the bowels. Then I remembered the oil in the engine.

I groped out into the night, down into the stern compartment, and loosed the crankshaft plug. I drained off half a pint of gurgling liquid and returned to the cabin where I stirred the thick gritty liquid and made ready to drink it down.

There are people who wonder how far a man will go when he is hungry. By hungry, I don't refer to the foodlessness of a day or even a week. Desperate hunger doesn't come until one has starved for at least two weeks after about a month of semi-starvation.

I turned the pan up and drank deeply and quickly. My throat was outraged. My stomach revolted. I blustered and nearly vomited. My head spun in a light swim and I grew faint and drowsy. I remember the knots tightening in my stomach and the far away ringing in my ears that seemed to come close and go away again. And as I dreamed I found myself in Sydney Harbour. There were the harbour bridge, the skyline of Kings Cross, and the Manly Ferry steaming into Circular Quay. Then I wakened; the same darkness, the same slapping of water in the bilges, the same soughing of wind in the rigging, the same feeling of a weak stomach.

In the waning dark I scraped at the spear point with my small file. Hour on hour I wore away at the weapon, sprinkling mites of steel on my swollen feet. By mid-morning it showed a cruel, knife-edged point and two jagged flanges. Before noon it was a formidable weapon, heavy, unbreakable, sinister. I looked past it to the shark. I had nothing for a shaft, but the last of the oars had gone to jury-rig a mizzenmast. Shark spearing had priority over sailing; so down came the little mizzen.

With four heavy screws, I tightened the spearhead to the long oar handle. In addition I bound it with a wrapping of shroud wire. In the opposite end of the shaft I drilled a hole with my knife to secure fifty feet of line, bending it to the heavy cleat at the cockpit coaming.

I stirred the water a bit and the shark sped straight in, giving me the once-over. We sized each other up and squared off. He loitered purposely, turned lazily. Exposed to me was his whole side. I saw a likely point midway between the dorsal and ventral fins. Bone, flesh, vital organs lay there – everything to bed a spear in. I glued my eyes to his open flank, and drove the spear hard down. The blade hit what felt like rock, but it penetrated. The shark lurched in a spasm. I was shoved upward, off my feet. I held to the spear and thrust it back. The great fish threshed and writhed. I felt the spear push deep into his flesh. My hold weakened and I saw the rope paying out as he lunged at the end of the line, tautening it with a slam. He spun around – plunged, and I couldn't see him for the boiling he made, but I could feel his might as the decks jerked.

He flailed the surface white. Tail up he fought his way downward, curving back toward the boat. As slack showed in the line I took it in and twisted it around the cleat. The shark shot under the keel, coming up on the opposite bow.

I sat down watching his useless battlings against death. I knew the spear had a killing hold in his vitals. When his blood gave out he would come to terms. In a moment he lay on the surface wallowing gracelessly. The shark was stirring only feebly as I dragged him in. Suddenly with explosive fury he shot to the end of the line. In a moment he grew limp, like a dead weight. Then again he came to life, or so it seemed, and bolted away, and then again relaxed. I watched him closely as I towed him in. Another shark was entangled in the line, then a second shark fouled himself with the line. As it yanked tight I saw everything. The sharks weren't tangled, they were tearing at the carcass of my shark!

A third and fourth shark darted in as I heaved frantically. Whenever the line showed slack, I wrapped it with mad haste around the cleat. Every pound of flesh the gluttonous pack was tearing off was vital to my chance of life. One of them bit into his tail, spinning him around in a half-circle and racing to the bow till the line flew tight. There I could hear a terrifying snap of jaws as the four set to ripping at him. Great holes showed in my shark as he was thrust and pushed and torn.

I worked the mutilated mass of sagged flesh as close in as possible. The thing now was to hook him and somehow get him on board. The four sharks were thrusting back and tearing from side to side, pulling in opposite directions. My big shark was bent S-shaped. Rusty, blood-filled water nearly hid his attackers. Like hungry hogs, they were eye deep into the carcass. I tried to fit the grappling hook into the gills of the dismembered victim, but weakness felled my arms to my sides.

The grisly feast dropped down to keel depth; and then beneath the keel to *Pagan's* other side. Through the soles of my feet on the deck boards, I could feel the vibrations of the strained oar. I peered over to see what was happening, and from out of the water came a muffled snap. My oar bobbed to the surface and below me, gradually sinking, was the gory feast. I watched it glimmer, and when it no longer glimmered I fell back and lost myself in remorse. I have never been at a lower moment.

Water was gone. *Pagan* was able to make one knot given a fair breeze, and there were hundreds of miles yet to go to land.

Caldwell was saved sooner than he expected because, after dead reckoning for upwards of a month, he was hundreds of miles adrift in his navigation. Less than a week later he piled up on an outlying Fijian reef. The people of the remote community nursed him back from near-death, and he made it to the love of his life via an island schooner and a transport aircraft. The couple removed to the United States and in 1967 he opened a hotel on Prune Island, now Palm Island, beside Union Island in the Grenadines. He, Mary and their family ran it for the next 30 years. John Caldwell died in 1998. His book Desperate Voyage *has become a classic of human endurance.*

WOMEN WRITERS

Life on the wild side at 70° North Winifred Brown

A child of the sea Lis Andersen

Clueless cruising in a different world Ellen Barbara Flower

Downwind drama Constance Buel Burnett

LIFE ON THE WILD SIDE
AT 70° NORTH

Winifred Brown

Duffers on the Deep

Peter Davies 1939

Win Brown was a fearless lady aviator of the old school in the early 1930s. Born in Manchester, she won the King's Cup round England air race in 1930 and, in search of further adventure, canoed the length of the Amazon. Her father had been a yachtsman who named his boat Elwin *after his wife and Win, so perhaps it was that memory that spurred her on to go sailing. Whatever the motivations, she does not stress them in her book,* Duffers on the Deep. *The facts are that in 1935 she opted to give up flying and invest her resources in* Perula, *a 45ft fishing boat which someone had converted badly into a sort of yacht. Fortunately, Brown was a woman of taste as well as remarkable Lancastrian tenacity, and she had the boat transformed into a fine motor sailer by the original builders, Dickies of Bangor in North Wales. As soon as she had completed the refit, Brown signed on a gentleman friend by the name of Ron Adams and squared away for the Norwegian Arctic. Neither had any significant seafaring experience.*

The voyage north to Spitzbergen was by no means without incident, but it was on the way back to the Norwegian mainland that the weather really dished up the dirt. I love this book for its gritty, British humour. As a child of our time, I am also perplexed that so unstoppable a lady would choose to place herself a very firm second when it came to action on deck on grounds of her sex only. I met her on board Perula *fifty years later and we laughed even more than we drank. She clearly hadn't changed, because in* Duffers, *it is always the fun that carries the day.*

We join Win Brown and Ron Adams in the high 70s of latitude between Svalbard and Bear Island. Adams has recently had to make a bold sortie out of the wheelhouse to the deck to save the meat safe as it was being washed aft from its stowage on the foredeck by a huge wave. Brown's comment was,

'Well, you are a "BF". Risking your life for a dozen lamb chops and a pound of butter!'

*J*UNE *30th, 1935, 2100*:

At 9.40 last night the wind backed NE and started to blow really hard. The glass fell another two points and things began to look nasty. Fortunately we had got round the worst of the ice, but a few odd pieces were still crashing about. We throttled the engine right back, but we were still going too fast. We debated about getting the mainsail in and as usual left it too late.

We were taking the seas on the port quarter, and water poured over the wheelhouse. I looked at the mast; it was bending right over and the track slides were tearing out of the sail. I looked at Adams.

'I'm sorry, Ron,' I said, 'but the sail will have to come down.'

'I know,' he replied. 'I'll go and do it.'

'Can I help?'

'No, I don't think so.' We both knew the half-frozen canvas, the strong winds and flying spray were beyond the strength of a woman.

I sat miserably at the wheel trying to heave-to and keep *Perula* as steady and dry as possible as Adams struggled with the sail alone. He was soaked to the skin and blue with cold. One minute I'd see him working for'ard, then a wave would come and blot everything out. Sometimes I shut my eyes not daring to look at a deck I felt certain would be empty. But there he was, his arms tightly wound round the mast. The suspense was awful; I felt helpless and useless.

'Oh, hell!' I groaned. 'Why am I a blasted woman?' I think I drank about a quarter of a bottle of neat rum while he was out there.

At last the mainsail was down and Adams safely back in the wheelhouse. He staggered below to change, for he had not dared to go out encumbered by oilskins and seaboots.

We proceeded under mizzen and staysail. It was not a bit of good; the wind and sea were beyond description. I really think we were doing about 8 knots under such reduced canvas. We tried to back the staysail and heave-to. We had never tried this before and found that the sail was too big. *Perula* swung broadside and I had to use the engine to bring her back. I was doing this when there was a horrible jolt. The engine faltered. We looked at each other.

'My God!' said Adams. I pushed open the throttle; the engine roared back to life.

We went on; the weather got worse and worse. Even if *Perula* could go on, her crew could not; we were both completely exhausted and sat in miserable silence. At first I tried to make bright conversation; it sounded inane. As wave after wave crashed on the wheelhouse I began to wonder what we should do if it carried away, how we should block up the hole. Then I realised that if the wheelhouse went we should probably go with it.

It was the first time I had wondered what the end of things would be like. Once or twice in the air the ground had come up to meet me, but there had been no time to think – I had been too busy trying to save my 'plane. Strangely enough, I don't think I was very frightened now. Of course, I'd had a lot of rum, but I have always been horribly afraid I would be afraid.

It is rather a blow to one's dignity to realise the world will go on quite well without you. On this occasion I thought to myself, 'Perhaps it won't be so bad, at least we shall not have to fight any more.'

I think that Adams too was thinking on the same lines. He sat at the wheel, very silent and looking utterly wretched. He was not afraid for himself, I know that, his actions on deck proved it. He was thinking of his people at home; of me, perhaps. I staggered to my feet, put my arms round him and said a few daft things, but he took no notice, except perhaps to look even more grim. I sat down again and had another rum.

Then we remembered the sea anchor. We had never used one before, but read up in a book what to do. Ours was a hefty affair specially made for us by the Fleetwood Trawler Supply Company, with 4 fathoms of half-inch chain, 15 fathoms 4½-inch warp, and a canvas drogue 6 feet in diameter. In the Menai Straits they had laughed at it, asking if we thought we were the *Queen Mary*.

By 5 a.m., after a fearsome session on deck, the sea anchor was out, the staysail down, and the engine stopped. It was now a full NE gale, but *Perula* lay remarkably well under sea anchor and mizzen. For a few moments we watched, then having done all we could, we staggered below and fell into our root bunks.

'I don't want to dishearten you, Win,' said Adams, 'but while I was on deck I found the mainsheet over the side.'

I remembered the faltering engine.

'How much has gone?' I asked.

'I should think about 3 fathoms,' he replied.

'Three fathoms of 2-inch yacht manila round the propeller,' I groaned.

'It may not be round the prop,' he said. 'The engine has run for an hour or two since.'

'Was the end chewed up?' I asked.

'Yes,' he admitted.

'Oh, well,' I said, wearily, 'what the hell does it matter? Time enough to worry if we see this lot out.' With that we both went to sleep for nine hours.

We have been riding to the sea anchor now for almost 17 hours. One gets quite used to it. We are both in our root bunks; it is the only safe place. We sleep, read, eat and sleep; actually it is the best rest we have had all the cruise! Sometimes I stagger up to the wheelhouse to look at the barometer, but it is depressing. Waves seem to tower up, almost to the height of the masthead; the saloon is infinitely more reassuring. We have drawn the porthole curtains and turned the wireless full on to drown the shrieking wind, but if it doesn't give gale warnings it plays hymns.

The words 'sterk kuling' (fresh gale) have come over the air from the shore stations, but I really feel that, exposed as we are to the open sea somewhere WNW of Bear Island, we are having the 'benefit' of a good full gale. Fortunately, it is a long sea, but sometimes a wave breaks on deck with a sickening crash that makes *Perula* shudder. One has just forced the skylight open and a cascade of water has descended into the saloon. I had to laugh. Adams sat up quite peeved, and exclaimed: 'It shouldn't do that with a sea anchor out!'

The wave filled my box of chocolates with sea water and Adams says I'll be sick; but think of it, here I am, in an Arctic gale, eating chocolates from London. It is a funny world.

Sometimes to cheer ourselves up we sing our 'theme song'. It is strange how a song helps you along, as 'Tipperary' did in the war. On the Amazon we had 'Ol' Man River' and 'Ain't it grand to be blooming well dead' – with modifications of course!

For this cruise we decided on 'I've got my love to keep me warm', but we have changed 'love' to 'rum,' and with due apologies to the composer, our version runs:

Duet: *The wind is blowing, The snow is snowing, But we will weather the storm.*
No matter how much it may storm,
We've got some rum to keep us warm!

(pause for action)
Adams: *I can't remember*
It's worse in December. Just watch those icicles form.
Brown: *What do we care if icicles form?*
We've got some rum to keep us warm.
(pause for action)
Duet: *Off with our oilskins, our boots of gum,*
We don't need wrapping up, we're burning with rum.
(more action)
Brown: *My throat's on fire, The waves rise higher,*
Duet: *But we will weather the storm.*
What do we care how much it may storm? We've got some rum to keep us warm.
(no action – bottle empty)

I think I'll go to sleep again, my novel is no good anyway, I've never read anything so depressing, everybody is dead or dying. I don't know how the author will finish it.

July 1st, 8 p.m.:
When we woke this morning it was blowing as hard as ever. We managed to get some breakfast and went back to our bunks. By afternoon conditions improved enough for us to go on deck and examine the propeller. The rope is round it, three blasted fathoms of it.

'What are we going to do?' said Adams.

'Sail,' I said somewhat grimly. 'But first we must get the sea anchor in, and how we are going to do that without any engine to manoeuvre, I don't know.'

We went for'ard, seized the tripping line, gave a mighty heave and nearly went over backwards.

'Hell!' said Adams. 'There's nothing there.' We sat down on deck and laughed until we cried.

The sea anchor had gone at the bridle and with it its lifebelt float bearing *Perula*'s name and yacht club. She had ridden out the gale with nothing but a mizzen and a trailing warp...

A CHILD OF THE SEA

Lis Andersen
Lis Sales the Atlantic
George Routledge & Sons 1935

This remarkable book was written in 1930 by Lis Andersen, aged 12. A couple of years earlier, her father finally admitted he was bored with life working in a Copenhagen shipping office. He sold up the family home along with most of their possessions and ploughed the funds back into the Monsoon, *a 59ft plumb-stemmed ketch, built in 1895 in France as a smack. The Andersens sailed from Copenhagen to Cape Town by way of Rio and Buenos Aires, then home via St Helena, Ascension, the West Indies and New York. The dramatis personae of Lis's book include her parents, her two little brothers, Sigurd and Jan, her dog, Luf, and a number of colourful characters who signed on variously as cook and what one must assume were paid hands. Reading her book is pure, innocent delight. This is a girl who has had a proper childhood.*

The work needs no further introduction. We join Lis and her shipmates as they leave New York, homeward-bound on what turns out to be an eventful Atlantic crossing.

Many of the things I saw in New York seemed to me marvellous and beautiful in their way, but they were nothing compared with the breakers at Ascension, the rollers on the blue Atlantic, and all the real thrilling adventures we had had. At half-past two we were once again out in the sound with all sails set, and when we were going at a good pace Father and Christensen jumped into the boat with our film camera, and Father filmed the *Monsoon* when she was coming towards them in full sail. As soon as they were on board we hoisted the boat and lashed it fast, for now we were sailing out into the Atlantic Ocean and it was autumn weather.

Next morning, when we couldn't see land any longer, we saw a coastguard which came hurrying towards us. No doubt they thought that we were smugglers and quickly came right up to us, but since we sailed on calmly they probably realized they were mistaken and went on their way.

Now we were on our way to Denmark and hoping to make a record voyage, but just wait and you will hear what happened!

When we got out into the open sea we were met by a head-wind, and the day after we ran into a storm. If only the wind had been favourable, it would have been marvellous with that storm – but of course it had to be a head-wind. Nevertheless we thought that we should soon get a favourable wind, for at this time of the year there is nearly always a west wind blowing across the North Atlantic and the North Sea.

The barometer fell and the wind got stronger so that we had to reef. The wind was getting stronger and stronger and every five minutes we looked at the barometer. Luckily Sigurd was only two days sea-sick, but Mother was very ill. We others weren't sea-sick, only a bit uncomfortable the first day. On that day I didn't have any lessons, but then the school had closed down, as Mother said. The worst thing about school was when Jan had to practise good handwriting, for that wasn't so easy. Sometimes the inkpot fell over and the ink was spilt all over the book so that it looked like the sea on a map.

Mother was always longing for fish and fish rissoles, and for that matter we all did, so it was a pity not one of us really knew how to catch fish. But the nice Alfred knew what to do. He invented many new dishes. For example, he made an 'Atlantic Ocean Pudding' from rice, soaked rye biscuits, baking powder, some prunes and jam and other left-overs, which he boiled first of all and then baked in the oven, and this dish he had invented himself, so no one could part with it into the sea; but it was the fish-balls we were all longing for.

He put the tinned crayfish – by the way, they tasted like boiled bandages – through a mincer, then treated them just as one treats ordinary fish when one wants to make fish-balls. These fish-balls tasted almost as good as the real ones.

After we had had stormy weather for about three or four days something awful happened. We had a terrible accident. One night the goose-neck on the main-boom broke and it took us three whole days to mend it, for we had almost nothing to mend it with. We were forced to use both our kevels and take our winch to pieces to make a jaw, and we also had to use up a couple of thick boards we had. You must also remember that we did all this during a storm, and of course we had to take down the mainsail and lash the boom to the mast and so on.

When the goose-neck broke, the boom fell down on the roof of the W.C. with a huge crash and the roof fell in. Karl had to do a lot of work there before we could go to the W.C. at all. At last we succeeded in mending the main boom, but now the end of the boom split and we had to make it tight with some bits of iron which had been left over from the rudder when it was mended in New York. It took us a whole day to mend the boom, for we had to do a lot of filing on the iron before bolts could be passed through.

We had several more accidents on this voyage, but they were only small accidents compared with these others, for example, when Sigurd broke two panes in the skylight, so that Christensen had to put canvas there instead. Otherwise Sigurd was quite good.

One day Christensen had put Sigurd at the helm and ordered him to keep a good look-out because Christensen had to go and do something else ; but Sigurd hadn't yet learnt to steer properly, although he had tried before, and he swung eight points off the course up into the wind, and before Christensen had time to prevent it the *Monsoon* turned round. Something might easily have gone wrong. We might have capsized, but all went well as usual. Father shot up on deck in a hurry and we got the mainsail over on the other side.

The storm lasted for nearly twenty days, with a head-wind the whole time, before finally we were off the Newfoundland Banks. It had driven us so far south that now it would take us much longer if we sailed round the north of Scotland, as we had at first decided to do, and so we decided to go through the English Channel instead.

Now at last we got a favourable wind, and you can imagine how fast we sailed across the Atlantic. In ten days we were in the Channel. A few days before I had been on watch together with Father and Christensen, and I have never before seen such a beautiful phosphorescent wake as I saw that night. At this time I was playing the mouth-organ a lot, for Sigurd had sold me his old one for six pieces of chocolate. Every day we got a piece after lunch, and sometimes two, because we had had such a lot given to us in New York.

After thirty days' sailing we were just outside the Channel, according to Father's calculations, and we were all waiting excitedly, as all sailors do when they are going to catch their first sight of Europe for ages. In the morning Jensen sighted land and we were up in the rigging like one man. Yes, there was land plain enough, and one could see the tall white lighthouse which rises up above one of the Scilly Isles and is called Bishop's Rock. We couldn't help being pleased because the voyage had gone so well.

Now there was only a thousand miles left to Copenhagen, and those we didn't count. In my heart of hearts I was very sad that day, though, for that was the last day we saw the Atlantic.

The day before we saw land we were taking soundings all the time. The first time we took our soundings we got 102 fathoms. We were therefore almost at the 100 fathoms' bend now, and Father didn't need to take the sun any more, for we could sound our way along and find out sufficiently well from the chart where we were. The day Jensen discovered land Father said to Mother immediately after lunch that he thought Jan and I ought to have a holiday from lessons, because all sailors had a holiday from lessons when they were running before the wind into the Channel for the first time for ages; but Mother wouldn't give way. Father tried all sorts of ways, but nothing helped. Finally Father sent a message that when Noah's Ark was running before a spanking south-westerly wind into the Channel, all the animals were given a holiday from school. That, Mother couldn't resist. Jan was excused from scrawling in his exercise book, and I from swotting German with my poor brain.

In the night Jan, Ture and I were going to hold Channel watch, but it was blowing so hard that Father only called me, because he thought that I at least must be allowed to see the Eddystone Lighthouse which was almost abeam of us. When I came up I asked Father if I might be allowed to stay up for two hours of the middle watch, and I was allowed to do that. At first we saw a lot of trawlers and steamers, but as the wind freshened to a real storm the steamers and trawlers disappeared or hove to and hoisted two red lanterns as a sign that they couldn't steer in the rough weather.

With all sails set we flew on wings, and it was real sailing. Finally we were forced to take in the balloon-jib and the topsail and shorten the mizzen.

I also saw Land's End, the Lizard and other points; but of course it was only the lighthouses on these points which I saw because it was pitch-dark and every now and then the rain came pouring down.

I kept watch from twelve o'clock till two with Father and Christensen. The wind got stronger and stronger and the weather was steadily getting worse. It was a proper Channel gale. We ran before the wind with close-reefed mainsail and stay-foresail, and the barometer fell 40mm in twenty-four hours so that one might have thought there was an earthquake happening somewhere. We only had a board knocked out of the bulwarks aft, and that wasn't worth talking about compared with the high seas and what might have happened.

There was plenty to do on deck and the crew and Father were dead beat. They hadn't slept much for the last forty-eight hours, because it isn't all play to run before the wind in the Channel in such a storm. We were now almost right opposite Dover and decided to sail into this port and wait for good weather, for Father said that there was a storm blowing in the North Sea from the northwest and north, and there was no point in going out there and wearing ourselves out and having the *Monsoon* spring a leak. First we sailed past a small town called Folkestone and there it was very beautiful with high cliffs. We saw several trains which went straight through the cliffs for a long way. When we were abeam of Dover we saw in time that there was a wreck lying in the east entrance to the harbour. So we had to sail through the other entrance; but we had to wait a bit because the current ran strongly out to the North Sea and we had a following wind. So we tacked once out into the Channel and lay there for some time tacking till the current grew less strong.

Out there we could see the French coast at Calais, but not very clearly for it was very cloudy – real Channel weather.

When we came in again towards Dover's high moles we were sailing fast and we almost flew round the mole; but then it suddenly took the wind away from us and we had an exciting moment. But we cleared it and half an hour later were riding safely at anchor in Europe again.

The authorities came on board and they opened their eyes very wide when they heard that we had come from New York. They told us that if we had come the day before we wouldn't have recognized Dover, for the high moles which surround the harbour were quite hidden by the waves. It was the worst weather they had had for many years.

CLUELESS CRUISING IN A DIFFERENT WORLD

Ellen Barbara Flower
Under Jane's Wings
Edward Arnold & Co 1936

It is a mistake to wear rose-coloured sunglasses when considering vintage yacht cruising. Those people inhabited a world without GPS or auxiliary power, and some of them performed miracles of seamanship. Others were more human. In a book of this era written by a man, doubts and errors are often downplayed. After all, many of them had fought in the Great War, where sympathy for weakness was in short supply. Reading Under Jane's Wings *by Ellen Barbara Flower gives a different perspective. Her husband lived for golf, yet for reasons that remain obscure, the couple bought a paid-off Bristol Channel pilot cutter in 1921 and sailed her two-handed, via every small port in Western Christendom, to Marseilles.*

Jane *was an engineless gaff cutter, 50ft on deck, 8ft 6in draught, 30 tons displacement, with a 30ft boom that weighed 400lb or more. Their experience was minimal; navigation consisted of a few old charts and what Mrs Flower frequently describes as 'Sailing Directions', so getting lost was commonplace. Just operating the boat was a major challenge and disaster was always round the corner. I know from my own experience that two competent men can manage such a vessel, but to think of Ellen Flower and her 'Lord and Master' – who appears to spend much of his time taking his ease while 'the lady wife' attends to the business of saving themselves – let loose on the high seas is another matter.*

That they made it to their destination does credit to those powers who smile on gamblers. Under Jane's Wings *must be read with tongue in cheek, but it reminds us today of just how far yacht cruising has come in a hundred years. We join the Flowers off the Biscay coast of France. Quite how we all make it through the night remains a mystery to me.*

IT was evident our little cat was very ill. He had been hiding all night and he emerged from his place of sequestration very sick and weak. Then he did a very strange thing. He got into the white enamel basin that is placed under the cistern tap, curled himself up and stayed there in a cold bath for three hours. I took him out, dosed him with castor oil, dried him, and placed him on cushions in my cabin, feeding him now and then with spoonfuls of milk and white of egg. He lay there very nearly dead. Remembering his remarkable recovery at Roscoff, I still did not give up hope. But preoccupation over his illness prevented me from studying the charts and the Sailing Directions as thoroughly as I generally did.

We sailed through the tail end of a thunder-storm. There was no wind and the current was against us. We had passed the Rocher d'Antioche and rounded the Pointe de Chassiron, the most north-westerly point of the Ile d'Oléron, when dear little Puss-cat died. That was at 3.30. Half an hour later we were still off the Pointe de Chassiron, though round the corner. It was intensely hot. We noticed how flat all the islands are in that group, and how thickly peopled. A quarter of an hour later, a fine head wind sprang up and *Jane* sailed for all she was worth. It was too late though, we feared, to make Royan that night. The glass was still falling. At 5.35 we judged we were about five miles off the shore of Oléron.

At 6.25 we picked up La Cotinière lighthouse. The coast was piled up with high sand-dunes covered with pine-trees. We were now sailing very much closer inland. The skipper understood from the French charts that we could approach the island to within half a mile, and he judged we were about two miles off. It was strange, I commented, that I could not pick up any of the landmarks mentioned.

As we drew opposite the fishing village of La Cotinière, it was already 7.30. A calm set in. The sky looked threatening, promising thunder. The wind began to rise. Rather than be out all night in bad weather, we decided to try and seek shelter in the little fishing-port. The skipper fixed the Union Jack under our burgee and I worked our foghorn to attract a pilot. As it was ebb tide we realised that it would be impossible to get into the harbour, but we hoped to get advice as to where best to anchor in the Roadstead. The Sailing Directions spoke of a white mooring buoy. We could only see one buoy and it was red. The skipper was positive that it could not be the buoy that was meant. As we were making towards it, close off our starboard bow we saw a long ominous-looking dark line

just below the surface of the water. With all haste we put about. We had been close upon Le Grand Rocher – a very real danger in approaching the port. We were now close to the buoy and saw that it was reddened through rust and that it was indeed the 'white' and only mooring buoy. *Jane* was travelling quickly. We saw two rowing-boats pushing off from the shore and making towards a small sailing-boat anchored just outside the port. We wondered whether they were going to come to us or just going off on their own. We had left the mooring buoy behind and were making our way up the channel marked by black and by white beacons. If we were going in to port, I had to see to it that our cat was buried at sea. I ran below and wrapped his little stiff corpse up in canvas with a pigot of iron. 'Leave that,' said the skipper. 'Get the glasses and see what those men in the boat are doing. Are they coming towards us or not?' I did as I was bid, having first thrown poor Puss overboard. That was at 7.30. 'They are coming toward us,' I announced. Afraid of going any further up the channel the skipper decided to gybe *Jane* round. With the glasses still on the men, I saw that they were signalling frantically to us to put about on the other tack; which my husband hastened to do. But too late! In manoeuvring we had put ourselves on the wrong side of the beacons. We were already on the rocks! 'Nous touchons!' I called to the men, as they rowed up to us.

At 7.45 they were all on board. They said they saw us sailing amongst all the dangers and thought we must be some local boat doing it to scare them, and that we were sounding the foghorn as part of the joke. No one, they said, ought to sail nearer than four miles from the island! A glance ashore showed me the skeleton of a boat – an English boat, they told us. She had gone ashore off the rock we were on. We had nothing to fear for the present as the wind was a land wind from the north-east and the rock was flat. But the tide was falling. We should have to wait until *Jane* righted herself. Then she scrunched as she rolled on her keel. Dark night now enveloped us, enlivened with an occasional flash of summer lightning. The men got to the pump. *Jane* began kicking a good deal. Then followed a horrible scrunching and crunching, bumping and jumping. Oh! How I prayed she would not be injured!

If the sky had not looked so threatening we should not have thought of seeking shelter in that little port. Our old plan of keeping out to sea in bad weather was the best! Thousands of such vain regrets chased themselves through my mind as I listened to poor *Jane* in torment.

No more of the sea! If once we reached La Gironde safely we should rest satisfied. God! How she crunched! My husband said never a word. He sat in his deck-chair in the cabin and waited. I sat in the cockpit with the men and talked. They had put out an anchor. *Jane* was lying on her side with the surface of the water on a level with her bulwarks. There were rumbles of thunder and flashes of lightning. The men told us that once off the rocks there was nothing to do but to put out to sea. A boat of our size would lie badly in the port, and if the weather got bad we should need two chains out forward, and in that wind (which had changed to SW) we could not lie on the buoy. We tried to arrange that one of the men should come on with us to Royan but the sum they required was excessive … for we should have to make more than good a whole day's fishing.

At 11.20 they said we were free but *Jane* was still bumping terribly. They put up the sails. Oh! Those knocks! At 11.37 we were bumping still – but less. They got the small anchor on board. At 11.45 we were really free. One man went ashore in our dinghy to fetch a boat to take the others off. I had no remembrance of them taking their boat away.

At midnight we were lying to, waiting for the men to come back before putting out to sea. At 12.30 they got our punt on board. In a few minutes my husband and I should be alone again out there in the deep and the dark. I was feeling very tired and sick. My husband paid each man handsomely before they left us. Out of the black darkness they shouted to me at the helm to keep her five minutes as she was and then steer west. Off we went, following their directions as near as the wind would allow.

I felt some anxious qualms about setting on to other sunken dangers. A thunder-storm broke loose with much noise and vivid flashes of lightning while a whipping rain lashed our faces. To add to the fatigue and anxiety, I was now assailed with sea-sickness. It seemed a long, long night. But at last the weather cleared, bringing a nice wee breeze.

At long last the dawn broke and the day crept in, dismal and grey. We were well out of sight of land when a fog encircled us. We had to find the red and black buoy of Pertuis Maumusson so as to know where we were. Towards 9 o'clock, to the skipper's immense satisfaction, we passed the red and black buoy close on our port bow!

Not long after that we saw a lone fishing-boat, the only one we had met. The crew of three men were busy laying lobster-pots. We shouted out and asked if one of the men would come with us as pilot in to Royan. They signalled their assent. There was a fairly big sea running and *Jane* was travelling fast. My husband had to get the dinghy overboard and row off to fetch the skipper of the fishing-boat, so I was left alone on *Jane*. I kept her head to the wind, watching my husband appear and disappear in the dinghy amongst the waves. Soon he was back bringing the fisherman – a big burly fellow of tremendous strength. He brought several freshly caught soles as a present. Right glad was I to give the tiller over to him. My husband went below to sleep in the deck-chair, telling the fisherman to take *Jane* through the safely buoyed Passe du Nord. I was left on deck to watch, seated with my back against the afterhatch, but sleep overcame me.

I awoke suddenly, to find that our steersman had taken us in, almost amongst the rows of formidable breakers off that long straight sandy coast. He had never taken the channel through the Passe du Nord! Now he was anxiously looking out for the wreck of a Spanish boat whose prow, he said, showed above the water. He was leaving the buoy that marks the wreck on the starboard and seaward side but as yet he had not spied the little projection he was on the lookout for. Suddenly, in the hollow of a wave just ahead of us, I saw it: a black prow sticking up above the water! A very big sea was running but there was no wind.

'I don't understand it,' I heard our pilot mutter, '*une si grande mer – et point de vent!*' He could not get *Jane* to answer, which was very obviously worrying him. Then he exhibited one of those feats of strength which were continually surprising us in the French fishermen. He took our great heavy boom between his two hands and lifted it from one side of the boat to the other. Next he got out one of the sweeps and pulled… It was then I called my husband, who came and took the tiller.

We were now opposite the great sand-bank that forms a wall against the breakers for La Bonne Anse – a wall that is strewn with wreckage. Skeletons of ships of all sizes lie in profusion on that sandy ridge, washed up by the irresistible waves. Upon it in two pieces lay the wreck of a great English boat that had met its fate there the preceding year. But *Jane* had slipped out of the grasp of those turbulent breakers, and we were headed out to sea and safety. I went below to prepare lunch. Soon we were enjoying hot soup, delicious fried sole, red wine and bread and butter. About 3 o'clock we were in La Petite Rade of Royan.

DOWNWIND DRAMA

Constance Buel Burnett
Let the Best Boat Win
Houghton Mifflin Co Boston 1957

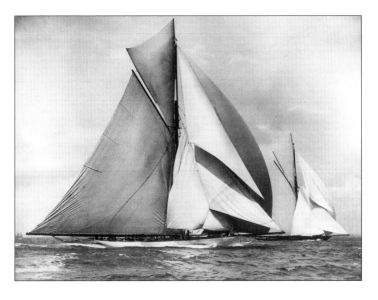

The eighth British attempt at the America's Cup took place in 1893 when the Royal Yacht Squadron issued a challenge on behalf of Lord Dunraven. The challenger, Valkyrie II, *met the 124ft defender* Vigilant *in New York Harbor.* Vigilant *was designed and built by Nat Herreshoff who, up until this time, had made his name in steam yachts, so the selection of his centre-boarder was controversial to say the least. The first race, which* Valkyrie II *was well set to win, was abandoned when the light airs died altogether. We join the series at the start of the rerun of Race 1. Race 2 was an unspectacular victory for the defender, but in Race 3 these colossal gaff cutters generated some of the most desperate seamanship ever executed during an inshore event. The world of yachting is indebted to a spectator, Constance Buel Burnett, for this thrilling account transcribed from her book, 'Let the Best Boat Win'.*

As usual, at this sort of international event, hundreds of spectators in excursion boats and private yachts were milling around the starting line off Sandy Hook. Americans were not too hopeful of the outcome. Herreshoff was a new name in Cup defence history. It was doubtful to many whether a steam engine expert knew enough about sail, and word had preceded the British challenger that she could travel fast in light or heavy weather, as she had demonstrated two days ago.

The great black sloop, *Valkyrie II* looked an impressive rival as she drifted lazily back and forth behind the starting line. The white ensign flew proudly from her gaff. Ten thousand square feet of snowy canvas soared above her dark topsides. Her topsail raked the sky. Three triangular jibs floated like graceful kites over her bow.

'You will note,' bellowed a yachting fan, hired by one excursion boat to impart items of interest through a megaphone, 'that *Valkyrie* flies the white ensign of the Royal Navy. This is a unique privilege bestowed only on yachts belonging to the Royal Yacht Squadron – Britain's leading yacht club.'

'Hear that?' a girl on one of the excursion boats teased her escort. 'The English have so much style! *Valkyrie* looks like a queen. I almost hope she wins.'

'Style – that's all a woman cares about. I didn't bring you here to cheer the wrong boat.'

A man near the couple was studying the big English cutter through his binoculars. 'There's plenty of power in that black hull, though I'll lay my last dollar on Nat Herreshoff.'

'Ladies and gentlemen – look to starboard!' roared the megaphone. 'The United States' Cup defender, *Vigilant*, is the latest thing in boat construction. Her hull is metal – the first to be coated with Tobin bronze.'

'They tell me,' said the man with the binoculars to the couple, 'that *Vigilant*'s syndicate bought up all the available Tobin bronze in the country to keep competitors from getting it.'

'Ah!' The girl was not listening. She caught her breath as the *Vigilant* swept silently by. The lines of the white Cup defender had been refined down to such ethereal proportions that her hull seemed hardly able to support the great pyramid of her sail. Under its massive splendour she moved like a disembodied cloud.

'She's unearthly – a mirage,' whispered the girl.

'Note *Vigilant*'s amazing spread of canvas,' the megaphone broke in with statistical facts. 'The Herreshoff defender carries one thousand more square feet of sail than *Valkyrie*. To offset all that weight above decks she has a centerboard weighing four tons which drops through a slot in her keel. Her crew numbers seventy men. You'll have a chance to see them used as live ballast in a freshening breeze. They lie flat on the windward deck to cut wind resistance and hold her down.'

It was obvious now, from the manoeuvres of the two yachts, that they were jockeying for position. The start was at hand. Spectators, watches in hand, counted the minutes.

'There will be only one gun – at exactly 11.25,' the voice on the megaphone quickened sharply. 'As you can see for yourselves, the first leg of the race will be run dead before the wind. This start should be exciting. Both yachts have professional crews trained to splitsecond performance. Their captains are professional sailors too.'

'Rats!' said the man with the binoculars, giving *Vigilant* a careful scrutiny, 'the man at *Vigilant*'s wheel happens to be her designer – Nat Herreshoff. I understand *Vigilant* didn't do so well under her professional captain, so they asked Herreshoff to take the helm. I'd stake him.'

The crack of a pistol drowned the rest of his sentence and a puff of white smoke hovered over the starting line. 'They're off!' the shout went up.

During the next tense seconds watchers hardly breathed, though here and there a groan of dissatisfaction rose. *Valkyrie II* had crossed the line first.

The following wind was very light and the British yacht immediately broke out a light muslin jib that resembled a balloon. Close on her heels came *Vigilant*, raising a spinnaker of gossamer weight. For the better part of seven miles there was little change in the position of either boat. But suddenly the breeze freshened. The American boat, being in the rear, caught it first. No momentum was ever lost with Nat Herreshoff at a wheel. The defender began to move fast. In a matter of minutes she was abreast of *Valkyrie II*, then she had passed her. When she rounded the outer mark *Vigilant* was eight minutes and six seconds ahead.

The course home, due to a shift in wind, was one long windward tack. This was the challenger's opportunity and she made the most of it. Letting her sails take the full weight of the wind, *Valkyrie II* dug her lee rail under and settled down to eating up the distance between herself and *Vigilant*. Her advance was steady and dangerous.

But Nat, with his instinct for keeping on the edge of air currents, kept moving too. Like a jockey coaxing his mount to the inner side of the track, he nosed the Cup defender higher and a little closer to the wind with every favoring puff.

'He's pinching her!' An over-tense excursion passenger thumped the rail in protest.

The man with the binoculars gave him a glance of withering scorn and moved away toward more knowledgeable-looking company.

When there were but three miles left to go the British yacht was still gaining, but *Vigilant* was in a safe dominating windward position. It was now Nat gave the order to ease sheets and the foam under *Vigilant*'s bow whitened as she surged suddenly forward. The race was hers, no doubt about it. Boat whistles shrilled triumphantly as she crossed the line. They blew again 7 minutes and 36 seconds later for *Valkyrie II* who had sailed a game race. But this was only the opening one of the series.

The second race was unspectacular and won by the Americans, leaving the next encounter to decide the cup. It was scheduled for Friday, October 13. Superstitious sailors looked for anything on such a date, and sure enough, when the fleet of spectators arrived off Sandy Hook, storm warnings had been hoisted. Landlubbers wrapped comfortably in warm overcoats talked optimistically about the reported 'gale' and hoped something sensational would happen.

The wind obliged early in the proceedings by carrying off one of *Vigilant*'s throat halyard blocks half an hour before the start. Since the mainsail had to be lowered anyway to make repairs and the weather was worsening, the crew put a reef in the big sail. Working with dispatch, they were ready and behind the line at the required time, although the men were still struggling to lower the centerboard which had chosen this moment to become balky.

Lord Dunraven had been rather high-handed in his demand that each race start on the dot of 11.25, no matter what happened. Late contestants must take their chances – or default. He must have regretted it later, because at 11.25 on this day *Vigilant* was ready and *Valkyrie II* was three miles away still shortening sail. The Race Committee concealed their amusement behind a polite gesture. A launch was sent out to tell Lord Dunraven they would wait for him. As it turned out, the delay of an hour gave *Vigilant* time to get her centerboard pried loose.

The course for this third race was set for two legs. Wind and sea were making up at a great rate and the two big sloops were a magnificent sight as they raced full tilt for the line at the crack of the gun. The American Cup defender stole the windward position and Captain Cranfield of the *Valkyrie II*, fearing his boat would be trapped again under *Vigilant*'s lee, acted quickly. He shoved his helm suddenly hard over. The push shot *Valkyrie II* into the wind and her way carried her forward. When she fell off again it was she who was to windward of *Vigilant*. It was a quick-witted manoeuvre, skillfully executed.

During the whole of that first leg – a gruelling thrash to windward, with lee rails buried in suds and *Vigilant*'s crew stretched flat on her windward deck – *Valkyrie II* outfooted the American boat. She had to fight every inch of the long, fifteen-mile stretch, however, and rounded the outer mark 1 minute and 55 seconds ahead only.

The race back was the most thrilling in Cup defence annals. *Vigilant*'s crew now faced the most disheartening of all racing tests – a stern chase after a powerful opponent streaking down wind like a witch pursued by furies. The British challenger had raised two light spinnakers one after the other as soon as she rounded the mark, only to have each torn to shreds. To shake out her reef during that mad run before a strong easterly wind was to court disaster. As a last hope of holding the gains they had made, her crew hoisted all they had left – a small balloon jib topsail.

Behind the challenger sped *Vigilant*, her vast white wings outspread like those of an albatross. The slight, alert man at her wheel began to give quiet orders that were carried out with mathematical precision. One of these orders was to hoist the spinnaker. *Vigilant*'s was tied in stops after the American fashion. Once broken out, it was sheeted quickly home without tearing. Heaving seas and decks drenched with spray made every manoeuvre difficult.

Her balloon jib topsail was hoisted next but the wet halyard fouled. Instead of cutting the sail down, a man went aloft to clear it. Watchers gasped. Could that overloaded swaying mast carry one more pound of weight? Being Herreshoff-built, it did.

And now came a display of seamanship while the great American sloop was in full pursuit that made even old sailors shake their heads.

A life line was rigged from the masthead and made fast to a volunteer who began inching his way out on the plunging, outspread boom. As he went he cut the reef points one by one. Meanwhile, clinging to gaff and mast, two other men lashed and lowered the working topsail and cleared the upper rigging of all unneeded gear. Then the mainsail, its loosened folds bulging with wind, was sweated up to its entire height. It took the manpower of all hands. After that, they triumphantly raised the last bit of rag they had – a small club topsail.

A great many spectators had perspired freely during this performance, expecting momentarily to see mast and men go overboard. They breathed deeply when it was over.

'You've just seen something that will go down in racing history,' a veteran yachtsman said to his wife. 'The slightest miscalculation in steering would have tumbled those boys into the sea and snapped *Vigilant's* mast. No one but Nat Herreshoff could have done it. Dunraven has lost the race and it's rather a pity. One would like to see the English get at least one.'

Many Americans felt that way, though to look at them one would never have guessed it. Hundreds of them were on their feet in their rocking boats, yelling themselves hoarse, flinging sanity to the winds along with their caps, tin horns and red, white and blue paper streamers.

The two yachts were now parallel to each other, boiling over the last half mile of water wing and wing. *Valkyrie II*, minus a spinnaker to balance the weight of her heavy boom and mainsail, yawed dangerously in the lumpy seas. She held her own precariously for a while, and then, unable to match the driving onrush of her pursuer, she began to fall back. The end was near. Propelled by the mighty push behind her spectacular wingspread, *Vigilant* soared rather than sailed over the finish line, winning by the narrow margin of forty seconds. The eighth British attempt for the famous trophy had failed.

WORKING BOATS

Two gentlemen yachtsmen take a surprising holiday SGW Benjamin

Exodus DH 'Nobby' Clarke

Street credibility Michael Frost

An unwelcome rescue Frank GG Carr

Shoal water Bob Roberts

The First Fisher of Portugal Alan Villiers

TWO GENTLEMEN YACHTSMEN TAKE A SURPRISING HOLIDAY

SGW Benjamin

From an original article edited by Tom Cunliffe,
for inclusion in Pilots Vol 1

Chatham Publishing 2003

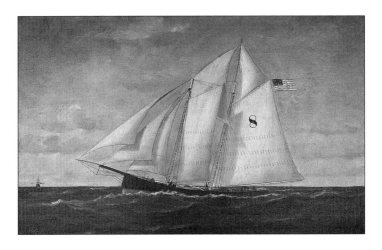

Much is said and written in Great Britain about the arduous lives and superb seamanship of the sailing pilots of the Bristol Channel, but they were not the only men engaged in this perilous year-round trade. From time immemorial until steam finally ousted sail around the First World War, pilots around the world were boarding ships from small boats carried to sea in craft ranging from 30ft to 120ft. Because of a strong element of mutual competition, the mother vessels generally had more in common with yachts than with fishing craft. Perhaps the most charismatic of them all were the pilot schooners of the East Coast of the United States. The bloodline of these rakish flyers developed directly through the America, *which was skippered and crewed by New York pilots and pilot hands when she scuppered the Royal Yacht Squadron*

in 1851. Their routine work was hazardous beyond all reason, and the pilots would take almost any risk to make their daily bread, but these hard-case sons of the tempest were not given to the written word, so few first-hand accounts have come down to us of life on board.

Fortunately, one winter in the 1880s, two gentlemen yachtsmen were invited to sail aboard the New York schooner Caprice. *One of them, a Mr SGW Benjamin, published an article about his experiences in* The Century Magazine, *giving us a priceless glimpse of a long-departed world. The extracts below are taken from the first volume of my own work on pilot schooners of North America and Great Britain.*

Benjamin and his shipmate Burns joined the pilots at the commissioner's office on the corner of Burling Slip on an ugly-looking morning. Between a pair of windows stood an ornate chronometer featuring a thermometer and barometer. As they straggled in, the pilots each peered at the 'glass' and watched the mercury plunging below 29 inches.

Down at the Caprice *Mr Benjamin describes his home for the next fortnight as a 'graceful little craft'. He must have been quite the toff, because the schooner was 96ft on deck, 20ft in beam and drew 11ft under her rudder post.*

T HE cabin was cosiness itself; a stove was firmly fixed in the centre, on a brightly burnished plate of brass. On each side were a stateroom and two berths that could be closed by slides. The galley and quarters of the crew were amidships, divided from the cabin by a bulkhead. The crew included four able seamen, a swarthy lascar cook, a cabin boy and the boatkeeper. The latter commands the schooner, and takes her back to port after all the pilots have been put on board other vessels. But before that, the boat is under the direction of the pilot whose turn it is to board the next ship.

We put to sea with six pilots, the full complement being seven. These formed a joint-stock company, but while all were licensed pilots, they were not all of equal rank.

No sooner was the Caprice *underway than the pilots were seeking ships to board. By nightfall we find them hove-to under double-reefed mainsail while Mr Benjamin recalls something of the fearsome history of the schooner:*

We were now in the waters where the *Caprice*, at Christmas time two years ago, encountered the most frightful dangers. Every sea that came on board froze, until the ice on deck was twelve inches thick, and it was feared she might founder with the weight of the ice. Great blocks of ice grew on the furled jib, and could not be detached without tearing the sail. On New Year's Eve, William Wright, the boatkeeper entered in the ship's logbook: 'January 1st and a happy New Year!' Five days after that, another hand entered on the pages of the same logbook the following terse but tragic record: 'Thursday, 6th. Blowing hard from N.E. At 4am hauled the jib down. Lost a man off the bowsprit. Hove the yawl boat out and lost two men and the yawl; then hove the other yawl boat out and lost her. Lay around tacking till daylight, and kept a lookout on the masthead till 8am. Then started for town at 1pm.' One of these poor fellows was Wright, the boatkeeper. One month more, and he would have been licensed as a pilot!

Two years before this, the *Caprice* was hove on her beam-ends in a terrific squall, losing both masts and a man who was in the rigging. On still another occasion she was tripped by a huge wave and nearly filled. Momentarily expecting her to go down, the crew took to the boats and were picked up. The schooner survived the gale, however, was towed into port by a passing vessel, and was repurchased at auction by her former owners. On another occasion she was run into by a steamer, cut down to the water's edge and sunk in shoal water, from which she was raised again. She seems to lead a charmed life, but her career well illustrates some of the hazards of piloting – which are so well appreciated by the underwriters that they charge 10 per cent premium for insuring pilot boats.

In the morning a race for a steamer is lost to another boat. On the third night it is blowing a gale when a steamer's lights are sighted:

'Give her a torch!' was the order that instantaneously followed the discovery. A tub containing turpentine was brought on deck; a ball of cotton was dipped into this and set on fire. It resembled the contrivance used to light cigars, except on a larger and ruder scale. The torch was so held as to illuminate the large numbers on the mainsail. Nothing more picturesque can be imagined than this contrast of light and shade – the dark figure in uncouth oil suit standing on the low, reeling deck, fiercely whirling the ball of fire over his head, and the ruddy sail and rigging clear-cut against the impenetrable blackness of night, while the wind whistled through the cordage and the foam seemed to turn into blood as it washed on board.

This attempt at boarding also reaps no reward, but later in the week, the boat has worked and raced her way down to the east of Nantucket Light when…

… a steamer was reported heading directly for us. Immediately the cards were flung aside, and in a moment every soul was on deck. The pilot whose turn it was to board the next vessel, after a hurried survey of the steamer, exclaimed: 'Boys, good-bye. Finish the game for yourselves!'

He then dashed below, and in all haste put on a 'boiled' shirt and a Sunday-go-to-meeting suit, and packed his valise. It should be remembered that these steamers are rather more 'swell' than sailing ships, and seem to demand a corresponding difference in apparel. In the meantime, the torch was blazing on deck in the liveliest manner. The needle-like points of light representing the steamer gradually approached, and at last the huge, vague form of the vessel herself could be defined. But she already had a pilot, and paid no attention to us. The game in the cabin was resumed at once, and the 'boiled' shirt was once more folded up and laid away carefully in the locker. The precariousness of steamer-catching is well illustrated by this matter of dressing to board them… There is a tradition of a pilot who dressed seventeen times before success crowned his perseverance.

All day the gale blows, with the schooner snugged down to 'a three-reefed mitten with the thumb brailed up', but still she maintains her position in the shipping tracks.

The sun went down over one of the wildest scenes I have ever witnessed at sea. With some difficulty we managed to get supper, while the deafening roar of the howling winds and the thunder of the surges pounding on deck almost deadened the conversation that went on uninterruptedly below; yarns were told, and intricate problems with cards were discussed by men in oil jackets and sou'westers, while the cook served out rations of hot coffee. Any moment a terrific catastrophe was likely to overwhelm us, but it is not in the nature of the sailor, after he has taken every precaution, to borrow trouble about possibilities.

By morning, the decks are sheathed in ice, and that afternoon the wind has eased, but with frightful squalls. Just as a particularly violent one is enveloping them, the lookout discovers a couple of steamers and a pilot boat to the eastward.

The wildest excitement ensued. Reefs were shaken out, notwithstanding the squall, and the little schooner flew before the blast as if bewitched. The 'boiled shirt' was put on again, winds and waves were defied and everything was forgotten except the great fact that we must snatch the steamers from the clutches of the rival pilot boat under our lee. When the dense pall of gloom finally passed off to leeward, the southernmost steamer was discovered to have been boarded by our rival. Every effort that skill could devise was then put forth to catch the other steamer. As we lessened the distance, the *Caprice* was hove to and awaited her approach. Slowing up, the great Cunarder gradually drew toward us, majestically mounting and plunging on the vast surges, while cataracts poured from her hawse-holes as the bow soared skyward. At this exciting moment an enormous whale, little, if any, shorter than our schooner arose close alongside the *Caprice* and spouting as if to salute her, dived again into the depths.

The yawlboat, only sixteen feet long, was now launched over our lee side into the frothing waters, and with two seamen and the pilot started for the steamer, then a quarter of a mile distant. I confess it was a thrilling spectacle to see this mere cockleshell, with her precious freight of three lives, now lifted far above us on a mountainous billow, and now descending out of sight into the depths of a hollow vale, and hiding there until it seemed as if she would never appear again.

By slow degrees the yawl succeeded in reaching the lee side of the steamer. There again the greatest prudence was required to prevent her from being swamped by the action of the mighty hull, rolling deep in the turbulent sea. At last we saw the pilot, the merest speck, spring on the ladder and creep up the side of the steamer. Then came the yet more difficult task of picking up the yawl. The way it was done was by keeping her head to the wind, and allowing her to drift down toward the schooner. By wearing, we kept directly in the track of the yawl; she slipped across our stern, and pulling up under the lee side, was hauled on board.

Later, and nearly back at the Ambrose light vessel, the schooner is beating around in the fog when she sights a sailing ship heading up for New York, perhaps in need of a pilot.

Edging away toward her, we lit our torch, and had the satisfaction of seeing her send up a couple of rockets in response. At the same time she backed her reefed main topsail and hove to. Running down on her lee side, we also hove to very near to her, and proceeded to launch the yawl. It was a wild scene as the little boat vanished into the darkness, perhaps never to be seen again. But her crew carried a lantern with them, and after they had left the pilot on board the ship, we were able to shape our movements by this little glimmer bobbing up and down like an *ignis fatuus* in the misty dark.

The story ends in another violent storm with the schooner running up through the Narrows under bare poles. 'And so,' as Mr Benjamin observes with the understatement of a true Yankee sportsman, 'ended a most delightful and entertaining cruise.'

EXODUS

DH 'Nobby' Clarke
East Coast Passage
Longman 1971

In the 1950s, DH 'Nobby' Clarke was living with his wife, Mollie, his 10-year-old son, Kester, and his dog, Sym, on the engineless Thames sailing barge J & M. *Having survived the Second World War as a fighter pilot, Clarke later made a name in multihulls and took up a job with Airworks, Ltd, doing initial flying training in Tiger Moths. Later, he cruised his barge north to the Humber in search of quiet. There, the barge had been home for five years, but work opportunities were few and it became clear that they must sail south once more, to the old barge's homelands. In his book* East Coast Passage *Clarke describes the massive physical tribulations of refitting a barge without power of any sort. Aided only by Kester, Mollie and Sym the dog, he prepares the vessel, then sails her with the family to the Walton Backwaters in Essex. In these days of casual circumnavigation this may seem a trivial voyage, but to understand it, one must consider the nature of the vessel and the fact that*

her people were entirely alone in shocking weather with an ancient barge not really fit for the job.

As we join them south of Orford Ness on the final leg of the trip, we see that this was no yachting jaunt. It was an exodus of near-biblical proportions. The hero, for my money, is the lad, Kester, but a child of ten is not merely himself, he is also the sum of the love and attention his parents have given him. This is extreme family sailing that humbles and inspires any fortunate enough to read it.

Now that we were running before the wind, and not battling against it, it no longer seemed quite so antagonistic. The hot sun quickly dried the decks, which minutes before had been knee-deep in swirling water. Kester propped open the main entrance, and Sym staggered wetly on deck. (Everything must be soaked down below, I thought suddenly.)

I had no doubt that many of the holidaymakers on the Felixstowe beaches would be watching our seemingly distressed condition. The part-brailed mainsail bulged six red, round caverns from peak to foot between each semi-confining brail, and the topsail bellied and flopped in the gusts and eddies like an expiring lung as *J & M* pitched and lurched and reeled along in a smother of foam like a clipper ship in the Roaring Forties. She must have looked quite a sight from a distance, but all the gear was holding up to the strain and we were in no immediate danger.

The only real bother was the mess down below which we would have to clear up. But in this hot sun it would soon dry out...

I reckoned we must be making at least twelve knots over the ground with the tide...

And she no longer griped. She was steering easily now... The sun was so warm, so comforting...

'You know,' I said dreamily to Mollie, 'I wouldn't half like a nice cup of tea.'

'All right, I'll go and make some.' Then, anxiously: 'Will there be time?'

I awoke to my responsibilities. It was so easy to drift away into a semi-somnolescent state – and so difficult to face up to the brutal fact that somehow I had got to stop this mad charge downwind. I felt I could sit here for hours in the hot sunshine, just steering dreamily and watching the racing seas... It was glorious! Come on, old girl, show 'em on shore what you can do.

Will there be time?

No! Of course there won't!

Reluctantly I dragged my mind back from its happy depths of silent contemplation to the present urgent realities.

The speed at which we were being driven downwind was awe-inspiring, frightening, and a little hypnotic. I tried to think...

The thought of bringing this gale on to our starboard beam, which would have to be done if we turned into Harwich Harbour, was too frightening to consider. I told myself that it would only be a matter of minutes before we were behind Landguard Point and into sheltered water where we could anchor, but I just could not bring myself to turn and face the wind anymore. The wind had beaten me into submission at last; I had faced it fairly and squarely for three days and two nights. Now I was finished. I couldn't take any more.

Walton Backwaters was the simple way out. The entrance lay more-or-less directly ahead of us, and we had been in there several times before, so I knew what it was like. We could anchor behind Stone Point (a misnamed place if ever there was one, because Stone Point was made up almost entirely of soft sand), or up Hamford Water if the Walton Channel entrance was too difficult to attempt in this wind. The only problem was to locate the Pye End buoy amidst the confusion of spindrift and spray which seemed to be getting worse and worse as we charged along.

We drove past the Cork lightship like a demented runaway horse. The crew lined the deck. They all waved. I had the impression that they were cheering...

Then we were on the last leg, heading towards an embayed lee shore with absolutely no hope whatsoever of spotting the hidden entrance to the landlocked haven unless we could see the buoys which marked the channel through the shallow Pye sands which covered the whole of Pennyhole Bay to port, and the Dovercourt shore to starboard.

Just in case, I took one last precaution. I lowered the starboard leeboard.

I sent Kester up forward with the binoculars. 'Any buoy,' I told him, 'just yell and point.'

We thundered across the entrance to Harwich Harbour. The Pitching Grounds were aptly named.

Somewhere dead ahead we should soon be seeing the Pye End buoy. Dovercourt began to close in to starboard. We were now inside the bay; there was little or no hope of escaping...

The wind seemed to increase; the flung spume made a wet mist across the whole wave-tossed bay, which restricted visibility. Mollie, to port, searched desperately for the Pye End; Kester must have been doing the same... Not a sign.

I altered course to port, knowing the danger of going too far to starboard and ending up on the Dovercourt Beaches. Between holding my barge right on the point of a gybe, and peering towards the flat sandy shore for some indication of where the entrance lay, I, too, was searching to port, to starboard – anywhere for the sight of a buoy. Any buoy!

The minutes passed...

Now the shore ahead was so close that I could see a solitary man walking along the beach...

I knew then that we had lost the fight. I had made the fatal mistake of allowing Nature to bully me into an unseamanlike action. I had risked everything in a mad dash to leeward, towards a lee shore, because I was too tired and too frightened to turn against tempestuous forces any more. Now came the automatic pay-off for such indiscretion. All that was left for me to do was steer *J & M* straight up on the sandy beach dead ahead; but the water was shallow, and the tide flowing: soon she would refloat, the wind would swing her stern, the seas would pound against her side... Shipwreck!

The port leeboard touched the iron-hard sands, and the pendant rattled on deck. We had less than two fathoms under us! I was beginning to freeze in anticipation of what would happen to us in a few seconds time...

And then Kester yelled frantically. 'Nobby! Nobby! A buoy! To port!'

He was pointing urgently: off the port beam. I peered round the bulging mainsail. There it was! No more than a hundred yards away. It was a channel marker.

I gave her a little port helm – she didn't need much as we were already sailing very nearly by the lee. For the first time since I owned her, *J & M* seemed to question my decision: she hung for a moment on the verge of the shore breakers and refused to go.

'Go on, girl,' I breathed. 'Gybe. There's no alternative. You've got to go.'

She lifted her stern to the next wave and started to bore round to port. As she began to turn, so did I begin to meet her on the helm – we couldn't afford to broach-to here. For one appalling second she hung almost parallel along a trough between breakers, and then she gybed and rolled at the same moment. I had a momentary glimpse of the spreet – that Sword of Damocles – whipping across the sky like a gigantic windscreen wiper, followed by a teeth-rattling THUD as it was brought up all-standing by the wangs, then we were heeling to starboard, over, over... The roar of agitated bilge-water rose above the din; I felt the additional jerk as it woo-o-o-shed against the starboard side. She dipped her rails... A wave smashed against her exposed bottom, sending an explosion of wind-driven spray over us.

Then, viciously, she reverse-rolled – upright and over to port, so that she gathered more water over her port rail. The spreet swung across our heads...

'Quick,' I shouted to Mollie. 'Take in the slack: port wang!' She let go of Sym and uncleated the fall, heaving in the rope hand over hand.

'Watch out! Cleat it!' I had no time to say more. I was desperately fighting the wheel as I watched the bows swinging. The spreet hung to port aimlessly for perhaps two seconds, and then crashed across again to starboard. Mollie had caught a turn around the cleat, but at the precise moment of the next roll to leeward her feet slipped on the spray-wetted deck and she went down with a wallop. As we heeled she slithered to leeward, beating the deck with her fists in sheer frustration. The starboard wang met the strain of the spreet just; the port wang blocks screamed agony as the fall was ripped through the sheaves.

Again J & M lurched sickeningly to port in a rapid reverse roll. Mollie was still struggling to get up when Kester jumped over her and hurled himself at the uncleated fall. In the few seconds available he overhauled the festoons of slack, and as the next roll to starboard commenced he caught a double turn on the cleat and held it with professional exactitude...

And we were in. It was as close as that.

Suddenly the seas were just choppy. I glanced briefly around. We were just inside Hamford Water. I didn't bother about any fancy anchor work.

I up-helmed as fast as I could wind the wheel and ran forward. On the way I let go the foresail halliard. J &M began to round up into the wind, but with very little drive from the sails she was crabbing across the channel towards Horsey Island. I humped the foresail folds from off the windlass, whipped some slack chain across the barrel with my right hand, whilst I prevented the anchor from dropping by holding two turns pinned to the welts with my left, waited until we reached the south side of the Channel, and then let the anchor go with a run. I gave her fifteen fathoms. Then I waited. She continued to crab sideways towards Horsey as she took up the slack. There was an almighty crunch as the chain bit into the welts on the windlass barrel; the chain rose bar taut from the water; *J & M*, at the end of the tether almost flicked into wind; the mainsail and topsail began to flog; we were safely anchored!

With Kester helping, I brailed the main, stowed the topsail and lashed it to the shrouds, brailed the mizzen, and wound up both leeboards – working leisurely in an ecstasy of blissful relaxation after some sixty hours of continuous pressure. Apart from thanking him for his prompt action which had undoubtedly saved *J & M* from a dismasting (for the single starboard wang would not have held a second time against the appalling force of the free-swinging spreet), I could not speak. Mollie had gone below, no doubt to contemplate the disasters in her department, and Sym, scenting the land, whined unhappily, forepaws on rail.

J & M was safe enough now. We were anchored just in Hamford Water, behind the mud bank (now covered by the rising tide), which marked the bend to port into Walton Channel, and behind Stone Point on the other side of this narrowest part of the channel.

'Come on, Kes,' I called suddenly. 'Let's get the skiff in the water and take poor old Sym ashore.'

I called to Mollie, and answered her protests automatically: 'Half-an-hour won't make any difference, and a walk on dry land will do us all good.'

We unfastened the lashings, made fast the painter, and eased the skiff into the choppy water. Kester jumped down and unhooked the falls. Mollie did not have to urge Sym into the boat – he hurled himself down in a scrabble of joy. We rammed the thole pins into their holes – Kester at stroke, me in the bows; Mollie hung on to Sym in the sternsheets. It was only a short row.

We landed on the steep-to beach which miraculously is never washed away. There were no yachts in the little bay up-channel behind Sandy Point. We were quite, quite alone.

Sym went urinating-mad, beginning as soon as his paws touched land. Kester ran and ran, around the Point and into the full weight of the wind, pounding into it and then turning and flying downwind until an extra puff sent him sprawling in the soft, hot sand; again and again... I joined him. It was marvellous. My pent-up repressions began to flow out of my body as I lost control of both muscles and mind. It seemed that only a frightful expenditure of physical energy could cleanse away sixty hours of continuous strain. I rejoiced in the wind – the hated, terrifying wind; now I loved it; I thrashed into it, and revelled as it smashed and battered at my straining body; I wafted with it, light and airy, down the sand-slope, with scissoring legs unable to match the speed of my descent. I crashed, hilariously, in a smother of sand, only to scramble back again and again to repeat this mad dance of happy salvation.

Until, finally, I flung my exhausted body down alongside Mollie where she was sitting quietly at the top of the slope. To leeward, *J & M* strained at her anchor and looked every inch the queen she was. At that moment I loved her, as I loved Mollie and Kester and Sym and life itself. It was good to be alive.

Many thanks to Kester Clarke for permission to print this article.

STREET CREDIBILITY

Michael Frost
Half a Gale
Kenneth Mason 1981

The late Michael Frost bought the thoroughbred 30ft oyster smack
Boadicea *a couple of years before the outbreak of the Second World War.*
She was built in 1808 and seems to be the sole survivor of a type that was
superseded 50 years later by the famous, yacht-like oyster smacks built for
the fisherman-yacht hands of the Essex creeks. Two centuries on, she was
still sailing with Mr Frost's family.

A dentist by profession, Frost could only manage to work her as a fishing
boat on a part-time basis. His book Half a Gale *tells how his relationship*
with the hard-bitten professionals of the Blackwater developed alongside
his seamanship skills. This extract describes his growing respect for a
man by the name of Juggens French, one of the unofficial leaders of the
longshore community.

After an explanation of how Juggens is keeping him in line, the action
begins with Boadicea *dried out on the hard at West Mersea for antifouling.*

She is now trapped on a worsening lee shore. There is little space for manoeuvring in the immediate offing, while out among the moorings only a narrow run of clear water leads to the open river beyond. The smack has no engine. By our standards, her gear is heavy and awkward, but she possesses the ability to behave herself without too much help. The trick, as it turns out, is to think laterally and give her the chance to do what she does best.

This is not a tale of human fortitude in the face of life-threatening conditions far from land. It is a description of a young fellow confronting a test that will define his dealings with the fishermen. Readers unfamiliar with the specific vernacular of the Essex creeks will need to know that 'wending' means 'tacking', and that smacks feature a handspike windlass running athwart the foredeck. The anchor chain is passed around this and, in order to make room for more, is 'fleeted' across. The jib sheets are tended from the foredeck.

THE first warning of trouble would be a hail and the sight of Juggens French hurrying down Wyatt's slip with his arm partly raised. When this happened I would usually know what I had done wrongly and, summoning fortitude, would walk up to meet him. He was always right but having rebuked he did not carry on about it and this I respected. Gradually my corrections had become a form of friendship.

Juggens was a smacksman born and bred. He was a big man and rather fierce to look at. Talking to him was none too easy, partly because the tremendous volume of his voice made ordinary speaking somehow out of place but also because he had a quick way of using words as though distrusting them, and having spoken he turned away as though glad to have done with it. As a mentor on sailing matters he was an asset and I learned this very early on.

Soon after Manny French had sold me *Boadicea* she needed scrubbing and, perhaps because she had been so long in the French family, Juggens took an interest. With some trepidation I brought her on the hard single-handed one Thursday afternoon and he came to make sure I had moored her safely. Satisfied that all was well he left me to it. By dusk the hull was still too damp to paint and I decided to leave her on the hard and delay the antifouling until Saturday morning.

Friday the wind came in westerly and it was clear that unless it eased by the next day I was in for a tussle getting the smack off. I debated finding a crew to help but knew that although this might be forgiven it would never be forgotten. The smack was on the hard and if I deserved to have her it was up to me to sail her off as any smacksman would.

On the Saturday morning the wind was still just as strong and I went down very anxious about the troubles which lay ahead. Before starting with the antifouling I walked out the bower anchor to the full scope of its chain and took good care to dig in the fluke well to ensure it holding on the shingle. With that I brought the kedge back on board and stowed it with the feeling that this committed me and there could be no turning back now. I then started the painting and while I worked kept an eye on the weather hoping the wind would ease but knowing in my bones it was much more likely to blow harder as the tide made.

By the time I had done, the water was round the smack's keel and I went on board to wait. Just before she floated I unshipped the legs. The longer I left it the rougher the creek would be and I decided to get away quickly.

After pulling down two reefs in the mainsail ready for hoisting I brought out the storm jib and bent it. I then sat on deck for a few minutes working out the plan. With the wind onshore I would have to sail out the anchor in the approved manner which in itself was no problem. The anxieties would begin at the moment the anchor broke out because then the smack would be away with at least two fathoms of chain still to be hauled in and no time to do it.

If I tried to sail off the hard before the chain was fully hauled in the anchor was almost bound to pick up at least one dinghy cable or more likely several, and that would mean disaster because I could not hope to clear them in the short time I was able safely to leave the smack with her helm untended. If only the wind would lull that would more than double the time I could afford to stay up forward. A hopeful glance at the sky to windward showed me that reprieve was unlikely so, making the best of a bad job, I decided I would just have to get the anchor to the davit as best I could. If it did collect a dinghy I would make a short tack over the creek and then bring up on the Middle Ooze to get things cleared and make a fresh start from there.

With nothing to be gained by waiting, I set up the mainsail and sheeted it in to about close-hauled position. At this it slammed back and forth heavily but that was no harm and could be ignored. After stowing the halyards carefully so they would be clear for free running in emergency I carried on and set the jib. The moment of starting could not be delayed much longer but, still hoping for a lull, I paused to study the lie of the boats round the smack and plan my route of exit.

While doing this I saw Juggens sculling off. He was still on the far side of the causeway and although already well out in the creek he was heading into wind using long powerful strokes of his sculling oar. I guessed at once that he was coming off to help me and in a moment or two would bear away to scull into tide while the wind drove him inshore toward me. With the urgency of the situation now gone I watched with a glow of gratitude.

As I expected, he did swing the boat's head round and then with the wind over her quarter swept down toward the smack. He rounded up alongside and in a single flowing movement laid down his oar and gathered up his painter as he came on board. After letting the boat go aft he made her fast and then strode up to the foredeck, timing it so he could ignore the boom altogether. He glanced round quickly and then told me the sooner the smack was off the hard the better. He said this in a conversational tone and in these surroundings his voice had a clarity an orator might have envied. Quite unperturbed by the noise and wind he pointed out the avenue the smack must take on her way out and then in his quick way of talking went on to add, 'shorten in your chain by half and sheet the jib to starboard. She'll do the rest herself.' To my astonishment he then strode away aft and pulled in his boat. A moment later he was gone.

My first reaction was swingeing disappointment. The help I so much needed had come to nothing. Juggens was now sculling up to weather not far away and perhaps realising my dismay he raised his hand and called across, 'shorten in your chain'. I began to realise that by coming off he had changed the situation. I was no longer a tyro taking foolhardy risks but was instead a pupil doing as I was told. I began to understand why he had come off and why he had not stayed. I raised a hand in reply and began hauling in.

When I had shortened in the chain I sheeted the jib to starboard as he had told me and answering to the pull of it the smack payed away easily, hove-to on the starboard tack. The furious slamming of the mainsail stilled as though by magic and moving forward slowly the smack began fore-reaching southwards, ranging to her anchor. For a few moments she continued, and then the chain began checking her as it drew out bar-tight nearly at right angles to her course.

Answering to this new pull quietly she began to luff and I quickly fleeted the chain across the windlass barrel so as to be ready for hauling in after she had wended. She came round easily and with her jib now drawing she was sailing on this tack without curb. She headed away west by north with the chain coming slack beneath her. Now was the time to shorten in again and with the windlass pawls ringing merrily I hove in by hand taking up the slack as she won it for me.

Soon would come the question as to when I should stop hauling and this was something I had to judge for myself. The lie of the chain was straight ahead and clearly I must break out the anchor as the smack wended this time but because of the lack of searoom I must on no account break it out before it brought her round. I stopped hauling at what I hoped was the right moment and a second later the smack snubbed sharply. She came round to lie hove-to again, and now I had to haul in at full stretch. At all costs the anchor must be broken out before she snubbed again. The chain was coming home too easily and something was desperately wrong. It dawned on me that somehow I had misjudged things badly. At that moment the chain did snub with a force which winded me. The anchor was at the davit.

Collecting my wits I took stock of the situation and felt a wave of relief and pleasure. Juggens had said the smack would do the rest herself and she was indeed doing just that. Fore-reaching down the lane he had indicated she needed no help from me and I simply stood by watching her.

I woke up to the fact that by now every oysterman in sight would be watching and judging my next move and realised that I must begin thinking ahead quickly. The Juggens manoeuvre must not be spoiled at this stage and when I did break away from being hove-to it would need to be cleanly done. I would wait a few moments longer and then go aft to bring up the helm. When the smack had payed away about half a point I would lash it and move forward to let the jib draw. If I judged it right the smack would then hold her course and I would not need to go aft again to tend her. All being well, she would find her own way out while I leaned in the rigging ready to intervene if need be. In the event it did not quite work out but the smack did sail herself more than halfway down toward Packing Marsh before I was forced to go aft and begin steering. Juggens did not speak of the incident afterwards but it remained between us.

Reproduced with permission of Kenneth Mason Publications.

AN UNWELCOME RESCUE

Frank GG Carr

A Yachtsman's Log

Lovat Dickson & Thompson 1935

The account you are about to read is perhaps less of a sailing yarn and more of a reflection on the social structure of Britain between the world wars of the 20th century. On the one hand, we have a highly competent gentleman sailing with his wife and a friend suffering a minor inconvenience but remaining in complete control. While they are minding their own business, a crowd of longshoremen powered by lust for profit and the opium of popular acclaim man the lifeboat and come to their 'rescue'. To understand the nuances of the situation, it may help to consider one or two facts about the dramatis personae.

Frank Carr, our gentleman yachtsman, became the second Director of Britain's National Maritime Museum in 1947. Through his lifelong research into the nation's nautical history, his work remains a major authority on ships and men of the sea. Carr was an active cruising sailor from his mid-teens, beginning with tiny boats on a very limited budget. In 1926, after reading law at Cambridge, he acquired the 25-ton Bristol Channel pilot cutter Cariad. *Faced now with a vessel of some significance, he took six months out to study the old Board of Trade Yachtmaster's*

(Deep Sea) Certificate. Anyone who sat for this qualification even as late as 1970 will feel for him when he states in his book, A Yachtsman's Log, *that most of what he learned was entirely irrelevant to small craft. After passing the brass-bound examinations, therefore, he walked down from the Minories to the Thames and shipped on a sailing barge to become a practical seaman. When we discover that he spent the Second World War serving in the RNVR as lieutenant commander, we begin to feel some measure of a remarkable man who understood sailors from all backgrounds.*

The lifeboat crew were raised in a different school altogether. Rough-handed beachmen all, they would have spent their working days in the famous open yawls of East Anglia. These were long, narrow, clinker-built vessels of tremendous speed and minimal stability whose life-saving heroics were mingled with salvage jobs known as 'hovels' that sometimes verged on piracy. For them, a life preserved might also mean a profit turned on goods they could grab from a wreck. And wrecks there were in plenty. The charts of this coast indicate a series of offshore shoals, many out of sight of land, all capable of sinking a fleet of good ships. Before GPS, with seamarks in poor supply and bad visibility common, the pickings were rich.

We join Frank Carr and his crew aboard Cariad *cruising peacefully northwards past Great Yarmouth one spring evening in 1934.*

T HE season began with an unexpected adventure, for to our complete amazement we had a real lifeboat of the RNLI sent to our assistance! The circumstances were so ludicrous that although we were extremely annoyed at the time, we had many a hearty laugh about it afterwards.

Our first passage of the season was from Pin Mill to Hull, as I wanted to take some photographs of the old square-sailed Humber keels and to collect information about other local types of craft. We sailed in the morning, and had a fresh westerly breeze all day until evening. At 7.50pm we were passing the Britannia Pier at Yarmouth, and the wind had fallen very much lighter, so that we were carrying our big jib and topsail. The north-going tide was nearly finished, and as it looked like falling a flat calm, I decided to save as much distance as I could by going through Hemsby Hole and inside the Scroby Sand. If the wind dropped completely we could anchor at any time until the tide turned again in our favour and although I knew that some shoaling had taken place here, I thought there would be water enough for us. In any event if we did take the ground, it was so near low water that we should neither be there long nor come to any harm, for there was no swell and hardly any wind. A small fishing boat was going through ahead of us under power and we followed under sail. It seemed a good opportunity for trying this inshore passage in ideal conditions.

At 8.15pm we felt her touch. She sailed on to the sand just as easily as if she had been in a river, a slight hump, and there she hung. We hauled our sheets flat in to try to list the ship over and thus reduce her draught, but there was not enough wind. We started the engine, but there was too little swell to lift her heel from the sand. She lay there as if she had been in a pond, upright and without bumping. Low water was at 9pm.

'Well, here we are, chaps!' said I. 'It's a pity, but it doesn't matter. We shall at least be able to sit down to dinner all together.' We did not trouble to lay out a kedge, we should not need it. We left all sails standing; there was no wind.

The mate returned below to serve up our dinner, and I followed her. Ralph remained on deck to enjoy a peaceful smoke. Suddenly a shout from him brought me on deck.

'They're sending the lifeboat out,' he said.

'Nonsense,' said I, 'don't be so ridiculous, Ralph!'

'It's true all right,' he answered. 'Look over there!'

I had come up on deck, and following his outstretched arm I saw that the shore toward Caister was black with people. Then I saw the lifeboat, close in to the beach. With her sails set, she was being tracked along by hundreds of dark figures on the shore. I could now hear them cheering. I remembered that it was Whitsun Bank Holiday, and I understood the crowds. Here was excitement indeed to round off a jolly day on the sands – the lifeboat going out to a wreck!

There was not enough wind for the Caister sailing and pulling boat to stem the last drain of tide, whence the need of the trackline. There was no lack of willing helpers. When opposite, she cast off, and stood out across the stream towards us. I armed Ralph with a marlin spike and the mate with a heavy ivory fid, with instructions to rap the knuckles of the first man to put his hand on our rail. I stood by with a megaphone, and my hand in my hip pocket. We could see the bowman coiling a rope ready to throw. The boat looked as crowded as an excursion steamer; we found it difficult to believe all these could be lifeboat men.

'It's all right, sir, we're coming,' sung out the coxswain cheerfully when they were within hailing distance.

'The first man to step aboard this ship, I shoot with a revolver,' I yelled, 'and if you touch my topsides, I'll report you to the Institution!' I had no revolver, but the effect was the same. There were grunts of surprise; she sheered off, anchored just above us, and veering down on her warp, lay a few yards away between us and the shore.

Then followed a wordy battle, in which I cursed them roundly for coming off, wasting the funds of the Institution, when they could see that there was no possible need for their services. I told them that they couldn't go home soon enough to please me, and there was a good deal of unpleasantness when I explained quite candidly that they were not going to make a 'hovel' of us. They enquired the name and nationality of our ship, and the mate heard them muttering that we 'couldn't be British, no British yachtsman would threaten to shoot the lifeboat men.'

I then tried a little enticement. 'What time do you reckon it will be low water?' I asked anxiously.

'That'll be three hours yet the water will have to fall', came the answer in awesome tones, 'you'd better let us come aboard and lend you a hand.'

'Strange that my almanac should make it nine o'clock,' I replied innocently.

They were nettled. 'You've got seven wrecks round you, where you are,' said someone, 'you'll like as not have a hole in your bottom directly.'

'Strange,' I countered, 'that none are marked on my large-scale chart.'

'We're not pirates,' they protested, 'we're only lifeboat men doing our dooty.'

'Do your duty if you like,' I answered, 'but don't come any nearer to do it. We are now going to eat our dinner.'

After we had fed, we felt in better mood, and I let them sheer a little nearer so that I could pass them out some cigarettes and tobacco in a bucket on the end of the boathook. I thought a set-off to our rather unfriendly reception was indicated. They had by now got over their disappointment at not having a good salvage job, and were ready to accept the smokes as the next best thing. They were sure at least of their pay from the Institution.

A final attempt was made before *Cariad* floated, when they asked if they might lay out my anchor for me 'as we are here?'

'No thanks,' was my reply, 'I shan't need it. If I do, I can put my own boat over.'

With that all their hopes were dead, and at three minutes to ten, *Cariad* floated, and we proceeded on our way, going out by the Cockle Gat. With a cheery 'goodnight' we left them, and thought no more about it.

Some months later a friend sent us a copy of *The Lifeboat*, the journal of the Institution. In it was the following official account of this incident.

'Caister, Norfolk. – On the evening of the 21st May the lookout reported that a small cutter-rigged yacht was ashore, about one mile south of the station, on Caister shoal. A squally W. wind was blowing and the sea was smooth. The yacht was not in immediate danger, but she was ashore at a very dangerous point, and it was thought that she might capsize on the ebbing tide. The pulling and sailing lifeboat *Charles Burton* was launched at 8.30pm and found the yacht to be the *Cariad* (*sic*) with a woman and two men on board. She stood by until the yacht refloated and went on her way, and then returned to her station, which was reached at 11pm – Rewards...'

'A squally west wind was blowing.' Ye Gods! and with all sail set, we could not get the ship to heel over at all. 'It was feared that she might capsize on the ebbing tide.' And the water dropped at the most nine inches! It never uncovered the red antifouling below the green boot topping. A twenty-seven-ton pilot cutter in danger of capsizing with a fall of nine inches in a calm sea! The time that the lifeboat was back on her station is proof enough that the water could not possibly have continued to drop for the 'three hours' her crew had predicted.

Had I not been wise to the manner in which attempts were made to render service to yachts with the intention of preferring heavy salvage claims, I might have been worried enough to accept help for which I should have had to pay dearly. I would like to offer the strongest possible warning to yachtsmen never to accept help from longshoremen's boats, or even lifeboats, unless they are in actual peril of life itself, or threatened with an otherwise almost certain loss of their ship.

SHOAL WATER

Bob Roberts

Last of the Sailormen

Routledge & Kegan Paul 1974

Anyone who has sailed the waters of the Thames Estuary will have seen the surreal, almost prehistoric sight of one of the 20 or so remaining Thames sailing barges at sea. For centuries, these unique craft kept London supplied from the fields and small industrial sites of Kent and East Anglia. The sailing barge developed into its full flowering late in the 19th century, after which it changed little until its final eclipse in the increasingly mechanised years following the Second World War.

At 80–95ft on deck, the Thames barge was one of the most highly developed of all working vessels. To be economically viable, she needed to ship 100 tons or more of dry goods. Her loaded draught could not exceed 6ft – up to 14ft with her leeboards down. In ballast she was said to float on a heavy dew. The ability to dry out on the tide was critical, and the wages of her labours would not pay more than two or, at most, three men. Lateral resistance for her flat bottom was supplied by one leeboard each side, a centre board being out of the question for structural and, perhaps, cultural reasons, since the Thames is not far from Holland, the ancestral home of the leeboard.

The barge's rig remains a lesson in the ingenuity of unsophisticated men. In the first place, the whole unit had to be readily lowered by the crew, sometimes when approaching a bridge underway. To drive her considerable bulk at speeds up to 7 or 8 knots close-hauled and at ten or more off the wind demanded as much as 5000 sq ft of heavy flax canvas. This was controlled without power of any sort other than 'Armstrong's Patent'. The secret was a permanently rigged sprit which enabled the massive mainsail to be kept hoisted. This was furled, to shorten sail either partly or fully, by means of brails operated by a simple winch. The sprit also supplied a sheeting point for an oversized topsail which could, as a result, be set independently of the mainsail. This made for flexibility and helped the barge manoeuvre among buildings by standing far aloft in clear air. For headsails, a coasting barge set a triangular foresail on the forestay. She also carried a long bowsprit for a working jib and a jib topsail. The bowsprit could be hove up out of the way to shorten the barge for berthing after first casting off the bobstay, a chain affair tensioned with a wire tackle, which held it down against the pull of the sails.

Operating a barge can be back-breaking, but feats of seamanship we might consider extraordinary were routine to the men who sailed them all their lives. In the incident described here, we join the late skipper Bob Roberts and his crew aboard the Greenhithe in the 1940s. Roberts was the last man to work a barge under sail. He was a writer, a squeezebox player, a singer of no little talent and he also sailed an engineless, 28ft smack to the Pacific with a chum from the London River just for adventure, only to lose her on Cocos Island. He narrates the following incident from his barging days in his book Last of the Sailormen. The standard of deck work and his own fine judgement speak eloquently for themselves.

W ITH Hazelton as mate and his young friend Jim Godfrey, also of Ipswich, as third hand, I had as good a crew as any barge skipper could wish for. Hazelton was sensible, workmanlike and experienced while Godfrey (unlike many third hands in barges) was clean, obedient and a good cook.

We were a happy ship. They relied on me and I knew that I could rely on them.

It was while they were my crew that we once made a spectacular entry into Lowestoft harbour in a gale of wind on a Sunday and made a lot of people late for church. We had flour in for the wharf in the Inner Harbour and had made a fast night passage from London in rough weather. Between the North-east Gunfleet and Southwold so many seas had peeled the full length of her deck that she was as clean as a new pin. The ship was, but the crew were not. We had had no time for such luxuries as washing and shaving and in any case we were too anxious to get into harbour to worry about what we looked like. It took two of us to steer and the gallant Jim, wet and weary, emerged periodically with mugs of steaming tea or cocoa and sandwiches which can only be described as hefty, each one being a meal in itself. In between times he saw to the navigation lights at night, kept an eye on the lashings and wedges, tended the leeboard winches when required and carried out the many duties which the mate did not have time to do when helping me at the wheel.

Approaching the South Barnard buoy, which was rearing up and down like a kid's Jack-in-the-box, the wind backed to the south-east and it was obvious that the gale was likely to become worse. But I had a plan in mind and I knew of a low way across the Barnard shoals into Pakefield Road, which runs close under the cliffs to the south of Lowestoft. Once in this in-shore channel we could run close to Lowestoft pierheads and see if conditions were fit to take the harbour. If not we should have to run on through Yarmouth Roads and probably round the Cockle to find shelter off the sandy beaches along by Winterton and Haisborough.

The Barnard shoal looked white and wicked. The seas were steep and curly, too much like the breakers on a sandy beach to feel comfortable, even though I was confident that there was enough water for us. Young Jim, being a better third hand than most, was trusted with the lead because I wanted the mate to help me at the wheel. He was a good helmsman and when I needed to step clear of the wheel house to judge my bearings he struggled manfully and kept her from gybing or broaching-to.

Jim called three fathoms, then three again, then two and a half, not quite two and a half (I stopped breathing for a bit when he said this), then two and a half again, thank God), three, three and a half. All was well. We were in Pakefield Road.

We eased our mainsheet a little and sped along by the beaches towards the stone walls of Lowestoft harbour. The seas were thundering on the pierheads, sending up clouds of spray and presenting to us weary mariners a fearsome aspect. But we were looking at the worst side, the windward side, of the harbour entrance, and with a free wind such as we had I knew that she ought to go in. She was nicely loaded, being not too deep and a bit by the stern, and was travelling at such a rate that she would batter her way through the broken water in the opening.

Hazelton looked at me inquiringly. He was a bit anxious – and he had reason to be by the look of the spray flying over the south pier. I told him that we would take the harbour.

'Down jib and up bobstay as soon as she's inside, and get your anchor off the bow.'

I had the pair of them pull in the mainsheet as far as they could, up to their backsides in water at times, and then heave the weather vang in on the crab winch. With everything trimmed ready for either a luff or a bear up, I ran her offshore a little and then headed in for the entrance.

It was not so bad as it had looked. She careered through the confused and broken water in the entrance like a bronco and as we gained the welcome shelter of the harbour walls I saw two men on one of the inner piers vigorously beckoning to us to keep coming.

'They're ready for you with the bridge,' they yelled. This was indeed a great slice of luck. Instead of performing intricate manoeuvres within the confines of the outer harbour in order to get the sail off her and probably let go the anchor, we could now go surging up through the cutting right into our berth. The older men on the swing bridge, which carries the roadway through the town, had in days gone by been accustomed to making a quick swing if they saw a sailing smack taking the harbour in rough weather and unable to check her way. There used to be a big fleet of splendid ketches belonging to Lowestoft and my forbears had owned and sailed in them. I had sailed to South America in one of them and although she was only fifty-seven feet long I had kept my feet drier than I did in the old *Greenhithe*.

Heeling over with the weight of wind in her topsail, the barge glided swiftly up the narrow cutting, through the bridge hole and into the Inner Harbour. We were so busy with our own affairs that it was only then that I noticed we were being watched by a great crowd of people. Apparently we had virtually split the population of Lowestoft into two sections, marooned on each side of the opened bridge.

It transpired that when the harbour master saw that we were safely within the outer walls he had stopped all traffic and got the bridge open in good time. There everyone was compelled to stop and watch our little struggle, whether they were interested or not, and I have to confess to a little touch of conceit as we went sailing up between them and through the centre of the town.

Things had to happen quickly while this was being done. I rapped out orders to the mate and third hand and they jumped to it like a couple of heroes. It is on occasions like this when an inefficient crew can bungle the whole affair and cause the ship, themselves and the master's reputation a deal of damage.

Down jib, up bobstay, anchor off the bow, brail up your mainsail, down foresail, down topsail, clew in your topsail sheet, lower the boat in the water, swing your davits in, fenders ready to go alongside. I will hand it to Hazelton that I have never seen a mate fly round a barge's deck as fast as he did during the few minutes he had to do all these things. But, with Jim's help, he accomplished it.

I learned afterwards that when the crew were recognised ashore that evening there was more than one pot of ale stood up for them – 'for the lads in that barge what took the harbour this morning'.

They deserved it, too, for they had been a credit to the old *Greenhithe* that day.

THE FIRST FISHER
OF PORTUGAL

Alan Villiers
The Quest of the Schooner Argus
Hodder & Stoughton 1951

Those of us who go to sea in yachts maintain our status among sailors from larger ships on the grounds that our extreme closeness to the water confers a unique immediacy to our seamanship. There is more than a grain of truth in this but, whatever our chosen way of life, there will always be somebody whose experience leaves our own in the shade. For many, it will be the Grand Banks doryman.

Cod-fishing on the Banks of Newfoundland and Greenland began in medieval times, partly in response to the Roman Catholic Church's dictum that Friday would be fish day. The salt cod that resulted provided a vital source of protein for the whole of Europe centuries before refrigeration. Many countries took part in the trade, including the United States, Canada and Portugal. The last dorymen on the grounds were the Portuguese.

The banks were fished from 18ft, flat-floored open dories propelled by a simple sail and a pair of oars. The schooners that carried them to the fog-ridden shoals of the Canadian North Atlantic were vessels of great charisma. Those from the North American ports of Gloucester and Lunenburg achieved legendary status for their speed, beauty and the way their crews cracked on sail when racing home with their catch. Twenty or so dories were carried per ship in the early days. By the end of the fishery, up to 70 nested in neat piles on the decks of purpose-built steel vessels.

Each dory had her own fisherman, and each fisherman his own line up to a mile in length, bearing numerous baited hooks. Awkward when she was launched off carrying only her one-man crew and his gear, a dory was fished with single-minded dedication in fair weather and very foul until she had no effective freeboard at all. She then had somehow to be worked back to the schooner, often in poor visibility and a rising sea.

Multitudes of dorymen of all nationalities were lost on the banks. They have no headstones except the grey waves that still kick up against the

currents, no witnesses but the summer icebergs drifting south to melt away,
yet their legacy of supreme seamanship is one no sailor should forget.

In his 1951 book, The Quest of the Schooner Argus, *Alan Villiers,*
square-rigged seaman and hands-on researcher extraordinaire, describes
a voyage in the twilight years of the schooners. In particular, he tells of the
First Fisher of Portugal. The description of who he was and how his life
was lived offers an important insight into the minds of simpler men than
us, now virtually disappeared, who knew the sea better than we can ever
hope to emulate.

FRANCISCO Emilio Battista, called Laurencinha (a family name) was
First Fisher of Portugal and more likely than not, of the world. He
was a lithe, slight man, without an ounce of superfluous fat, with a
strong, dark face, and fierce, imperious eyes. He had strong wrists, great
hands and a ready smile despite the hardships of his chosen life. Above
all he had an infinite capacity for thoroughness in all he did or thought
of doing, singleness of purpose and the ability to go straight for what
he aimed at, and to keep going despite all difficulties. His energy was
boundless, and his strength of will indomitable.

He was born in Fuzeta on the Algarve, on the fourth of August, 1914.
His father and uncles were away on the Banks at the time. He was the
youngest of four brothers, all destined to become Arctic dorymen. He
had no schooling. None was available for fishermen's sons when he was
a boy. Even if there had been a school, it is doubtful whether he would
have attended it regularly. Fuzeta men preferred the school of life. This
was provided for him abundantly. He could sail a dory as soon as he
could walk, and he was a fully fledged paid hand in a small *caique* when
he was eight. When his father and uncles came back from the Banks
they always went fishing in the small sailing vessels from Fuzeta. These
were swift and narrow craft, lateen-rigged, splendidly seaworthy but
allowing no fool to handle them, just the sort of little ship to develop
brightness and the qualities of good seamanship in a lively boy.

Laurencinha was marked out as a doryman from the day of his birth.
At near-by Olhao, at Faro, at all the lovely Algarvian ports where the little
ships touched to sell their fish, the talk was always of great adventures
on the distant Banks, of hazards faced and overcome, of famous captains
and their deeds, and of the miraculous escapes of fortunate dorymen.

An uncle, lost in a fog somewhere on the Banquereau, had turned up in Fuzeta years later when he had long been mourned for dead. He had been picked up by a big sailing-ship after being adrift four days. The weather was bad, the sailing-ship did not intend to lose time on an already long voyage by looking for a fishing schooner in a Banks fog, and she was bound for China. To China the doryman had to go, and it took him years to get back again.

When Laurencinha was thirteen years old, his father took him as deckboy in the three-masted schooner *Rio Lima*. In those days there were no such things as auxiliary engines or even power windlasses. The *Rio Lima* simply sailed from Lisbon, went to the Banks, fished there for five months, and then sailed directly back to Lisbon. It was a bad season, with much bad weather and the cod far from plentiful. Deckboys were not allowed to go in the dories, and he soon realised that he would learn more about fishing by continuing in the local craft at Fuzeta. So from the voyage in the *Rio Lima* young Laurencinha went straight home, and stayed there for the following five years. Working a dory on the Banks of Greenland and Newfoundland was no life for a boy.

At eighteen, Laurencinha went back to the Banks as a doryman in his own right. His father was an old man then, and dying. His elder brother José was Second Fisher of the schooner *Hortense* and it was customary for Fuzeta men serving as dorymen to recommend relatives and friends to their captains when opportunity occurred. José recommended him to his skipper, and a word from José was enough.

At the end of his first season – again, a tough one – he ranked fourteenth of the thirty-eight fishers aboard. He made two more voyages in the *Hortense*. On the second, he ranked fifth. On the third he passed his brother to become First Fisher of the *Hortense*, and he remained a First Fisher ever since.

He had six children, four boys and two girls. All would go to school. His ambition was to save enough to buy a boat of his own, preferably with an engine, to fish from Fuzeta all the year round, and to come to the Banks no more. When not thinking of his work, sometimes quick thoughts of wife and home and children came into his mind. Like all the dorymen, he was much attached to his distant home and family. He hoped the day was not too distant when he might buy his boat, for a man past forty ought not to be an Arctic doryman in a big hand-liner. But for the time being, he was happy.

He had not yet been wrecked, or foundered, or sunk a dory; nor was he obliged to swim for any reason on the Banks, nor was he ever lost overnight in fog. That in itself is a remarkable record, but his way was not made easy. A remarkable exponent of a dangerous and exhausting craft, his success is entirely due to himself.

I watched him, for once near the ship. There was a threat of foul weather, and he had shifted closer in to make a third shoot for the day with his longline, to be safer if the sea got up. Some dorymen were not making a third shoot at all, some had shortened their lines. Other dorymen hauled in their lines slowly, taking a little time over each fish. The First Fisher always hauled in his fish boldly, hand over hand, as rapidly as he could, no matter how the dory was jumping, flinging them with a flick of his elbow into the dory and, with a second rapid, practised flick, coiling down line, snood, and hook clear in the tub. One look of his fierce brown eyes was enough to tell him whether big cod were securely hooked in their mouths, or held only by a prick of their rubbery lips or by the loose skin of their cowlike faces. He gaffed them in when necessary, losing no more than a few seconds, and so he continued until the whole long-line was in, without pause, though it must have been a great strain on his arms. Then at once, setting his little sail, he sailed the line out again, all hooks clear, rebaiting quickly with a piece of catfish or fresh halibut as the unbaited hooks came to the top. As soon as the line was shot again, he set to work jigging, a line in each hand.

I asked him how it was that he could always fill his dory. He knew no answer except work, but it was more than that. Work indeed, but work and a clear head; work and magnificent hands, with the true fisherman's sensitive fingers to receive all the messages flashed lightly from thirty, forty even fifty fathoms down; work and the indefatigable determination of a strong-minded, magnificently fit man, who would have been a success at anything. And, as a background, centuries of the same tradition. No one knew how long the Fuzeta men had been fishing, possibly for thousands of years. And behind him, too, was the shield of a great religion, a sure belief in God. Francisco Emilio Battista was a simple man, an illiterate, and consequently debarred from entry to the U.S.A. and my own land of Australia. Yet he was a man whose knowledge was his own, gained and secure in his own mind, a man educated by life and not misled by nonsense, a man who knew and got on with the job for which he was fitted, a man untroubled by political slogans, uninhibited by any confusion of besetting doubts, unhampered by theories, complacent or destructive. His way of life was set, and for him and his happy kind it was enough: his feet were upon the earth though half the year they trod the frail planks of an Arctic dory. He was a man, I thought, very close to God. Down upon the sea, his life in his hands, he knew the way of the sea and the way of the Lord. And, knowing these things, he was fortunate.

All the dorymen in the schooner *Argus* were the best of friends, though fierce individualists in their dories. At cleaning and salting fish they worked splendidly as a team, but when well-meaning people with safety in mind began to promote the notion of larger, two-man dories, they all spoke out for the traditional solo version.

'No two men are alike,' Laurencinha said.

'Aye, aye, the two-man dory might be safer, I'll grant that,' said Jacin to Martins. 'But we're used to this. We'll keep it this way.'

'My dory is my sea-horse,' said Francisco Martins. 'I don't want any rump-riders.'

'I will catch my fish myself,' said Joao de Ohveira.

'There have been experiments with two-man dories,' old Antonio Rodrigues recalled. 'They make sense. I have seen many new ideas tried in my time and they have nearly all been good. Maybe the two-man dory is good, too, but we are accustomed to fishing alone and we'd like to see things stay that way.'

The truth was that they were as conservative as they were courageous. New ideas in the ship were acceptable and the dorymen could see their great advantages. But new ideas in the dories were entirely different, and not to be tolerated. The ship was something in which they lived and slept and cleaned and salted fish; but their dories – why, they were their lives.

PICTURE CREDITS

ACKNOWLEDGEMENTS

The author humbly acknowledges the heroes themselves who have shared their experiences with us from either this world or the next.

He is also grateful for inspiration, help and assistance from: Andrew Bray, without whom none of this would ever have happened; Liz Multon for commissioning the work; Penny Phillips and the rest of the team at Bloomsbury.

He would like to thank all those who have so willingly provided material, in particular Tony Adams, Clare Allcard, Kester Clarke, Bob Comlay, Tony Dixon, John Gore Grimes, Val Howells, Bill (Swampy) Marsh, Adrian Mulville, Jennifer Scott Hughes, Alvah Simon, Colin Smith, James Wharram, the Catboat Association and the Diaper Heritage Association.